$89.95

BUSINESS

UNDER THE BALLS

HOW TO BE A SUCCESSFUL PAWNBROKER

By P. TAYLOR-FLETCHER

FOURTH EDITION

ACKNOWLEDGEMENTS

Of course, to my family. While writing this book, they have met the monster and they have retreated. This shows how great wisdom flows like the tides of the Nile when motivation *to get the hell out of my way* is inspired by fear and common sense. And, again ... sorry.

Always and ever to my wonderful husband, the original, the one and the only Wimpey! I am one lucky lady, indeed. I hold him directly responsible for everything I know about the pawn business ... and a lot of things *not* about the pawn business.

To my beautiful Delta Dawn, the one lovely and fragrant flower in our lives. Although I am the mother, I still want to be just like her when I grow up!

And to someone new and special in Delta's life, her new husband, Greg. Sorry fellas ... Greg wins, you lose. There's a lot to be said for a man who insists on marrying the only daughter of a dragon lady ... the blue-faced beast who chains herself to her computer, spewing forth vile obscenities whenever her cage door is rattled. I wonder if he will recognize my face without monitor reflections cast upon it. *Sigh.*

To Jerry ... a toast. May we both get rich...er!!!!!

Last, to my wonderful friend ... my fellow *ditto head* and political ally, Michael *Mitch* Mitchner who thought up the title to this book and who introduced me to the world of computers. I miss you terribly. May your soul rest eternally in the arms of God.

Library of Congress Catalog Number: 93-92693
ISBN 1-883103-01-0
Printed in the United States of America

Published by Jerry Stokes
P.O. Box 18646
Charlotte, North Carolina 28218
(704) 536-3214
1-800-422-PAWN (7296)
FAX 704-532-5602

Direct Inquiries and/or orders to the above address.

Printed by Delmar Printing Co., Charlotte, NC

Publisher's Cataloging in Publication
(Prepared by Quality Books Inc.)

Fletcher, P. Taylor.
Business under the balls : how to become a successful pawnbroker / by P. Taylor Fletcher. -- 4th ed.
p. cm.
Work also issued in paperback as: Pawnbroker's operations manual.
Includes bibliographical references and index.
ISBN 1-883103-01-0
1. Pawnbroking--United States--Guidebooks. I. Fletcher, P. Taylor. Pawnbroker's operations manual. II. Title.

HG2101.F54 1993 332.3'4
QBI93-684

DISCLAIMER

Due to continuously changing legislation, new innovations, and human error, the author, the publisher, the Collateral Loan and Secondhand Dealer's Association and the National Pawnbroker's Association are not responsible for the contents herein. The reader is advised to follow up on this material by checking with their city, state, and Federal agencies that regulate secondhand dealers and pawn shops.

FOREWORD

When I wrote the first edition of *Business Under The Balls,* I received a lot of good feedback on it. There was one question people asked of me more consistently. They wanted to know why I would want to share this information so openly. They wondered if I worried about teaching the trade and then finding those I've taught in direct competition with my own stores. The answer is NO. I am not afraid of competition. A little competition keeps us on our toes and makes us want to take that extra step to treat our customers with courtesy, dignity, and respect.

I would like to take this opportunity to thank you for purchasing *Business Under The Balls.* This book is not just a one way street. If you find any error within these pages, please feel free to contact me and let me know about it. My goal is to always make future editions of *Business Under The Balls* better.

The reason WHY I wrote *Business Under The Balls* was NOT the money! I'd hate to be forced to depend on its income for my support. The book is too specialized to become a nationwide best seller ... although I argue that pawnbrokers would benefit if the general public would learn about how to deal in pawn shops. Because of its specialty, the printing costs are very high. I can't run off the deep end ordering 100,000 copies printed. The laws change before I can get a few hundred out the door.

I began writing *Business Under the Balls* first because I am a writer. Secondly, I am a pawnbroker. As a pawnbroker, I have had many occasions where I had to hire new clerks and train them to follow a complicated set of procedures that were crucial to our business.

The thought of dealing with new clerks is always distressing. There are always many applicants. The job of weeding out those who seem to be the most capable, eager to learn, and who would be most trustworthy is a cinch, if one is psychic. Barring that, it is a burdensome task.

Finding a person with the combination of honesty, intellect, common sense, coupled with a burning desire to clerk in a pawn shop is not a very realistic expectation on the part of any employer.

Many good and hardworking people overestimate themselves and find the job to be more difficult than they'd anticipated. The position of clerk in a pawn shop is not exactly like selling hamburgers at Burger King.

Only too often, after an employee is hired and trained, they come to the realization that, except for pay raises, the position isn't one that offers much in the way of a future. There are few promotions, no benefits, and absolutely no chance of career advancement within the pawn industry. The need for employment is, sometimes, so great that the perspective employee doesn't think it through to a logical conclusion.

With this in mind, I blew the dust off my trusty typewriter and began outlining the job description of a pawn shop clerk. We handed these out to new applicants and they seemed to work quite well. They knew what was expected of them ... and they knew what they could expect from the job.

We finally managed to hire several very good clerks who were happy with the job because they came in with realistic expectations. They stayed longer and their enthusiasm for the job was much improved.

Then I decided to write a training manual as reference for our clerks so that they didn't have to keep asking when they forgot certain procedures. I wanted a manual that was more than a cut and dry procedure manual. I wanted to explain the 'why of things' ... to help the new clerks understand the reasoning behind each procedure that was required of them.

Actually, this idea stemmed from an incident that happened to me as a young teenager when I was hired on in the mail order invoice department of Montgomery Ward in Kansas City, Missouri.

I was new to the whole state, as well as the job. Between that and because I was so young and unsure of myself, I felt like I was on pretty shaky ground from the beginning. I recall a supervisor sat me down and directed me to sort pink invoices in one pile and white invoices in another. I was supposed to do something different to each invoice which included stamping them and marking something in the upper right hand corner for some reason.

There I was, sitting at a desk with invoices piled all around me. I saw no rhyme or reason behind my job. I didn't know where the invoices were coming from and I had no clue as to where they went when I finished doing whatever it was I did to them.

In my earnest effort to do a good job, I worked myself into a lather of writing and stamping and sorting. Needless to say, I soon confused the pinks with the whites. For two weeks, truckloads of useless paper was stuffed into envelopes by downline employees and mailed nationwide. Monkey Ward was not happy.

I regret to say, I can't remember if I was fired or if I quit. All I know is that it was mutually consensual. I was glad to get out of there and they were happy to see me go. I still can't tell you what that job was all about.

The final reason for my latest effort to make *Business Under The Balls* even better than before is this ... My experience in this past year has proven the philosophy of "what goes around comes around," "givers get and takers lose," and "do unto others" has proven itself true over and over again.

Business Under The Balls has opened many doors for me to make new friends (both in and out of the pawn business) and to create the opportunity for other pawnbrokers to feel freer to open up, sharing their thoughts and their ideas with one another, as well as with me.

There have been many new sharing experiences for me. For instance, I have been asked to do a number of radio talk shows and that has been a real growing experience for me. I might be able to communicate with my pen and I even do well in forum. But as soon as I am the only one under the spotlight, I die! I am the original Toastmaster's dropout! It was through those talk shows that I did a lot of growing. I doubt I will ever come to like it under the spotlight, but at least now I know I can do it.

I never minded so much when some callers put me on the spot, but I must admit that there were a few times when some of the talk show hosts made me flinch. For the most part, they were very kind and helpful and it was only a rare occasion or two when the host jumped on the caller's side and did the team attack number on me. The good news is, I survived. The worst part of the ordeal was a few hosts who thought it was cute to label me "The Princess of Pawn." That's not funny. I beg your pardon!

Mom and Richard

P. Taylor Fletcher

THE PAWNBROKER'S NATIONAL ANTHEM

Pop Goes The Weasel is a tune that most American and British children learn at a very early age. 'Pop Goes The Weasel' was written in the year 1853 by W.R. Mondale. 'Pop' was an English slang term for 'pawn' and a 'weasel' was a small hand-iron that was common in most homes. 'Pop Goes The Weasel' was sort of an economic commentary written at a time when the commoners were struggling harder than usual in their pursuits of making ends meet on a day-by-day basis. Today, there is still the age-old problem of 'too much month at the end of the paycheck.'

Today's 'weasels' have changed from irons to televisions, stereos and VCRs, which is further justification on the accuracy of the old adage,"The more things change, the more they stay the same."

POP GOES THE WEASEL!

W. R. Mondale, England, 1853

A penny for a spool of thread, a penny for a needle,
That's the way the money goes ... Pop! goes the weasel.

All around the cobbler's bench, the monkey chased the weasel,
The monkey thought 'twas all in fun ... Pop! goes the weasel.

Potatoes for an Irishman's taste, a doctor for the measles,
A fiddler always for a dance ... Pop! goes the weasel.

Blood-pudding for a Dutchman's meal, a workman for a chisel,
The tune that everybody sings ... Pop! goes the weasel.

Major Wood has put the rum sellers through, the Maine law's sad and evil,
We cannot get our toddy now ... Pop! goes the weasel.

The butcher, when he charges for meat, sticks in bone and gristle,
But that's the way the money goes ... Pop! goes the weasel.

From round about the countryman's barn, the mice begin to mizzle;
For when they poke their noses out ... Pop! goes the weasel.

The painter works with ladder and brush, the artist with the easel,
The fiddler always snaps the strings at ... Pop! goes the weasel.

*Up and down the city streets, *in and out the Eagle*
That's the way the money goes ... Pop! goes the weasel.

**Pub or bar*

CONTENTS

PAWNBROKER'S OPERATIONS MANUAL

ODE TO THE PAWNBROKER

P. Taylor Fletcher • First Edition

Uptown or Downtown
the goal is the same,

Collateral Lending's
the name of the game.

Guitars and Wetsuits,
Drums and CDs,

Golf Clubs and Diamonds
and Color TVs,

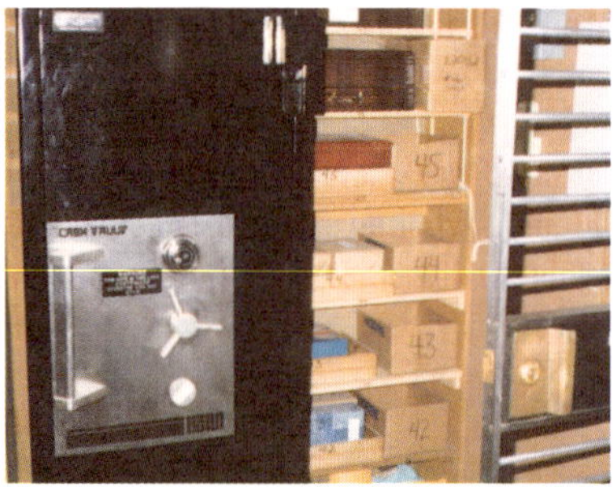

Security Vaults with
time locks and bars,

Or an old combo safe
stacked with used drawers.

Fancy spotlighting
all sparkle and class,

Or piecemeal shelving
and Windex the glass.

Streamlined and modern
or simply make-do,

High tech or low tech
the reflection is YOU.

A pawnbroker's a pawnbroker,
they-re born and not made.

It runs in the blood,
they're proud of the trade!

CHAPTER 1

A BRIEF HISTORY OF PAWN SHOPS

If you think **THE IDEA OF PAWN SHOPS** isn't an age old concept, you might be interested to note that one of history's most significant pawns was recorded in the late fifteenth century. Not only that ... it was this pawnbroker who was responsible through his financial contribution for the discovery of America!

Almost any fifth grade student can tell you that it was, indeed, a pawnbroker who took the Queen of Spain's (Isabella of Castille) royal jewels as collateral. This was done in order that she might finance Christopher Columbus' expedition ships, the Nina, the Pinta, and the Santa Maria on their voyage of discovery!

A nineteenth century writer quipped that if the founders of our country would have thought about this, the mighty stars and stripes could easily have included the three golden balls.

Pawn shops date back to ancient times and are one of the earliest recorded lending institutions, according to one California pawnbroker (article published in the *Collateral Loan & Secondhand Dealers Association of California*, Fall 1990 issue of their quarterly report).

"To trace the history of collateral lending, or pawnbroking, we must go back to the earliest recorded history of the world, since the business of lending money on portable security is one of the most ancient of human occupations."

Charles Goldstone reports:

"The Chinese, the Assyrians and the Babylonians, the Egyptians and the Greeks and Romans of antiquity were all familiar with the practice of pledging valuables for cash. In fact, much of today's legislation on the subject is derived, in part, from Roman law.

"It was in the Middle Ages that collateral lending, as we now understand it, began. Its origins are closely interwoven with the social and secular activities of the church; the first true pawn shops were established by the authority of the Popes.

''These were primitive and relatively unregulated beginnings, however, and it was not until Pope Leo X told the 10th Council of the Lateran that ''the pawn shop is a lawful and valuable institution'' and threatened to excommunicate anyone expressing doubts on the subject that collateral lending spread throughout Europe.

''The Italians called their pawn shops ''monti di pieta,'' and the phrase was translated into most European languages. The words mean, literally, ''mountains of compassion,'' and to untold hundreds of thousands of borrowers, the phrase must have been extremely apt. For then, as now, pledging valuables to obtain needed money was an excellent method of funding without compromising credit.

''Monti di pieta became commonplace in Italy after 1464, for it was in this year that two Franciscans, Barnabas Lnteramnensis and Fortunatis de Copolis collected the necessary capital by preaching and opening pawn shops in Perugia and Orvieto under a papal patient issued by Pope Pius II. The town of Viterbo obtained a shop in 1469, and ten years later a new Pope, Sixtus IV, ordered a pawn shop established in his own home town of Savona.

''After the death of Brother Barnabus, another Franciscan, Father Bernardino di Feltre (who was later canonized) continued his work and established pawn shops in Assisi, Padua, Pavia, Mantua, and elsewhere in Northern Italy.

''From these beginnings, monti di pieta spread all over Europe. Ausberg adopted the system in 1591, Nuremberg copied the Ausberg regulations in 1618, and by 1715, the pawn shop as we know it now was a part of the financial life of all Europe.''

Prior to their disbanding around the 1350's, the early Christian Crusaders (who date back to the Gnostic people who were the direct descendants of Jesus Christ's disciples) were pawnbrokers of that time.

The Crusaders were notorious lenders on landholdings. What made them pawnbrokers was that as long as the Crusaders held a lien on the land, all of the earnings generated by that land went to the lenders, hence, making this kind of loan a pawn and not a mortgage!

During the late middle ages, the House of Lombard in Europe owned a group of pawn shops. During those times, prominent families of wealth and power were recognized as a 'house.' The family moniker was represented as the 'House of....' and whatever the surname happened to be.

It was customary for each family or 'house' to design and display their coat of arms. The coat of arms consisted of the 'colors' selected by the family, not much different from any sporting team. Many wars were fought among prominent families and they proudly carried their 'colors' into battle.

A traditional coat of arms might display a lion and a bow and perhaps a wine goblet. These insignias might symbolize their fierceness or perhaps some form of royalty because of the lion. The bow might indicate their sign for battle and perhaps the wine goblet would signify the sign of their trade or profession. The famous fleur-de-lis was the traditional insignia for royalty which is still very much in use today. The coat of arms that belongs to the British Royal Family depicts the fleur-de-lis among its illustrations.

The coat of arms that belonged to the House of Lombard took on the design of three golden balls. This sign is historically associated with the pawn industry.

The first early settlers brought the pawn industry to the shores of America. In those early times the pawn shop was regarded as the main source of consumer credit. The pawn shop fell by the wayside when the larger consumer credit organizations came into being.

Savings and Loan institutions, credit unions and the large consumer credit corporations abound worldwide. With the advent of such monolithic financial empires, the pawn shop was reduced to the lesser lending role. But the pawn shop still remains a vital element in the area of consumer credit.

The general public retains the ongoing need of being capable of borrowing less significant amounts of cash which the larger institutions are not willing to provide. The result has revealed a rising popularity in the once, almost extinct, pawnbroker.

What major financial institution would be interested in processing a fifty dollar loan for a 30 to 120 day period? The cost of processing such a loan would far exceed any interest that could be realized. In fact, just such a loan processing fee would prove to cost well over three to five times the entire amount lent and that's in the paperwork alone!

It is said that pawnbroking is the second oldest profession in the world. But this statement leads the inquiring mind to the question, 'Where did that first guy get the extra cash to spend on indulging as a customer in the first profession?'' It does cause one to ponder.

So, it is not only possible that the lowly pawnbroker is responsible for the discovery of this great nation; there is reasonable cause for us to speculate on pawnbroking as a strong contender for the world's oldest profession!

"I will assume the undertaking," she said, "for my crown of Castille, and am ready to pawn my jewels to defray the expenses of it, if the funds in the treasure shall be found inadequate."

Statue, "Columbus' Last Appeal to Queen Isabella," in rotunda of California State Capitol - c. 1855 Photo Credit: California State Capitol Museum

CHAPTER 2

INTRODUCTION TO PAWN SHOPS

MY OWN EARLY MISCONCEPTIONS

Pawn shops were an impressionable part of my youth; or at least my opinion of them was formed very early on. I was what one might call a mid-war, pre-baby-boomer kid, having arrived into this world eleven months short of the end of World War II.

During those times of *Mares Eat Oats and Does Eat Oats* (a hit tune of the big band era), the fabric of the American family was more closely woven. Public transportation was (and still is) more limited on the Pacific Coast. Automobiles were not as prevalent in California and the luxury of owning one was unthinkable for us, especially when an extra nickel for a streetcar ride was better saved for a rainy day.

People say life was more difficult in those days. Perhaps so, but life was also much less complicated, less turbulent.

In looking back, it seems that people were more inclined to seek pleasure in the most mundane daily tasks. Some of my fondest memories were created in the exhausting treks afoot to Cimmirusti's Poultry Mart or Wallgreen's Grocery. We kept in step and chanted the familiar military cadence, *"First she hired me, then she fired me, then by golly I left ... I left ... I left, right, left!"*

The supermarket conglomerates were not yet so firmly entrenched that they were the convenience that they are today. In our neighborhood if a person wanted poultry or rabbit, they went to Cimmirusti's. If it was vegetables they were after, Mr. Wallgreen was their man.

There was a neighborhood butcher shop and bakery. A milkman delivered our dairy products before dawn on the door step. The ice man came into our kitchen three times a week. I was just a little afraid of him because he looked so menacing with those large tongs gouged deeply into massive chunks of ice. He hefted each block over his shoulder onto a leather apron that draped across his back. The apron protected the flesh beneath his shirt from frostbite. After he put the ice in the box and let the tongs dangle loosely in his hand, he looked much less foreboding to me.

I smile inwardly as I recall my old thirdhand wagon. There's no telling how many coats of paint covered it. My uncle painted it bright red when he gave it to me. After several years of my abuse, the paint eventually oxidized and then began chipping away, exposing all the other paint jobs. My red wagon finally took on a kind of patchwork quilt design. I liked it.

The empty wagon bounced and clattered, trailing behind us over the uneven sidewalks, then rode in solid silence homeward, struggling and straining under the burden of our purchases – fruit, vegetables, a few pounds of ground round, sugar, and flour, and probably rabbit for a nice stew or a fat fryer for our family supper come Sunday.

On our way to run our errands, we had to pass by a strange little store that peaked my interest. I always tried to lag behind a bit so I could peer in through the dirty windows at all of the interesting things that were haphazardly displayed for sale. Each time I did this, my grandmother pinched me on the arm to hurry me along. She was clearly angry and the why of it was as mysterious as the forbidden store.

Once my grandmother's opinion was established on a subject, it was unwise to suggest anything to the contrary. This fact was firmly entrenched early on in my upbringing. Whatever possessed me to make such a fatal error in judgement will probably always elude me. I actually suggested (no, I'd insisted) that we stop to look inside.

Her face turned crimson with rage. I don't recall her heated words that fateful afternoon, but they made a distinct impression. After I had a thorough blessing out, she pinched me extra hard on my arm, then gave me the silent treatment for the rest of the day. That was Grandma's way.

I longed to go inside and look around that dusty old store because it looked a lot like an attic. My favorite thing to do was to rummage around in our musty attic. I must have made quite a mess whenever I did so I was banned from going up there alone unless it was a rainy day. My forced indoor confinement resulted in my being underfoot and it was a relief to the adults to be rid of me at any cost. It must have been easier to deal with the mess than to deal with a restless eight-year-old with no siblings for distraction.

I still love the rain. It reminds me of my childhood when great attic adventures were mine for the taking. I was the boss, the queen. I held total dominion over my own personal space above the heads of my family. I spent long, leisurely afternoons in that attic, free to explore as I pleased. Once they forgot all about me and only remembered where I was when there was a noticeably empty chair at the dinner table.

The vast treasures of my attic were hidden in trunks and cardboard boxes. Treasures like old photo albums to look through, ladies' clothing for dressing up in, and large feathery hats to perch upon my head. My baby crib was up there with boxes of baby clothes. There was an old blue and white lard can that was full of a colorful assortment of buttons and a Shirley Temple doll my mother got for Christmas when she was around my age. (I still have that doll.)

Of those treasures, the most precious of all were the books and old newspaper clippings. Several large boxes were filled with adult and children's classics. They had, at one time, belonged to my mother and her siblings. I digested the literature voraciously. Sunlight poured onto the pages through a louvered vent. It was by that illumination I became acquainted with *The Brothers Grimm,* the *Bobsey Twins, Mary Poppins, Tom Sawyer, Huckleberry Finn.* My favorite fictional character was Jo March in *Little Women* because she had an attic, too.

I was introduced to historical figures like Theodore Roosevelt, Abraham Lincoln, and Thomas Edison. I particularly enjoyed Theodore Roosevelt's game hunting safaris in the wilds of the African jungles.

Newspaper clippings related all the details of WWII, from Pearl Harbor to the Enola Gay at Hiroshima and Nagasaki. Then the famous headlines of August 1945. WAR ENDS! I knew as much about that war as any adult who lived through it.

That old attic probably had a lot to do with my penchant for appreciating the value in *stuff.* It also explains why *Fibber McGee and Molly* was my all time favorite radio show.

Fibber McGee had a passion for *stuff,* too. His *stuff* (i.e. golf clubs, fishing poles, a bowling ball, etc.) was crammed in the living room guest closet; which happened to be located right next to the front door. People were always dropping by to visit with Fibber and Molly. Without fail, one of the visitors mistook the closet door for the McGee's front door.

Molly was always at Fibber to clean out the closet and get rid of the clutter. His intentions were good. He began his project often but nothing ever got done. He found each item had a future use or a sentimental value. Instead of cleaning the closet as promised, he added more to the precarious pile.

Fibber's best friend was The Great Gildersleeve who was the unfortunate victim most of the time. He could be counted on to forget, opening the wrong door at least once on every show.

It was always a hoot when Molly yelled, "No...don't open that clo....." The sound effects were great! The fun was in the mental images such a din conjured. One pictured an avalanche of equipment tumbling on top of the unlucky victim. What a racket! Baseball bats, golf clubs, bowling balls, fishing poles, skis, ski poles, bob sleds, then the clatter of several rolling hubcaps as a finale. Everyone loved Fibber McGee — even my grandmother.

That was another reason I couldn't understand her attitude toward that store. Much later, I came to realize that it was just such a store that was the topic of her adult conversations with her cronies.

"Those shady old men lend penniless widows money on the few cherished things they own ... then if they can't pay the money back just when he wants them to, those greedy old rats just take their things anyway ... just like that!" She'd snap her fingers in the face of her listener to emphasize her point.

Those who had survived the great depression would grimly nod their heads in agreement.

She never mentioned the names of those who suffered such misfortunes. She always related her story in the third person, suggesting that she only knew about those *thieving places* because she, as she put it, "lived through the depression."

Although she never said, I eventually surmised that it was *Grandma* who was the penniless widow. My grandfather died in 1928 when my own mother was only four years old.

As I grew older, I began to understand that the forbidden store in which I longed to browse was a *pawn shop.*

My mind was made up without ever having experienced the reality. My grandmother's anger, the stories I read, the films I saw; each story contributed to the formulation of my opinion. Every reference to pawnbrokers was presented to me cast in the glow of negative light.

It doesn't take a doctorate in psychology to figure out how I came to equate pawnbrokers with the fictional character, Fagan. In Charles Dickens' book, *Oliver Twist,* Fagan was an evil man who preyed on homeless orphans. He taught them how to pick the pockets of the fancy ladies and the stylish fops in London's finest quarter. The children brought stolen jewelry and trinkets to Fagan in return for food and a warm, dry place to sleep during the freezing winters.

Rod Steiger's role in *The Pawnbroker* was very convincing. He played the character of a Jewish husband and father who was the sole survivor of his family in one of Hitler's death camps. The result of this experience caused him to reject his own emotions. His fear was that if he allowed himself to feel, he would go insane with grief. What other occupation would be more suitable for this poor soul than the occupation of a moneylender? The story had to show his interaction with desperately impoverished people. What better setting for this than a pawnbroker in a pawn shop?

The natural conclusion for the viewer, who is unfamiliar with the industry, is that a person would have to be a little deranged in order to be a pawnbroker.

My grandmother was never to know what became of me as an adult. She died when I was just out of high school. I often think about her when I am waiting on a new customer who is fearful of losing an item that holds a special sentiment for him/her.

Old *Grammy* would turn some soil if she knew I became a pawnbroker; but had she dealt with a pawnbroker like myself, she might have come away with quite another opinion!

MY OWN INTRODUCTION

It wasn't until I'd lost a very sentimental and expensive gold bracelet that I experienced my first visit to a pawn shop. I looked everywhere for it without success. Realizing that I'd probably lost it off my arm somewhere in town, I checked the police department to see if it had been turned in. They told me that sometimes when people find things like that, they sell them in pawn shops. They don't realize that what they are doing is illegal.

I was desperate to find my bracelet so I worked up the courage to go into one of the local pawn shops.

My discomfort must have been obvious when I walked in. At first, I looked in all the jewelry showcases in hopes of spotting my bracelet. When I didn't see it, I approached the pawnbroker, described the lost bracelet, and asked him if he'd seen one like it. He was very pleasant and anxious to be helpful. He didn't recognize my description but offered to call me if it came into his store. Once I realized he was actually a very nice man, I began to feel more comfortable. The store appeared to be a little junky but it really wasn't so bad. Really, it was quite interesting. I found myself browsing around out of curiosity, spending more time inside than I'd anticipated.

Once I got my feet wet, the rest of the pawn shops were easy. Finding my bracelet became a mission not so much for the bracelet as for the interesting variety of pawn shops I was discovering. They were fascinating!

It wasn't long before pawn shops became my new addiction. They were better than antique stores and swap meets. The fun was in browsing and the discovery of an occasional treasure. I collected silver souvenir spoons from all over the world and I found many of them in pawn shops, priced *only for the silver.* Antique dealers knew the value of collectibles. Pawnbrokers didn't care! Their only interest was in generating a profit on their merchandise. The rarity of the piece held no concern for the pawnbroker. This translated into a large savings for me. I became familiar with the pawnbrokers and I soon developed a good rapport with most of them. As this happened, they made an effort to take in the items which held my interest.

I quickly learned that pawnbrokers don't lend on just anything. If I were looking for something special, like the souvenir spoons, I made my desires known. Pawnbrokers tend to turn away items that don't normally move well. If a pawnbroker has a sure customer for an unusual item, he will bid on it if the opportunity arises.

In addition, I was meeting lots of interesting people. The pawnbrokers weren't such a bad lot after all. Some were a bit crusty, especially when I asked them about my bracelet. For the most part, they wanted to be helpful and all of them wound up wishing me well in my efforts to track down the wayward bracelet.

One day while driving through a nearby town, I noticed a pawn shop that I'd not been in before. I'd long since given up the idea of finding my bracelet. Besides, right now I was Christmas shopping. My budget was limited and a pawn shop was just the ticket to finding great presents for the least amount of cash.

I walked up to the loan counter to ask about a portable television for my brother. I started to speak to the pawnbroker when I happened to look down at his hand which was resting on the counter.

I looked back up at him and I was speechless. I just stood there, foolishly staring at him, unable to get the words out of my mouth. Finally, he asked if he could help me with something.

I regained my tongue. "My bracelet! God, I can't believe it! You're wearing my bracelet!" My treasured, sentimental piece was right there as big as life on the arm of this pawnbroker!

He said, "You're kidding! Is this really your bracelet?"

I told him that it was and he expressed surprise at the idea that such a large piece of jewelry belonged to a woman. Actually, I think he was a little embarrassed when he realized that he mistook my bracelet as masculine enough to wear himself.

He said, "We do all we can to keep this kind of thing from happening, but sometimes it does. You sure can have it back. Just give me what I gave for it and it's yours. I'm not interested in profiting off of anyone's loss, but I'm not willing to take a loss for myself, either.''

That seemed fair enough to me, so I agreed. He checked his records for how much investment he had in it and he even presented the paperwork for my inspection.

Just as an aside, shortly after that I met a man who was just starting out in the pawn business. We began dating and after several months he proposed marriage. I accepted. My acceptance made us obligated to each meet the family of the other. Neither of us looked forward to this protocol. As a matter of fact, we both dreaded it.

I took him to my parent's home for Sunday dinner and we announced our intentions. My folks were easygoing people by nature. They were very gracious, making my intended comfortable and welcome.

The following Sunday was my turn. When the introductions were made, I stood there like an idiot, speechless once again. While I knew my fiance had a brother who was in the pawn business, I had no idea that he was going to turn out to be the very same man who had adorned himself with my bracelet!

The moral of this story is that one can never be sure what one might find in a pawn shop! I found a lot of bargains – I found my bracelet and I found my husband!

PAWN SHOP BARGAINS

By staying out of pawn shops, I wasn't protecting myself from being taken, I was only insulating myself from some wonderful bargains! All of my prior purchases (i.e., stereos, televisions, refrigerators, precious jewelry) were made at top dollar retail prices. I did my shopping where most people do, in luxurious department stores and in the smaller stores housed in the local shopping malls. I was paying for television, radio, and printed advertising. I was paying for the beautiful displays, the showcases, the lighting, the escalators, temperature control, mood music, the exorbitant mall rent, all of the fancy trimmings that go along with luxury shopping in such pleasant surroundings.

Almost every item, save for clothing, could have been purchased new (or near new) from the local pawn shops and all at a mere fraction of what I actually paid.

Not only did I pay a premium price on everything I bought, I paid far more. Much of my money went toward the exorbitant interest rates I paid by charging the goods on revolving charge accounts.

I never want to know how much money I could have been saving over all those years. It might depress me to the point of no return!

You don't have the ready cash? Not to worry. Pawn shops offer lay-away plans and they take most major credit cards. Paying the interest on the credit cards isn't so bad when you are getting the item for half of what you'd pay for it elsewhere. Many times the items in the pawn shops are brand new and near new.

HOW DOES A PAWNBROKER DETERMINE VALUES?

Many people who are wary of pawn shops will admit that they are curious about how they work. They wonder how it is possible that the pawnbroker can figure out what to offer on such a wide variety of items. And they wonder how the pawnbroker can tell the difference between the genuine article like diamonds and gold and good replicas.

How does a pawnbroker tell the value of one television from another? One trip to Circuit City causes the blood pressure to rise when in just one department like the televisions. Twenty or thirty similar televisions are grouped together in one area and one looks pretty much like another, except for price tags that can vary by several hundreds of dollars! And that's just the *new* televisions! How can one determine between so many new TVs without the added confusion of older models?

Unless one is an expert in the field of televisions, all the average person can surmise is if the price of an item is higher than a similar item sitting next to it, the more expensive one must be better!

Haven't you ever wondered how a pawnbroker can tell a diamond from a zircon, or be certain the gold is genuine? I always thought it took a true expert in the jewelry business to know how to determine such things.

And now, with all of the new computerized items (i.e. video recorders and cameras, compact disk players, video games, word processors, etc.) that are constantly perfected and updated, obsolescence can be a major depreciation factor within only months!

My own home computer was state of the art less than two years ago and the price tag was pretty state of the art, as well. Today, with all of the money I have invested in upgrading the system, it is barely worth a fraction of the new price.

There is no year written on the back of computer terminals. One computer looks pretty much like another. Personal computers vary widely. Apple, Tandy, IBM, and then there are all of the Taiwanese clones that are just as good, but worth fraction of the name brands.

A PC clone is not considered good quality like the Apple or IBM, however, a clone can be worth as much or more than the name brand if it contains more memory with more bells and whistles than the name brand with only 1 megabyte of memory and no extra features.

Shouldn't it take years of experience before one attains enough knowledge to determine the values of such varied items? If one were to assume that it did, then one would be correct in that assumption.

It stands to reason that there must be some kind of short cut, some references that are made available to people like pawnbrokers. If so, then where can these references be obtained? Who puts them out? Why aren't they made available to the public?

Very few pawnbrokers are experts in any particular field. Those who aren't have learned to understand a few simple, basic rules and concepts. They also know how to find the information they need in order to be effective in their trade. These are the secrets that pawnbrokers *never* share.

These secrets are valuable to anyone, whether they are aspiring to become pawnbrokers or not. The decision to invest a few dollars in this book can save you literally thousands of dollars. Even if you choose *not* to open a pawn shop, you will always have the sources nearby which will make you just as knowledgeable as any pawnbroker. Armed with the facts contained in these pages, you will never again pay more than that which is fair for anything you purchase from pawnbrokers and secondhand dealers. You will have a pretty good idea of what they have invested in each item. With that knowledge, you will have the ability to make offers that are fair and reasonable for the dealer and for yourself.

You don't want to give the dealer fifty times his investment and it doesn't make him dishonest if you are willing to pay it. On the other hand, you don't want to insult him by ridiculously low balling his prices. Once a dealer is offended,there is little chance the offender is going to get any kind of bargain from him at all.

WHO BORROWS MONEY IN PAWN SHOPS AND WHY?

Who are the borrowing customers?

First, let's go over the popular notions of what kind of clientele pawn shops attract. What are the first things that come to mind? Junkies? Prostitutes? Dope dealers? Thieves? Derelicts? Depraved people, people down on their luck, welfare recipients; that sounds about right, doesn't it?

Wrong! You couldn't be more wrong. Oh, some of those people might come in now and again. Eventually, every kind of person imaginable winds up needing a small loan now and again.

Not long ago we gave a gentleman a sizeable cash loan on a very expensive utility truck that was brand new. He only bought it a few weeks prior to coming in. This man was probably worth more than anyone else in town. It just happened that all of his ready cash wound up in a large real estate transaction and he had several escrows going at once.

Being a very smart businessman, he understood that it would be very poor timing on his part if he borrowed the money from any source that would require a credit check. His big real estate deal could be placed in jeopardy if there was any unusual flurry of loan activity, whether from a lending institution or on his major credit cards.

TRW picks up that kind of information in a heartbeat and even if it didn't queer his deals all together, it would surely cause them to become bogged down by flagging the real estate loans for which he was applying.

That, in turn, could result in being faced with paying higher interest rates, points, and loan fees. Worse, it could result in a denial of his loans.

By going to a pawn shop, he got the cash within a few hours and by the time one figures all the points and loan fees that must be paid for a bank loan, he paid less in interest on the collateral loan in the pawn shop than he would have paid if he borrowed the money at his local bank. He paid the loan back in less than a week. It would have taken *two weeks* for the banks just to get loan approval.

We currently have customers that are in many professions — doctors, lawyers, bankers, prominent business people in our community; the same people we see in our local grocery stores and at church on Sunday. Why do they borrow money from pawn shops? It's quick. It's easy. It's confidential. It doesn't show up on their TRW and it is sound business!

What do people generally need to borrow money for?

It is common for many of the wives of these professionals to frequent pawn shops. Sometimes the ladies don't budget their spending money very well and they run up the credit cards higher than they'd planned. It is much easier to pull out a piece of jewelry they seldom wear, borrow the cash to pay down the credit cards, and return later to redeem their jewelry. It also saves wear and tear on the marriages!

And before you fellows get all puffed up about the ladies being less than honest with their husbands, you guys are the worst offenders! There are some of you who have made a few poor financial decisions (like maybe at the race track or in a card game) and robbed Peter to pay Paul without letting your ladies in on just exactly what you were doing! Isn't it nice that pawnbrokers are bound to keep their customers' business confidential?

I am able to reveal the identity of one famous borrower (not in my store, however) because she has already been publicly named in the press. I also have additional corroboration of this because I am a personal friend of someone who has been in her employ and who has been very closely associated with her for many years.

Would it surprise the reader to learn that the Princess of Iran is a customer of a very elite pawn shop in Beverly Hills, California? I reveal this solely to point out the fact that people from all walks of life utilize collateral lenders.

The Princess commonly pawns her jewels and I think she'd be very surprised to learn of the stigma it carries in this part of the world. This stigma is fairly limited to the United States and only a few European countries as well.

China is proud of its pawn shops. The bigger and fancier the pawn shops are in a city, the more wealth and the more social standing the district has in the eyes of their nation!

Are these professional people the usual customers?

No. They only make up a small percentage, but they are very steady customers, both in borrowing and in purchasing. Wealthy people didn't get that way from shopping in Beverly Hills! They love a good bargain just like the next guy.

Our most common customers are the ones who are living in varying degrees above the poverty level. Their average income ranges from $15,000 to $50,000 per year. They borrow money when they have unexpected expenses that crop up from time to time. Like the song says, *'Too Much Month At The End Of The Money.'*

Other common customers are the folks who are living on fixed incomes. They, too, have a tough time of it when they are faced with unexpected expenses.

Most people who aren't familiar with California's MediCal program (which is supposed to provide medical care for those who are on welfare) do not realize that California pays the doctor to diagnose the patient, but they don't provide for the prescription medication that it takes to get them cured.

This means the poor (including children) who are suffering from agonizing and even deadly diseases like cancer can get the diagnosis, the surgery, and even the chemo therapy, but they cannot get the pain killers, the antibiotics, and other prescription drugs they need even if it means a prescription drug that will keep them alive. If not for pawn shops, where would these people go? What would they do?

Pawn shops are becoming America's *blue collar lending institution.* The blue collar worker makes up the bulk of a pawnbroker's customers. They are honest, hard working people who are trying to tough it out in an economy that has been showing no mercy.

More and more we are seeing people who have been laid off from jobs that they have had for many years, especially in the aerospace industry.

The people who frequent pawn shops are as broad a section as you will find in any public place at any given time. The last people we see are those who are totally impoverished and indigent. In the first place, those poor souls usually have nothing to sell. When they do wander in, it is to ask for a handout. We don't encourage them by giving out money, but if they are hungry, we send them to a local businessman who owns a fast food restaurant. They give him one of our vouchers that is good for a free meal and the restaurant owner charges us only his cost.

Whenever a new pawn shop opens, the pawnbroker can count on the local indigent to come by first. This is normal. They come in to feel out the new pawnbroker – to see if he can be *suckered.* They are very obvious and they can be used to the pawnbroker's advantage. We've opened three stores and found, without fail, that if we gave these people a dollar or two for some of their junk, the word of our store spread faster.

Soon, people with decent collateral hear about the new store that doesn't turn anything away and business is soon booming! As far as the accumulated junk goes, box it up and call out the Salvation Army or the Goodwill. It makes a great write off and you can't get any cheaper or better advertising!

New pawnbrokers who ran these people off found out too late that they acquired a poor reputation before they hardly got started in the business. People who hear the worst don't often ask where the information came from or what the circumstances were surrounding the event.

After awhile, when business picks up, the undesirable can be politely discouraged. They will get the idea and find some other outlet for their junk.

IGNORANCE IS THE ONLY THING TO FEAR

Ten years ago, I bought my first personal computer. The user's guide is meant to be an introduction of computers to the reader. I couldn't understand the first page of that guide. My first experience with the computer left me with the impression that whatever information I fed into it was mysteriously sucked up into some infinite black hole and it just kind of meandered around the vastness of my computer's memory.

Days after I decided that my input probably hadn't been memorized by my computer, I would accidentally push the correct sequence of keys and the data I previously entered would very suddenly and unexpectedly spew forth on the monitor screen. It was bad enough that I had to worry about never recovering the information that I'd previously entered without the added worry that I would push the wrong key and do the unthinkable; the dreaded *program crash* thing, whatever *that* was supposed to be!

Because I didn't understand computers and I certainly didn't have the faintest idea of what I was doing, I decided that I couldn't learn and that perhaps I'd even made a mistake in trying. Rather than ruin the computer, I put it away thinking that maybe I would take a class in computers some day when I had time. I didn't touch that computer again for nearly two years!

One day I was cleaning out my closets and I saw that poor little PC sitting all alone in a dark corner. I thought about what a shame it was that I paid such a dear price for something I couldn't use. I decided to give it one more fair shot before I put it in our pawn shop for sale.

I took out the user's guide and started all over again. I poured over that guide for several days. Each pensive move I made on the computer was not without reading and re-reading every single instruction until I was sure that I was carrying out each procedure correctly.

Pretty soon I began to realize that the truth of the matter is that programs seldom crash and there aren't any buttons on the keyboard that can crash them. In the event of a crash, all programs can be recovered if the operator backs up all of his information on the software.

Now I couldn't live without my computer. I feel silly when I think about how I packed away a perfectly good PC with a wonderful little word processor program that I could have used in my writing. Instead, I plugged away on my old IBM Selectric. It was like driving a horse and buggy with a new car parked in the garage!

I was frightened of my computer when I should have been frightened of my ignorance! It was ignorance that made me fight against what was really best for me.

DEALING WITH MISCONCEPTIONS

Everyone is fascinated with the pawn shop — even those like myself who have heard only the very worst nightmare stories and who never stepped foot inside a pawn shop door. Still, they can't help but wonder about what pawn shops *really* are, if they are really as bad as they are made out to be.

It is an enlightened soul who braves his way for the first time into the dark confines of the 'den of thieves'. The enlightenment is, nothing terrible happens!

I love it when a first time visitor enters our stores. I can spot them as soon as they walk in; after all, I was one of them. The body language shrieks from the hilltops — arms folded protectively across the chest, eyebrows knitted tightly together. They glance in every direction but mine.

Warily, they stand away from the showcases, maintaining their demeanor as they peer from a distance at the gold and diamond displays as if they were scrutinizing a cage full of rattlesnakes. Sometimes a piece catches their eye and they lean a fraction closer, arms still folded, eyebrows knitted, never budging an inch from where they planted their feet.

They are leery. After all, it could be stolen merchandise and they don't want to give the false impression that they would be interested in making a purchase.

Usually, their eyes fall on something interesting and they begin to loosen up a little, making some comment or other about the item to their partner. They always come in *with* somebody. That's so they have a witness there to testify that they were in the pawn shop only out of curiosity.

I just let them walk around and get the feel of the place. As they begin to loosen up more, they drop their arms to their sides and take a tentative step closer to the showcases. The eyebrows are firmly knit, still indicating their distaste for the store. That's where I come in. My job is to unknit those eyebrows!

Instead of offering to help them, I make a statement of observation that ranges anywhere from a comment on the weather to some added information about the item that is currently holding their attention. "That camera you are looking at has a zoom lens that comes with it."

Or, sometimes I'll ask them if this is their first time in a pawn shop.

The response is generally that they are only looking.

I just give them a big smile and tell them to take their time as we're not going anywhere. They return my smile when they realize I'm not going to hard sell them.

I've done my job. The eyebrows unfurl.

Soon their curiosity peaks and they feel more comfortable. Sometimes they will ask me how I know this stuff isn't stolen. Or they ask about what kind of people pawn their things. They even ask about how we tell diamonds from glass. I answer all of their questions honestly and with a friendly and open attitude. I invite their questions and they have a number of them.

My game isn't won by getting these people to buy something. It is won when they respond positively to what I can teach them about pawn shops. When they realize that pawnbrokers are honest people who are making a positive contribution to the community, we have won ourselves much more than a valuable customer. We have created one more informed individual who will openly share what he learned about the pawn industry with his friends and neighbors. I know this to be a fact because there have been countless people coming into our store for the first time telling us that they were sent to us by a friend who was impressed with us during their first visit.

No pawnbroker tires of hearing comments like: *This is really neat. Now I know where I can come to get a little extra money when we're running short. You have some great deals in here. I'm going to remember this place for my wife's birthday present.*

By the time they leave, I have made a new friend and hopefully, they will become another one of my good customers.

Pawnbrokers have had a notoriously poor image. They have suffered more unfair bias than any other profession. A popular misconception is verbalized in an old saying, "The word *pawnbroker* comes right before the word *prostitute* in the dictionary," – what a sad and misdirected commentary when the fact is, the pawnbroker should be held in high social esteem.

We may take the worst rap but we are not alone in our grouping with the bad guys. Since the Rodney King incident, cops are back at the top of the hit parade list and that list includes those who are sincerely good people.

Fine statesmen are maligned because of the few philandering politicians and those who cater to special interest groups instead of to their constituents. They trade votes for perks and large cash donations.

Let's not forget the decent barristers who must share reputations with those few lawyers who are winning ungodly settlements for clients who perjure themselves in the courts.

Good physicians suffer unearned stigma along with the exorbitant malpractice insurance premiums because others bilk the same companies by lying for their uninjured patients so they can collect undeserved settlements, or the doctors who steal from our own government by ordering unnecessary tests for their MediCal patients.

Insurance companies are ripping off the consumers with higher premiums and less coverage. Consumers are cheating on their taxes and Charles Keating gave everyone a bath!

The truth is, there are many wonderful and unbiased people who work in police departments all over our nation.

Many politicians really are humanitarians who want the best for their nation.

There are lawyers who donate thousands of free hours of their time to causes that they believe in and there are people who have been truly hurt through negligence on the part of another and they deserve to win a lawsuit.

Doctors often go into poverty stricken areas and give of themselves to help those who have no other means of medical care.

There are some insurance companies whose CEOs truly care about their image and not all bankers are into their profession for what they can steal.

It isn't difficult to gain a bad reputation and it takes a very long time to prove the general population wrong.

That is why *pawnbrokers, nationwide, are working together to make important image changes.* Not everyone cooperates and it takes some effort to convince old-timers that the new ways are better, but slowly they are coming to see that with a slight change of attitude and the acceptance of new ideas, they are opening up an opportunity for themselves to grow, both in self-respect and in financial earnings through developing better customer relations.

Consumer confidence increases only by getting out there and giving more freely of ourselves within our own communities. As a collateral lender, you have the responsibility to step forward in your community and show that you are proud of what you do. This is the best way to earn the respect and friendship of your community.

We must not excuse ourselves for what we do. We have no reason to beg anyone's pardon. What we do is honorable and it is an important and much needed community service.

WOULD I MAKE A GOOD PAWNBROKER?

Obviously, you are interested in the collateral lending business. This training manual is designed to give you the proper information on how to get started and (better yet) how to be as successful as you *want* to be.

I have heard from people who thought they understood the business, leased a store, and opened their doors, only to find out far too late that practically everything they were doing was WRONG!

The problem from the outset was over-confidence in their abilities because they were successful at swap-meeting and garage sales or because they had expertise in one particular field, such as photographic equipment, coin collecting, guns, etc.

There are some real horror stories out there. This manual is designed to help you make *your* story a story of *success.*

EXPERTISE IN ONE, OR MORE FIELDS DOES NOT A PAWNBROKER MAKE!

No one can become an expert in everything, but one can become educated in the overall process of buying and merchandising, no matter what the item.

Some pawnbrokers choose to remain in the field of their particular expertise. This is wonderful. There are many large pawn shops that specialize in musical instruments, sporting goods, cameras, computers, and firearms. But if they really want to be successful (especially in California), they *MUST deal in jewelry* as well. I'm not saying there aren't exceptions, but I haven't come across any of them yet.

If you balk at the idea of learning how to deal in diamonds and gold and your specialty is photographic equipment, musical instruments, guns, or sporting goods, I would suggest you **not** consider lending.

The lion's share of pawns are jewelry. Everybody has a ring or a gold chain to pawn. Top of the line 35mm cameras, IBM 386's, Martin guitars, and high power hunting rifles are just not commonly found in the average man's closet or in his dresser drawer.

Coin shops do a marvelous business when they move into pawning. But if they don't deal in jewelry, they won't be able to function.

Your location is another very large factor. There isn't much use in being an expert in scuba diving equipment if you are in Nebraska. Snow skis might not go over so big in Amarillo, Texas. It really isn't a difficult concept, just a little common sense.

A pawnbroker who specializes in musical instruments might make a huge success of himself if he locates in Hollywood, California or Nashville, Tennessee. But knowing everything in the world about guitars and nothing at all about snow equipment can't do him much good in Vale, Colorado!

Another consideration is metropolitan in contrast to the more suburban communities. While you might do well with a full service pawn shop in the more rural or suburban areas, the high rents that are commanded in the heavily populated metropolitan areas like Manhattan or Los Angeles would preclude the pawnbroker from the ability to deal in larger, more cumbersome merchandise. Many of the metropolitan pawnbrokers deal only in the smaller, more valuable goods such as jewelry and firearms. A pawnbroker can get a lot of jewelry and gun inventory into the same area that would be necessary for one power lawnmower!

Sometimes having an expert education in a particular area can do more harm than good. While the pawnbroker is wrapped up in his specialty, he tends to discount other items that might have even more value attached to them.

For instance, if a pawnbroker is a camera enthusiast, it would not come as a surprise if he turned away an old guitar because he thought the customer was asking a ridiculous price of $200 for it. It could be that our camera expert just let a $5,000 Martin walk right out the door. That's not very smart.

I've seen musical instrument buffs turn up

their noses at gem quality diamonds. If this is anyone's idea of being a pawnbroker, then I would suggest they seek out another area of business and leave the true pawnbrokers to the collateral lending. Otherwise, it hurts everyone.

These people waste their own time and their own money plus they add to the already poor image that haunts the industry, the image that pawnbrokers have been fighting so long and so hard to overcome.

A pawnbroker is a pawnbroker. He or she must be versatile, keep an open mind about values, and develop a keen sense of what items to take and which items should be turned away. What a pawnbroker does is loan dollars for any collateral of value. That's why I prefer to be known as a *collateral loan broker.*

In our stores, it is not unusual to lend on practically everything from cars to oil paintings. How we know how much to lend and how we discern what to take and what to turn away is part of what you will be learning in this training manual.

A good pawnbroker will have at least seventy percent of his pawners pick up their merchandise.

Of those seventy percent, thirty percent will pick up their merchandise within the first month. Another fifty percent will return for their items within ninety days. Fifteen percent will wait past the ninety day period and the remaining five percent will go right to the wire and pick their things up on the last possible day.

* * *

DEPENDING ON YOUR STATE LAWS, THE INTEREST AND/OR STORAGE ON THE LOANS WILL VARY. PLEASE NOTE: THE EXAMPLES SET FORTH IN THIS WRITING ARE APPLICABLE IN THE STATE OF CALIFORNIA ONLY. CHECK WITH YOUR LOCAL LAW ENFORCEMENT OR WITH THE STATE DEPARTMENT OF JUSTICE FOR LAWS APPLYING TO COLLATERAL LENDERS.

Here in *California,* by law a minimum of a twenty-day loan is given. A pawnbroker can give a longer loan, but most stick with the twenty days since the redemption period is so long. The redemption period in California is four months. So there is a twenty-day loan with an added 120 day redemption period. If, after the passage of the initial 20 day loan period and the 120 day redemption period, the customer hasn't returned to redeem his property, a notice of forfeiture is mailed to the customer. If he doesn't respond, his loan is forfeited at midnight on the 131st day.

The laws are always difficult for laymen to interpret and most borrowers get very upset at the idea of a twenty-day loan. So the Collateral Loan and Secondhand Dealers Association got together with the *California* Department of Justice and agreed that the loan broker may call his loan a ninety-day loan at a fixed interest rate with a two and a half percent per month penalty for two additional months. The time period translates the same — twenty days plus four months.

At the end of the time period of 20 days and 4 months, a **30 day window** legally opens for the pawnbroker to mail out a notice to the borrowing customer. This is to notify the borrower that he has 10 more days in which to retrieve his goods or his loan will be forfeited and title will be passed to the pawnbroker. Once title passes, the pawnbroker cannot revert the item back to a pawn. This notice must be sent by a *Certificate of Mailing.*

In California, the 30 DAY WINDOW is crucial to understand because if it lapses without the pawnbroker having mailed the 10 day notice to the borrower, the pawnbroker may *no longer* send a notice. He *cannot* take legal title to the merchandise, he *cannot* sell the merchandise, and he *cannot* collect any more interest on the merchandise. In effect, this means the pawnbroker is *legally obligated to hold the pawned merchandise forever.*

If all the legalities have been followed and the pawned item was forfeited to the pawnbroker, the pawnbroker may no longer treat the item as loan collateral but he must treat it as a sale. *Title has been legally transferred* to the pawnbroker. This means if the original owner of the item returns to redeem it, it must be treated as a *sale.* If there is a monetary exchange and a transfer in possession, then sales tax must be paid on the money collected for the transfer.

This one law alone is a good reason why a new pawnbroker must take the time to educate himself on all the state and local laws that apply to him. Some states are similar to California, other states are not.

Many times when I am dealing with a good customer who has always been fair and not taken advantage of the system, I will agree to sell the item to the customer for what he would have paid had he retrieved the item before title transferred. But the customer must also pay the sales tax. I will also allow the customer to put the item on lay-away if he can't afford to get it right away. If this happens, I usually raise the price about 10 to 20% over the redemption fees because the money is still out and we are no longer collecting interest on the loan.

The regulated interest rates in California are very low. Recognizing this, the State of California agreed to allow pawnbrokers to charge storage on any item over twelve cubic inches. The rate increases with the size of the item. The storage charge is for the full five months. Obviously, this makes the interest return on jewelry quite unattractive. But it is. You will understand these ideas in upcoming chapters.

AGAIN: BE ADVISED THAT YOU MUST OBTAIN THE LAWS WHICH GOVERN YOUR STATE. ALL OF THE STATE LAWS VARY. SOME STATES ARE FAR MORE LENIENT IN THEIR PAWN LEGISLATION AND SOME STATES ARE MORE STRINGENT. THE STATE OF CALIFORNIA IS, BY FAR, ONE OF THE MOST REGULATED IN THE NATION.

The trick to making dollars work best for a pawnbroker is in his ability to convince borrowers that it is to their advantage to borrow the least amount of dollars that it will take to get them by, and to return for their merchandise as soon as possible. As you can see, pawnbroking is a technique. I would even go so far as to say that *collateral loan brokerage is an art!*

Becoming a pawnbroker opens doors of opportunity. The first of which is that it can create an unlimited source of income. That is a desire that everyone can relate to.

A pawn shop can be as exciting as the pawnbroker wants it to be. The atmosphere is whatever the pawnbroker allows it to be. The art of merchandising is unlimited and there is no end to the new ideas once they begin to take hold.

The pawnbroker can choose to run a *mom and pop* operation or he can spread out as far as his finances and his faith in who he selects to work with him will allow.

Chains and franchises are cropping up all over the United States as pawnbrokers discover the limitless boundaries the business of collateral loan brokerages can offer.

In essence, there are virtually *no limitations.* There are collateral loan auctions and warehouse sales. Pawnbrokers are beginning to advertise on television here in Southern California and have been advertising on radio for many years.

In Lawton, Oklahoma, a pawnbroker airs live radio commercials right from his store which entices people to come on down while he is broadcasting in order that they might take advantage of some extra savings on various lines of merchandise.

Television commercials are common in Orlando, Florida. The slogan, "A slow nickel beats a fast dime" is a familiar catch phrase in the Orlando area.

Pawn shops can do well in any setting. Small town stores can be just as productive as pawn shops located in large metropolitan areas.

The business of pawnbroking can be as laid back and inconspicuous as it can be fast paced and action packed. What other kind of business can offer the same kind of versatility, with the fun of wheeling and dealing thrown in for good measure?

As you begin your journey through the pages of this book, I must remind you to consider that it is my intent to educate the reader in the very basics of pawnbroking. There is no possibility of making an expert pawnbroker out of the reader. Only time and hands-on experience can do the real teaching.

What can be gained from this reading is a broad overview of the business. The person who follows the instructions set herein can be assured that the possibility of attaining at least a reasonable amount of success will not only be possible but, quite likely, very probable.

The camera expert will no doubt scoff at the advice set forth in the camera chapter. But, at the same time, the expert must agree that if the layman follows the guidelines set forth, he will be less likely to make a crucial mistake that could cost him hundreds, even thousands of dollars.

Every piece of information is extremely conservative in every chapter. This is for the protection of the first-time pawnbroker.

As one gets to know the local market and attains a relative amount of experience, confidence grows and the new pawnbroker will slowly depart from the advice incorporated here. Why limit a loan on an item that you know you can turn over quickly?

This book is a safety net for the person who is not willing to risk the dollars in a higher loan market at first. It is a method of 'testing the waters' without getting burned on deal after deal.

At the end of each chapter, there will be listed one or more sources where additional information can be obtained. If it is not included in this writing, there will be references that will lead you into more detailed information. These references are as valuable as this manual!

Invest the extra dollars in as many catalogs as you can. This will enable you to have every bit of possible information right at your fingertips and will eliminate the stress of 'guessing' a value. The additional references are even more precious than one would imagine.

It took years of pawnbroking before anyone took the time to write a complete reference book on anything.

If you want to lay your hands on a musical instrument buying guide, just go out and try to find one. Do you think your local music store will part with their own valuable information? No! Their information is all they have in order to make money in their store. If the general public knew how and where to find name brand musical instruments at wholesale prices, why would a customer armed with this knowledge be inclined to deal with a retail dealer?

Hence, at the end of the musical instrument chapter, I have listed some sources for additional information. I am not adept in the music field and I find I must rely on pure instinct when certain instruments cross our counter.

Using the method of not investing more dollars than I'm willing to lose, I have grappled about, missing some great deals and not getting too hurt on the bad ones, all the while making a pretty decent living in the process. If I can do it, anyone can!

Today, armed with a reference library that is probably slightly paled only by the National Archives, errors in calculation are fewer and much further between. Be assured that if I don't know it, I will tell you where you can find it! That information alone is worth every possible success that one could imagine. Coupled with my most repetitious piece of advice:

IF YOU ARE NOT SURE ... THE ANSWER IS NO!
and ... WHEN IN DOUBT, SEND IT OUT!

Take this advice more seriously than you've taken any other piece of advice you've ever been given. In fact, this is excellent advice in every area of life. It is the wisdom of the ages and the philosophical foundation on which rests every successful pawn shop I've come across! There is a small addendum to this wisdom:

IF YOU ARE IN DOUBT BUT WILLING TO TAKE A RISK, RISK NO MORE THAN YOU ARE WILLING TO LOSE.

This is the secret to making money. Ask anyone who dabbles in real estate or in the stock market. This is the single tried and true method of allowing the fewest dollars to earn the most dollars for you. It is a way of making money while, at the same time, cutting your losses.

Currently, pawn shops play an important but unacclaimed role in our society as the only institutional credit source for the millions of Americans who are excluded from bank and finance company credit.

The pawn shop is an industry that is headed toward major changes. Large companies are opening interstate chains and pawnbrokers across the nation are working to change the popular image of the industry.

The pawn industry is growing rapidly, especially throughout the Sunbelt and the Central Mountain states.

It won't be very long before the major commercial banks will be taking a second look at the area of the lending industry that they once thought should be left to the little man. Well, those *little men* are making major bucks and large corporations don't like the little guys gleaning too much off of their leavings.

The best kept secret in the lending industry is slowly leaking out and the time is at hand for joining those who are bound for success. Remember those 'if onlys'. If only I'd invested a few hundred dollars in the hula-hoop, I would be a millionaire by now. Well, I didn't. Does that mean there won't be other opportunities?

Even a mammoth organization like McDonald's couldn't resist taking their franchise into towns with populations less than 3,000, creating the atmosphere of small town *folksy* eateries which offer more country type fare for the less refined palate. The yogurt and salad entrees are switched for chicken fried steaks and root beer floats.

It doesn't take an economic genius to understand that if an institution such as McDonald's sees a profit in such a venture, it won't be too much longer before the giant lending institutions notice what is going on in the pawn industry and formulate a method of creating a pawn business of their own.

This information should not be a deterrent to the new pawnbroker. If anything, a wise man might want to *make hay while the sun shines,* allowing this writer the privilege of coining at least one cliche.

Some would have us believe that pawnbroking is a vocation which is less than honorable. I submit to my critics – there are few people in any profession or vocation whose goals are much loftier than the almighty dollar. Pawnbroking is a truly genuine way of offering a much needed service to the larger masses.

Perhaps it isn't as prestigious as glass encased high rises with underground parking and mirror paneled elevators, but I haven't met a pawnbroker yet who doesn't enjoy a tremendous amount of personal satisfaction that is far removed from his annual profits.

No matter who you are or what your personal philosophies happen to be, the joy that is derived by helping people through the arduous times is intrinsic in mankind.

We generally tend to get involved in the process of achieving the great American dream and it isn't difficult to lose sight of the most basic principals. We know these things to be true, but the austere realities seldom touch our hearts much beyond a brief surge of empathy while watching the six o'clock news. Pawnbrokers get a little closer to the problems. They rub elbows with what the rest of society can only know as *statistics.*

There aren't too many vocations where the customers say "thank you" and "God bless you." We hear it all the time. Now *that's* rewarding.

C.D. PLAYERS
SPORTS
CAMERAS

CHAPTER 3

A PAWNBROKER'S PHILOSOPHY
(AN OVERVIEW)

All interest and storage charges quoted in this book are based on the charges that are allowable by the ***California State Financial Code*** *and are presented solely for the purpose of example. These reminders are repetitious and directed toward all readers who are governed by other states.*

Do not skip any reading because the laws do not apply to the state where you reside. *The laws pertaining to California are well worth reading, even if they don't apply in the reader's particular case. If these laws can be read and understood with a reasonable amount of clarity, then the laws governing other states (while even radically different from California) will be more quickly understood.*

Remember what kind of business you are in. The name of the game is **LOANS.** More than a few people try to get into the pawn business without really learning what the business is all about. It may not seem like it at the time, but *fifty dollars lent to Mr. Smith on his diamond ring can turn into the goose that lays the golden eggs.*

Too many pawnbrokers get greedy. They see Mr. Smith's diamond ring as a fifty dollar investment that could be turned for a quick couple of hundred dollars, thereby *killing the goose.* By allowing Mr. Smith every opportunity to redeem his ring, the initial fifty dollar investment can be turned into a constant regenerating profit. Of course, the ring could bring four to five times the fifty dollars but one fact remains. Mr. Smith now has no diamond ring to use as collateral for his loans.

If Mr. Smith becomes a regular pawner, it would be safe to say that the pawnbroker's fifty dollar loan to Mr. Smith could create a tidy little return on his investment.

Most regular pawners return for their merchandise within the framework of thirty days. If Mr. Smith pawned his diamond ring on the average of six times a year, this would create a forty-five dollar annual return for the pawnbroker. Double that figure if Mr. Smith is a 'monthly pawner!'

The state of California allows a minimum of seven dollars and fifty cents interest to be charged on each fifty dollar loan.

California interest rates decrease with higher loan amounts, making the *smaller loans of fifty dollars and under much more attractive than the larger loans over one hundred dollars.* The ceiling is $2,500 after which interest rates can be charged per each agreement. This law will be modified because it does not serve the best interest of the consumer.

A good pawnbroker refrains from making offers. Instead, they ask the customers what they need to borrow. Banks don't offer to loan willy-nilly. The customer must request a certain amount. Discouraging customers from borrowing top dollar better insures early redemption. Last minute pick ups bring the returns down for the pawnbroker.

The psychology here is to provide a service which will keep the pawnbroker's risk at a minimum and it will also reduce the customer's risk of losing his merchandise. The higher the dollar amount lent, the less likely the merchandise will be redeemed. Consequently, don't jump out there with big loans unless you are interested in becoming the proud owner of whatever you are lending on.

This is why, generally, pawnbrokers will ***lend about half the smelting value of gold.*** Most habitual pawners know they can get more for their precious metals if they sell to a precious metals dealer. Many times the customer just wants to sell the gold.

It is our policy to lend and buy for the same amount of money. We try to encourage the loan so that the customer has the option to return to redeem. I promote this by telling them that the gold market fluctuates and they might be wise to borrow on it because they can always get it back. If the market goes up, it will be worth more.

Sometimes customers think the pawnbroker is trying to get the items from them for nothing. Often, the pawnbroker is called upon to explain that he is interested only in lending and not in owning.

Sometimes, when the customer cops an attitude, pawnbrokers tend to *low ball* the loans so as to discourage future business from the troublemaker. If the customer takes the offer, then the pawnbroker feels justified for putting up with the inconvenience of the hassle.

Historically, we have found that when customers tend to drag out their redemptions to the final date, it isn't long before they eventually lose their merchandise to pawn. Sometimes the same merchandise comes in over and over again for several years. When this occurs, the averages say that sooner or later the owner gives up on redeeming and the pawnbroker will ultimately wind up with the item anyway. This is the reason *the pawnbroker should endeavor to loan and not buy, especially on jewelry.* The style might become obsolete, but there is no obsolescence attached to precious metals and stones! It also helps to create the proper image of the pawnbroker. It shows he is not out to legally *steal* the merchandise from the customer. The end results in the pawnbroker making more money on his investment while maintaining his reputation intact.

Even though the rate of pawn on the jewelry return is the poorest,[1] due to not being able to charge storage fees on small items, but[2] there is no real depreciation and[3] many times the value appreciates with the fluctuation of the gold and diamond markets. As of January 1, 1992, pawnbrokers are allowed to charge a $2.00 fee for every ticket written. This offsets the return rate on those items.

Stereos, TVs, etc. are another story. They don't get any newer.

Each time the customer returns with merchandise that can be devalued due to being dated and wear-and-tear, the loans should become smaller.

A brand new video camera complete in the original box with instructions might fetch up to two hundred dollars when the customer first brings it in. Six months later, the equipment has been handled and the loan might drop to only one hundred dollars. By the end of the year, a fifty to seventy-five dollar loan is more than sufficient on any video camera. Remember, the length of time you are required to hold it will render the item even less valuable. The element of time is often more crucial than the element of use.

Some pawnbrokers extend loans by charging a minimum of two and a half percent per month with no maximum loan time. Others will rewrite the loans at the end of the specified loan time (a hundred and twenty days plus a ten day notice in **California**). This is done by requiring the customer to pay all the back interest, a two and a half percent interest charge for every month (usually two months as in **California**) over the ninety days and all the back storage (depending on the size of the item).

CHECK WITH YOUR LOCAL LAW ENFORCEMENT AUTHORITY OR YOUR STATE DEPARTMENT OF JUSTICE FOR THE LAWS THAT GOVERN INTEREST AND/OR STORAGE CHARGES. THE FIGURES QUOTED IN THIS BOOK PERTAIN TO THE STATE OF CALIFORNIA ONLY.

Different states offer many different laws. In some states, thirty day loans are legal. If there are no laws governing pawn shops, the pawn shops are usually called *Buy Back Stores.*

The way a Buy Back Store works is on a thirty day loan basis. *Instead of a pawn ticket, the customer is issued an option to buy a contract.*

The contract states that the customer may purchase his items for a set figure (usually the amount borrowed plus ten percent) within thirty days. Most brokers allow a sixty day grace period after the thirty days so that the original owner may redeem (or Buy Back) the merchandise.

The pawnbroker charges ten percent for each additional month the borrower leaves his items with the pawnbroker. The 'borrower' (in this case the borrower is the seller who retains an option to buy back his goods at a preset price) may 'extend' his option on a monthly basis, ten percent per month until he is able to exercise his option.

The customer may extend his option for as long as he chooses to do so ... or until forever. This is not a bad deal for the pawnbroker because this generates a steady income in exchange for storing the goods.

Buy back stores were outlawed in the State of California several years ago. There are, however, many states that recognize the buy back store as a legitimate business as long as they report all of the merchandise taken in to their local law authorities and follow all of the guidelines of the laws set forth by the state.

Some states require an impression of the pawner's right thumb to be placed on the police copy of the ticket. The State of California adopted this law two years ago. Other states require the pawnbroker take a photograph of all new customers and keep a running file on them.

Jewelry can always be extended or rewritten but beware of extending *dated* items too many times. *As the time passes, the values drop.* Perhaps rewriting a television that was pawned five months ago at fifty dollars would be rewritten for only forty dollars. This can be done by the customer paying off all of the charges plus ten dollars principal on his loan.

Another method of allowing the customer an opportunity to regain the merchandise once it is lost to pawn is by placing it on lay-away for thirty days. This is done by agreeing on a sales price (usually at least all of the original loan plus all late interest and storage) and charging the usual state tax required by law. State sales tax must be charged because legally the title of ownership has transferred from the customer to you. This happens automatically when the pawn expires and the customer does not return for the goods. *Do not put an item back into pawn.* Many pawnbrokers do this as a favor only to find out that they've broken the law. The state must be paid the tax on the item because of the title transfer. Technically, you are no longer *lending,* you are *selling.*

This gives the customer an additional thirty days to retrieve his goods. We incorporate the latter two methods since we are not willing to extend loans indefinitely.

Every state has laws that provide for pawnbrokers. It is my suggestion that pawnbrokers abide by those laws. There are always ways to cheat, but it has been my observation that cheating never pays.

If you are going into this business over the long haul, you have a wonderful opportunity to build on your savings with strongly collateralized lending. It is like a working savings account and it will pay off better than any other investment you could think of. Within five years, it is entirely possible to have saved $100,000 and earn interest on it surpassing that of any other investment. This can be accomplished by conducting your business according to the laws and regulations set forth.

LOANS MADE IS MONEY SAVED!

It is difficult to understand this concept when your dollars are walking out the door by the thousands. Looking at the loans in the light of those loans being *'savings'* creates an entirely different picture of the pawn business.

If a pawnbroker has $20,000 out on loan, he should have (based on new retail prices) $200,000 worth of merchandise in his safe and/or in his warehouse.

Realistically, of course, $200,000 in retail merchandise must translate into only half. This brings the 'used' merchandise value into perspective. The 'secondhand' retail market runs at about half. In this case, $100,000.

For the sake of further argument, we can readjust this figure to allow for a 20% discount sale. The total adjusted secondhand inventory now carries a conservative value of $80,000.

During the first year of business, if a pawnbroker is doing his/her job properly, it is not out of the question for the loans to be approaching the $20,000 mark. In fact, I would have to question the pawnbroker's methods if the $20,000 figure has eluded him for a year! In order to illustrate my point I will use this $20,000 figure.

Using radical conservatism that is unrealistic, by any stretch of the imagination, let's assume that every single customer redeems his merchandise on the very last day possible. This leaves the pawnbroker with zero inventory for his retail sales.

Figuring in the most conservative numbers, the total annual interest rate average will be $17.50 per $100, per five month intervals. This translates to the lowest possible return of $45 per year on every $100 investment.

If $20,000 in total loans translates into two hundred $100 loans, then multiply $45 times 200 for your annual income on interest rates alone. This figures out to $9,000 annually. Where can one find that kind of annual return on a $20,000 investment? These figures are based on interest earned only.

If a **California** pawnbroker is only earning $9,000 on his $20,000 investment, then he isn't pawning anything other than jewelry! Remember, in **California** there is also a storage charge for any item over twelve cubic inches in mass volume.

Let's base the $20,000 on more realistic items. Half of the pawnbroker's loans should be in jewelry. This means that $10,000 is tied up in items other than jewelry. Probably another $5,000 of the total loans are tied up in firearms. There is no storage charge for firearms but there is a gun fee that amounts to $4 per weapon. If the pawnbroker averages fifty rifles and shotguns and another fifty handguns on pawn, a $4 (**California**) fee is added to his charges.

The worst happens and each firearm waits out the full five month loan time. There are two and two-fifths time frames in the year. Multiply $4 by 100 (the number of firearms) and then that figure twice plus two-fifths. The total cost conservative income from pawning firearms (based on a $5,000 investment) calculates to $1,000. Added to the most conservative annual interest brings the total to $10,000.

But that isn't all! We must allow for the balance of the $20,000 ($5,000 of which is tied up in larger items).

Let's say the pawnbroker has 10 console televisions on pawn ($9 storage fee), 10 large tool boxes ($9 storage fee), 3 large stereo systems each with 2′ x 2′ x 4′ speakers ($9 storage fees), 40 VCRs ($3 storage fees), 30 boom boxes ($3 storage fees), 50 guitars ($3 storage fees), 10 microwave ovens ($3 storage fees), and 3 mid-size cars on pawn ($1 per cu. ft. — the average car is about 5′ x 15′ x 4′ = 300 cu. ft.). This comes to a conservative total of $6,487 per annum in storage fees. Keeping three automobiles on pawn at all times creates the lion's share of the storage charges.

Remember, the state of **California** does not fix interest rates on collateral loans over the amount of $2,500 due to the high risk nature of collateral lending. This law is subject to change because there are the few who ruin it for the many by taking unfair advantage of their customers. Some pawnbrokers with a healthy cash flow lend on higher ticket items like luxury cars, boats, fine jewelry and works of art.

Add the annual storage fees of $6,487 to the $10,000 in interest and gun fees and you will see a grand total of $16,487 income on a standing $20,000 investment.

As of January 1, 1992, a charge of $2 per loan was legislated.

The smallest pawn shops write 25 loans per day. Add $6,000 to your $16,487 = $22,487, a pretty tidy annual return for your $20,000.

But wait! We've assumed that every single customer is going to return to redeem their merchandise on the last day at the most conservative interest, fees and storage possible.

Let's take this process one step further and say that of the two thousand people who each have a $100 active loan, one out of every twenty people loses or forgets to return his portion of the pawn contract.

As of January 1, 1992, a $10 non-refundable charge to customers for lost redemption slips has been included in state legislation. Out of 2,000 customers, 100 will forget or lose their tickets. Your income just rose to $23,487.

But we know that around 20 to 25% of the people do not return for their items. Now we must deduct the gross to $17,615. This means we have $5,000 worth of the loans to sell to our inventory stock, leaving $15,000 left in loans.

Remember, we loan ten cents on the new retail dollar. So $5,000 worth of pawned merchandise translates to the *new* retail price of $50,000. It is agreed that a nice, clean, late model item such as a stereo, television, VCR, tools and musical instruments should easily sell for *half of the original retail price* in a pawnshop. This means we have an inventory stock that is valued at $25,000. Figure in the 20% discount off the sale price factor (bartering room) and the bottom line is a minimum of $20,000 worth of good resalable inventory.

So out of an initial $20,000 investment, there is an annual return of $17,615 PLUS $20,000 in retail sales inventory. The $20,000 investment will bring a *most conservative* annual gross return of $47,178!

Don't forget, there is still a $15,000 pawn balance in your warehouse, assuming you don't make another loan. Your total worth in one year will come to $62,178 not counting the new loan charges that will be due on your new loans.

Most conservatively, you are looking at about $70,000 in total assets or a return of $50,000 on your original $20,000 investment in just *one year*! Do I have your interest now?

By investing in your own pawn shop, you have withdrawn $20,000 from your account at the local bank which (at this writing) offers a passbook account interest rate of .03% and a maximum interest rate locked in from 7 to 10 years at .0714%. According to my calculations, it would take over ten years to double your money. That's a long time to wait without access to ready cash. And it is a far cry from what kind of income can be derived from it by investing in your own lending institution. A pawnbroker takes control of his money by investing where he *regulates his own earnings.*

No cash in the bank? Judging from the figures I have laid out before you on these pages, it would seem a wise move to borrow on the equity in your own home. Why not pay 8 to 10, even 12 percent for money that will be offering you such a return? Equity never does any good sitting in a property. The only thing that happens is that we get to pay a nice high capital gains tax when we sell it off. I'd rather use the money I've earned in my equity now and pay interest rather than giving the government 35% of my gains when I sell. My equity is going to work for me – not for Uncle Sam!

It doesn't take a genius to see that you will make your money grow more in just *one year* in the pawn business than by leaving it in your bank collecting the most interest possible in *ten years.*

By investing those dollars in yourself, rather than the large savings and loan institutions (and we all know what great guys *they* turned out to be), *you maintain control of your own destiny. Trust yourself!* You will not be disappointed in your ability to multiply your cash. The best investment anyone can make is in themselves.

By owning a pawn shop, you are saving your cash on a daily basis. How do you save the cash? *Every pawn ticket that is outstanding is CASH IN THE HAND!* You can watch your bank account grow while earning many times the bank interest. You will build a well rounded inventory and earn a substantial living, all the while having fun. It's fun to buy, fun to sell, fun to trade and this makes it fun to go to work each morning. *If it's not fun, don't do it!!* ... especially if what you are doing involves the living you make for yourself and your family.

A true pawnbroker is a 'jack of all trades and a master at none.' If there is one obsession on the part of the pawnbroker it is that of turning the dollars and making them grow.

The ancient rite of 'bartering' must be the life's blood of the pawnbroker. Outside of the occasional curiosity that comes across the pawnbroker's counter, no one item should be of more interest than the other. There is value in everything and it is the wise pawnbroker who understands that concept. Some brokers specialize, and a few of them do quite well. But they are the exception, rather than the rule.

And it goes even further than the dollars. It is a game. The game is not to take something for nothing and sell it for nine prices. The game is to become an important and integrated segment of society, to gain a reputation of honor and trust and to offer an invaluable service to your fellow man – and, on top of all this, earn a remarkably good living while doing so.

Owning a pawn shop satisfies the basic need for buying. Man has an inherent need to *buy* or to accumulate goods, if you will. This is nothing more than human nature. This need exists within everyone to one degree or another. Perhaps it is a throw back to the *hunting and gathering* instincts that drove our ancient relatives. The pawn business is a wonderful way to satisfy this nature without squandering recklessly.

ALL FIGURES QUOTED IN THIS CHAPTER ARE BASED ON CALIFORNIA LAW. CHECK WITH YOUR LOCAL AND STATE LAWS REGARDING LEGISLATION FOR PAWNBROKERS.

LOANS/RENEWALS
E-Z PAWN
Rules For Pawn Loans
I.D.s Accepted
$300 +
LOANS
IN
3 MINUTES

CHAPTER 4

DOLLARS TO START

Obviously, the more ready cash you have available the easier it will be to begin to get closer to the PAWN SHOP operation of your dreams.

But what *are* your dreams? Do you want a metropolitan store that is a full service pawn shop? Or perhaps you are more inclined toward a friendly *mom 'n pop* store that is more suitably located in a more rural area.

Let's assume you want to carve your budget to the bare necessities. The first thing you will want to take into consideration is how much it will cost for you to maintain your usual responsibilities for a maximum time of two years.

If you can figure on carrying yourself for this length of time, you are already off to a good financial start.

The second consideration will be the cost of initial expenses in the business operation, keeping down to the bare essentials, the cost of leasing or purchasing a suitable building in which you intend to house your store. Most leases require a first and last with a deposit.

Utilities usually require deposits so don't forget to figure them into the cost of your initial investment.

Showcases and shelves are expensive and there are many places to find used store fixtures. Check your Yellow Pages under *store fixtures.*

Shelves for warehousing your larger items must be figured in. Lumber can be very expensive. Remember, they don't need to be pretty, just sturdy!

A safe is very important to your business. This is where you will keep all the pawned jewelry and it is wise to *lock up all handguns* when possible. Most gun stores lock all their guns in large walk-in safes.

Pawnshops unable to afford such luxuries utilize drawers located under the counters. They are stored for the night or weekend and padlocked. A burglar can get to them easily, **IF he can FIND them!**

You ***must*** have a *good security system.* If

you are going to splurge in any area, this is the area where the *no holds barred* attitude should apply. Too many first-time pawnbrokers skimp on the security in favor of lavish showcases and custom electrical signs. While very nice to own, these items will do you no good if your store has been cleaned out.

The *fewer* windows and doors in a building, the *more economical* the security system. Consider this when you are looking at buildings.

If there are windows, iron bars should be installed **INSIDE** the windows. Iron barred doors should be installed **INSIDE** *all* entries as well. See the chapter on security systems.

Don't buy into any advertising unless you can really afford it. As a pawnbroker, you will find that your biggest irritation can sometimes be the telephone, especially if you are trying to work a small store alone.

If you have plenty of help to take care of those telephone calls, that is great! But if you are alone in your store and trying to keep track of a dozen or more customers, the telephone is nothing but a distraction. You must list your address and telephone number so people can find you, but a large, expensive Yellow Page ad is unnecessary.

Keep your ad small and well within your budget. You will get plenty of exposure for a lot less money. When people are looking for a collateral lender, they will find you! If you want to emphasize anything, stress your low prices and aim for those sales! You can't make loans if you aren't generating cash!

Computers are a wonderful addition to a pawn shop. They make the work seem like a breeze. But they are unnecessary, also. Look into computers when the workload exceeds the point where you need to hire on additional help. This is where a computerized system will save you money! It is much cheaper to finance a computer and software than it is to pay another clerk!

Sales clerks. Keep your initial sales space down to a minimum so that you don't need too many pairs of eyes. Pawners are usually very patient and they will wait their turn politely.

Cash register. The most inexpensive cash register is your pocket! Keep your larger bills under the counter in a drawer or container. Hide money around in different areas behind the counter. If you get a good deal on a cheap register, go ahead. The best register is an old cigar box when you are just starting out! Don't tie up your money in some computerized monster that was designed for a department store. Those things are out there used and they are a dime a dozen ... and that is too much money to pay for them!

If you feel you need a register, go down to your local Price Club or CostCo., or to any discount warehouse close to you. For a few hundred dollars, you can get a register that figures up the taxes, figures change, and has an extra key or two for a clerk.

The KISS system — the only way to go!

Pricing stickers
Pens and pencils
Pawn tickets
Scratch paper for figuring
Cigar box for the cash

(Pawn tickets can be printed for about ten cents each providing the order is in ten thousand increments. Order early!)

For those of you who still haven't figured it out, the KISS system translates to

Keep It Simple Stupid!

If you are opening a modest pawn shop in a rural area, your initial budget list should look something like this:

1. Lease (First & Last)	$1,500.
2. Deposit On Lease	500.
3. Utilities (Deposits)	300.
4. Showcases (5 Used)	1,000.
5. Loan Counter	300.
6. Storage Shelves	500.
7. Safe (Used Single Door Burglar)	1,500.
8. Security Alarm (Installation)	500.
9. Pawn Tickets (10,000 + 1 X Set Up)	1,250.
10. Iron Bars (1 Window 2 Doors)	800.
11. Office Supplies	100.
12. Miscellaneous (Includes NPA Dues)	400.
TOTAL INITIAL EXPENSES	$8,650.

Using this method, estimated initial monthly overhead will look something like this:

1. Lease	$750.
2. Utilities	100.
3. Alarm fee	25.
4. Miscellaneous	75.
TOTAL MONTHLY EXPENSES	$ 950.
CASH ON HAND TO LOAN	$20,000.

The above figures are realistic within the framework of Southern California's more rural areas. Leases range from about $ .50 to $1.00 per square foot in the average lower middle class community where adequate zoning is available.

If you are considering a store in an urban or metropolitan area, the numbers are going to change drastically. Where one might get by with a base of $20,000 to $50,000 in a more rural area, it would take much more cash to open a full service pawn shop in metropolitan Los Angeles.

There are several pawn shops for sale in Los Angeles right now. Some of the pawnbrokers simply don't want to contend with any more possibilities of another riot. The average Los Angeles pawn shop that has a loan base of $150,000 and an inventory of around $75,000 usually commands $100,000 in good will. It is my understanding right now that some of these pawn shops are listed between the $350,000 and $400,000 range. This, of course, does not include the real estate.

There are many variables in purchasing an up and running pawn shop. One must take into consideration the forfeiture rates, the percentage of jewelry that makes up the loans, the percentage of transient customers as opposed to steady clientele, among other factors.

If you have selected an area that has a population base of 50,000 to 75,000, you should be able to get $20,000 out on the street in about 3 to 6 months. Some pawn shops take a little longer to get off the ground and others leap to the fore almost right away.

The stores that lag in the beginning often do as well, if not eventually better, than the pawn shops that came off like gang busters.

How quickly your money gets out on the street is not an indicator of where your store will be in five years. Many eager new pawnbrokers tend to loan too much money on poorer quality items. This is almost as bad as offering too little on quality merchandise. If it doesn't walk out the door, then you haven't made the interest on the item that you could have made if you'd made a more generous loan!

The idea is to be conservative to a point. At the same time, you must remain competitive. If you don't, you will be sitting on a sack full of cash that isn't earning you a dime.

In seventeen months, our second shop had a total of $100,000 out on loan. As you can see, I am being very conservative on the initial figures. Our newest store had $40,000 loaned inside of ten months.

The bigger the operation, the faster you will get the dollars working for you. Obviously, if you have property available to you and the financial means whereby you can make the loans, there is no limit to the amount of money that can be working for you.

In the state of **California,** any loan over $2,500 can be charged any amount of interest that is agreeable between the pawnbroker and the pawner. On top of the large amounts of interest that can be collected, the pawnbroker may also charge five dollars per day on storage.

Look for the areas incorporated within your state laws which will allow for a few extra dollars to be generated. At the same time, remember to treat your customers **FAIRLY.**

Forcing people to pay rates that are exorbitantly high because they have no alternative will net you a tidy little profit, **ONCE.** You can bet that they will never return to your store again. Not only will they never be back, they will let their friends know what you did and you would probably be very surprised at how much business you really lost in the long run. It just isn't worth it!

The more cash you have on hand to lend out and the less personal cash you need to take out of your store to live on ... the more loans you will generate at a faster pace.

Any investment venture that returns over ten percent per annum on the initial cash investment is considered a good, solid investment. In the state of California, the going rate on a $25 collateral loan is $7 for a five month period. This means that every five months a pawnbroker would make $7 on his initial $25 investment. If that is not enough, he may charge set amounts for storage if the item is one cubic foot or more in bulk. Let's say the pawnbroker is charging $3 to store the item for five months. This brings his return on $25 to $10. (Not bad!)

Let's assume the pawner chooses not to redeem his merchandise. It is safe to assume that the $25 pawned item originally sold for $250.

If the item is in good condition and working properly (is not too old), then it is not out of the question that the pawnbroker could sell that same item for probably half of the new cost and still give the buyer a very good deal. So in this case, the pawnbroker has a $25 investment in an item that he can easily sell for $125. (Pretty good! Department stores could only dream of such a markup). This gives the pawnbroker room to adjust his prices accordingly ... (is the merchandise lacking in some area or is it just a bit too old?) ... (is there a slick customer who wants a discount of 20 percent?) Fine. Price the item to $100. Four hundred percent is not a bad return!

Are you getting the picture now?

You can generate your loan dollars by smart pawning. Of course, the more you loan, the better off you are ... but there is a fine line between trying to get something-for-nothing and over-loaning. This is what this manual is all about. Most of the following chapters are designed for the express purpose to assist the new pawnbroker in determining proper loan values.

Thus far, we have outlined the approximate minimum cash flow that it takes to generate a new *mom 'n pop* store in a rural area.

* * *

My best story about getting started on a 'lick and a promise' comes from my own experience with my *pardner* 'an pal, Judie Calton, who is the most courageous and daring lady I have ever known. It was Jude who sat me down during the Christmas holidays in 1987.

Jude poured a drink for us and motioned for me to come sit beside her by the fireplace. I always love to be in Jude's home. The German half of her loves to putter around in her spicy kitchen, busying herself with holiday preparations. Her Indian (Shoshone) half loves the outdoors and she has found a way to bring the outdoors in, creating a fairyland of scented greenery adorned in white Christmas lights.

Like her Indian grandmother before her, who gathered up straw to weave it deftly into intricate baskets which now grace museums, she can pick up a handful of nothing and turn it into a miracle. Her eye lites on what my eye discounts as trash. When she is finished with the little piece of trash, I envy it! I am one of her greatest admirers.

On that Christmas holiday, we sat cozily by the fire while she turned me topsy-turvy with what she had to say.

"Patrish," she began (she's the only one who calls me 'Patrish'), "I'm tired of the beauty business. I've been at it for twenty-three years. I'm going to sell it."

Sell it!? Jude was going to sell her beautiful little business that she started on a lick and a promise over two decades ago. The business began by accident only because she styled her own hairpieces. Hairpieces were popular with the ladies back then. Her friends admired her talent and brought their own hairpieces for her to wash, color and style.

The ladies insisted she take money for her efforts, so she began by charging $3 apiece for her handiwork. Her little kitchen enterprise took off and soon there was a small, crudely printed sign nailed on the side of her house:

JUDIE'S WIGS
PLEASE USE THE SIDE DOOR – THAT-A-WAY

A carefully drawn red arrow pointed the way to her kitchen door.

When it got to where one couldn't negotiate their way through her kitchen for the drying wigs, she found a little commercial store to lease and the rest was history. Her business was part of *our* history as friends. Heck, it was ALL of our history!

Jude was practically a local legend. Dale Evans didn't want anyone else to do her hairpieces. Jude was the only person who could color Dale's hairpieces that incredible shade of pink! I always suspected the secret recipe for Dale's wig dye was some sort of root and tree bark concoction handed down by Jude's Grandmother Rosie, a Shoshone Indian squaw.

If I was topsy-turvy then, she blew me right out the door with her next statement!

"That's right. That is, if I can. I'm ready to do something else with my life and I know what I want to do, but I can't do it without you."

She had to be kidding! There are only two things I'm particularly good at and I knew that she wasn't talking about writing a book. Her writing efforts are clear and intelligent, but she's no more of a writer than I am a beautician.

She went on with what was now the inevitable. "I want to learn how to be a pawnbroker, and you can teach me. We'll do it together, fifty-fifty. You're not doing anything right now anyway. Later on, if you want, I'll buy your half at a fair price. If you want to stay in, then you stay in. But if you don't want to stay, I'll understand."

If I was shocked, the whole town and all of the surrounding area was horrified.

On July 1, 1988, because it didn't sell and she was feeling impatient, she closed the doors to her thriving little beauty business.

The next day I met Jude at her store. I couldn't believe what I saw. She looked like she'd traveled backwards through metamorphosis. Her spiked high heels were replaced with a pair of Nikes. I didn't think she ever owned a pair of sneakers. (You think you know someone!) Her false eyelashes were gone (along with the rest of her flawless makeup), and a faded bandana covered her head. After all those years, I'd forgotten – she was so short!

The men came in and I choked back reminiscing tears as I watched them dismantle her life and what had been a very significant part of my own. Not Jude. She jumped in there along with them.

Makeup tables turned into gun racks. A large tool bin replaced the designer showcases in the center of the store directly under the high tech chrome track lighting.

I remember when that track lighting was installed. It was put there so her artfully decorated showcases would become even more appealing. The track lighting made all the difference for the displays back then, but it sure didn't do much for the tools.

On August 1st, everything was done. Because she realized no cash from her store, we pooled our few resources and began with a sketchy amount of inventory. One week later we were ready.

We met at our new store that was put together inside of five weeks. From the business license to the last shelf, an old vault, and a whole lot of hope, we did it.

"Well, Patrish," Jude declared, "this is it! We are about to find out if I am cut out to be a pawnbroker."

With that, we opened the front door of Wimpey'$ II.

Two months later the beauty salon next door moved because they didn't want to be located next to a pawn shop and we nabbed that building to double our size. The original store was less than 900 square feet and it was only a few months before we couldn't move around in the back room.

Wimpey'$ II was the oddest little pawn shop I'd ever seen. We stored our pawned handguns in Jude's old wig dryers. In our haste, we even nailed up rough shelving over a beautifully handpainted mural that graced one of the store walls.

Flowery scents of perfume and colognes intermingled with the smell of mechanic's grease that lingered on the tools.

Jude had the only wig shop in the high desert. The local doctors had no alternative but to continue sending their chemo patients to her. Jude couldn't turn them away and I wouldn't expect her to.

Those poor chemo patients sat amid the air compressors and amplifiers peering into the one mirror Jude salvaged in case this should happen. It seemed undignified, but I don't think they really minded at all.

The San Bernardino County Fairgrounds are directly behind the pawn shop. A swap meet is held there every weekend during the summer.

The desert sun was not yet one hour above the horizon and already it was toasting bared shoulders on all the swap meet Saturdays. Jude could be found in the early morning wandering around the tables and booths.

She wore an enormous slouchy bonnet that shielded her entire profile. If one didn't know her bonnet, the only way to recognize the person under it would be to stand facing her, peering down the stovepipe tunnel.

She wore that old bonnet because everyone in town knew her. If she was spotted, she would lose time in her quest for the real bargains. Everyone wanted to waylay her; asking endless questions about the pawn shop.

I made a few of those trips with her, but because I had to drive over seventy miles one way to the store every day, it was difficult to match her early bird hours.

When I was able to get there early, I was never sorry. She was a hoot in that old slouch bonnet. She would find some old wide-brimmed hat to plop on top my head and off we'd go, floppy hats and sunglasses, strolling the swap meet incognito. Like two celebrities fooling the world we joked and giggled. We ate purple and green icies, compared tongues, and altogether forgot we were grown up.

I would wager that we never spent over ten dollars and I was always the one who spent the most. She found treasures for nickels and dimes. A rusty old can she found made a great display for a diamond bracelet. She never cleaned the stuff up. She has a way of displaying merchandise. A fifty-cent item she picked up in a yard sale appeared so desirable that a customer might pay twenty dollars for it and walk off with the prize thinking they got a great deal. They probably did!

Since then, we've both moved on. I miss those times now. But who knows? Maybe we aren't finished. Maybe there are more bargains to share and more icies to enjoy on hot summer mornings. Jude and I are pards an' pals. We always will be.

Wimpey'$ Pawn Shop II, Victorville, CA, the pawn shop that started on a lick and a promise, has since expanded to 3,600 square feet (taking up all four of the individual stores) encompassing the entire building.

SAFETY SENSE

Ways To Help Protect Your Business

"Think security." That's the watchword to help protect any business. Large or small, a safe workplace begins with *you.* Mechanical devices—locks, closed-circuit TV, alarm systems and safes—can function effectively *only* with the cooperation of the people they are helping to protect.

Here are 10 suggestions from ADT Security Systems, the world's leading supplier of electronic security systems, on how you can help create a safer, more efficient business. While some of the tips may not directly pertain to your company, most can be adapted to your needs.

- Use hinge locks, so hinges can't be easily knocked out.
- Limit after-office-hours access to your building to one monitored entrance only.
- If practical, provide an employee identification security system which requires staffers to insert an electronically coded card to enter certain areas.
- Provide a sign-in book for all visitors, specifying time, date and purpose of their visit.
- Use alarms on unprotected perimeter doors.
- If possible, use closed-circuit television systems to monitor entrances and exits.
- If you are using a padlock system, make sure it's made to your specifications, from adequate gauge steel, with multiple tumblers.
- If your office is vacant in the evening, leave some lights on to signal activity.
- Install alarm buttons on desks as well as on the floor, for more discreet use.

- Use equipment serial numbers or a similar system to keep track of valuable equipment.

CHAPTER 5

SECURITY SYSTEMS

The Los Angeles riots took place during this rewriting. This current issue could have been ready much sooner, but I held it back because I wanted to address the topic of security in more detail.

As so many other pawnbrokers, I have also changed my thinking regarding my ideas as to what good security systems really are.

Thanks to those pawnbrokers who experienced the L.A. riots first hand, we now know more than we ever did before. We have learned what possible disasters could loom before us and how we might cope with them in foresight rather than in retrospect, as many of our unfortunate cronies have been forced to do.

I would be hard put to relay the information accurately and with a proper amount of emphasis so that the reader might understand the reasoning behind why he (as a pawnbroker) should concern himself with some seemingly farfetched ideas regarding security systems. I, too, regarded those same ideas as pretty farfetched and neglected to incorporate them within the pages of the past printings.

There were very real horrors that happened here in Los Angeles which fairly boggle the mind when one first hears the telling of them.

What the news media depicted was just a small part of what kinds of terrorizing really went on. Had it not been for the media, most people would be hard put to imagine that so many people could come together in one mind ... in such hatred. And even worse ... the violence, the vandalism, and the looting that took place (not in anger or hatred but) solely for the reason that it was "fun."

Prior to the rioting, I couldn't comprehend the idea that even an animal would commit such atrocities for "kicks"...for the sheer glee of it, and because "everybody else is doing it." A new record for an all time low in human behavioral degradation had to have been set! "My God," I said aloud to the television ... "if everyone on the block was raping your sister, would the idea of standing in line for a turn become an acceptable concept?"

I'm not in the Stephen King business. My goal is to help my readers be successful in their endeavor to undertake the pawn business. It is of no value to me that I should make my readers squirm in uncertainty and make them wonder if they are putting themselves in undue jeopardy by entering into the collateral lending field. I want to encourage my readers. The pawn business is probably one of the most fascinating and interesting businesses a person can undertake.

There is no reason why anyone who honestly wants to cannot be successful in this enterprise. I want to let them know that they *should* go for it ... that they are *not* putting their lives and the lives of their loved ones on the line only for the sake of reaching out for that elusive brass ring.

If there was a way of telling the reader about good security without dwelling on any of the atrocities of the riot, I fear that the information might not seem as valuable. I have found that even when training the most intelligent and conscientious of clerks that a greater percentage of information is assimilated when they are made to understand *why* they are performing each function. When a clerk is told simply to do it and has no understanding of the reasoning behind the job, the percentages drop to an all time low for memory retention.

Hence, it is my intention to shock the reader into seeing the value of the ideas incorporated within this chapter. I can only pray that by relaying *all* of the information my students will reconsider some of the cost-saving corner cutting and carve out a secure and thriving business for themselves because some few precautionary measures were observed.

I want to focus more on the results of positive actions that were taken with foresight, rather than the grisly aftermath of hindsight. I find that I cannot do one effectively without the other. So fasten your seat belts. You are in for a bumpy ride!

(Thank you, Bette D.!)

All of the cost-saving ideas are still incorporated within these pages. But, as my first pawnbroker told me in our interview, "Tell them everything and what applies, applies." Good advice!

There are many unhappy endings from those of us who found out far too late that a penny saved is not necessarily a penny earned!

In the case of our three stores, location turned out to be what saved us. This does not mean that we were so clever in selecting the sites for our stores. It only means that the riots happened to skip over us. There were reports of rioting going on in towns located on all sides of us and we fully expected to be hit. Other than sleeping in our stores with shotguns or just driving by the stores every hour or so, we simply didn't know what we should do ... if there was *anything* we could do at all!

I feel strongly that our Azusa store was nowhere near being prepared for anything more than one to three bungling amateur burglars.

We might have overcome an electrical fire, but never could we have emerged victorious over a fire bomb or any kind of fire caused by an incendiary nature. We were so busy being thrifty and depending on being well located within a block of the Azusa Police Department and a half-mile from the L.A. County Fire Department that we didn't give much more thought to our system than the usual bars inside the windows, a silent security alarm and several double door fire safes.

Of course, nothing is for sure and we still could have lost everything in spite of being secured and armed to the teeth. But the chances would have been dramatically cut to a mere fraction of the possibilities we initially faced. At the point of the riots, save for manning the store with armed guards, we were as vulnerable as a newborn kitten without a mother. Beyond that, we could have been caught up in our own trap and killed in the process.

We made some very important changes and we are still taking very serious notations of our weaknesses. The more we look at our weaknesses, the more we find that our efforts to cut corners have been very foolish. Loss of property and loss of our own lives could have been the disastrous results.

I thought, "Here I am writing books on the subject of pawn shops." I have written endless dialogue and have appeared as a guest on radio talk shows, expounding on the merits of cost-saving security ... I have been negligent in driving home the point that your security is your business. Your security is your future. Your security is your life! I suppose I assumed that the reader would just figure that point out for himself. Well, maybe not. We didn't.

Now I must say, if you find you cannot afford a decent security system that is in keeping with the area in which you are opening your store, skip it and keep your old nine-to-five job. No material goods and no amount of savings is worth your life — not yours or anybody else's.

With that in mind, I will continue to incorporate all of the cost-saving ways to secure your store, but I will no longer allow the dollar savings to become the focal point. As our pawnbroker advised, "Keep all avenues open. Share all of the information and what applies, applies."

I cannot be your eyes and your ears. You could be planning on opening a ten thousand square foot chrome and glass highrise in the heart of South Central L.A., or a 'mom 'n pop shop' in ...(as Tom Cruse put it to Dustin Hoffman in *"Rainman"*) ... Bumblef--k, Nebraska. No disrespect to mid-westerners intended.

My first interview with a pawnbroker who was in the heart of the riot area was very informative. Because of where he is located and the amount of security he needs, he (understandably) asked that he and his store remain anonymous.

His pawn shop is located right in the heart of Korea Town. He saw the riots first hand and this is his recount of it:

* * *

"Our everyday common practices virtually saved our business. There are three things that are most precious in a pawn shop. The first thing is your pawned merchandise. The second most important thing is your pawn records. The retail inventory can take a back seat to the first two things. A good vault saved all of our merchandise.

We specialize in jewelry only. We do not deal in firearms, VCRs, televisions, musical instruments or things of that nature. For this reason, we are able to store all of our pawned and retail merchandise in the vaults. This is our common practice upon closing every single day.

Besides storing our merchandise, we also back up our computer on tape at the end of each week, using alternating tapes each time. I make it a practice to take the back-up tapes home with me. The tapes are *NEVER* kept on the premises at night.

When we saw the mobs coming toward our store, we scurried about picking up all of the jewelry and backing up our computer information.

The only difference was we did it all just a bit faster than usual and we closed the store much earlier than usual. The jewelry was locked in our cement vaults and the tapes went out the door with me.

We got ourselves out of the area as fast as we could. Myself and everyone of our twenty-two employees made it to safety. That was the first and most important thing.

The bars of the pawn shop were lifted up into the air and every single piece of glass was broken. The computers were the first to make it out in the arms of the looters. Every scrap of paper disappeared and what wasn't looted was broken beyond repair. Every single thing that was not inside the vaults was gone or destroyed.

Even with all this, we were up and running as soon as the rioters dispersed and it was safe to reenter the area.

It didn't take any longer than to pick up a new hard-disk drive, some computer keyboards and monitors. The debris was cleared, the new computers were connected and re-fed the vital information that was saved on the back-up tapes. Except for the inconvenience of the workmen laboring around us and several days of lost time, we were up and running effectively, and it was business as usual.

Of course, it took a little more than that to get our store back to where it was. My computer people had to add to and refine our programs and equipment while our security cameras and tape recording equipment all had to be replaced.

If you are located in the thick of an area where incidents like ours might happen to erupt, the best thing you can do is leave. The better part of valor is discretion. This was especially true in our case where an angry mob of 3,000 strong were charging down the streets toward us.

In a riot situation you must try to determine where you are in the riot area. If you are in the middle of it, do what we did before you become too entrenched in it.

If you start shooting at people and then realize it is a lost cause, you are going to have to escape through those throngs of people that you were previously shooting at.

I don't know how gracious they will be about allowing you to retreat. In our particular instance, we did not even try to attempt to protect the location because they were coming at us by the thousands. It was like a wave of people.

No matter where you are, there comes a certain point where you must make a decision. Do you want to be shooting into a number of people trying to scare away the masses?

If you are in the outskirts where you have the smaller numbers of roving gangs and opportunists who are looking for the easy target, then, by all means, stay and defend yourself ... I would suggest, however, that you get a repeating rifle or a multiple shotgun and not a revolver — something that looks ominous — a 16 gauge pump shotgun, an M-16 or something along that line so that it not only sounds ominous but looks ominous as well.

I would also suggest that you don't stay by yourself. Get four or five friends because the more resistance it looks like you have going for you, the more successful you are going to be.

There were three Korean jewelers about a mile from my store who decided to protect their location. The problem was that they were going up against the Crips. They lost and two of them were shot execution style and the third one was forced to open up the safe. They lost 3 million dollars in jewelry.

Had they left, all that would have happened was that the store would have been turned upside down and pretty much demolished like our store was. Maybe they would have even been set on fire. It's better than what happened and the vault would have had a protection factor against the fire. Instead of losing some, they lost it all, including two lives. They had a TRTL30-6 vault and the rioters would have never been able to get it open anyway.

It was interesting coming down here in the aftermath. Originally, there were a number of vaults that were out on the sidewalks and a number of vaults that were in residential areas. The mobs had pulled them with tow trucks (they actually hooked the safes up to the tow trucks and yanked them right out of the stores) and brought them down the streets. They dropped them a few times on the concrete in an attempt to get them open. They were immediately successful with the fire safes, but they were not successful at all in opening up the TR30-6's.

All of the double door safes without exception ... all of the fire safes that I have heard of in pawn shops and in jewelry stores were opened up successfully. These guys all had enough time to pry them open, to yank off the doors ... they had cutting torches. Unless you have a TR30-6, I think you're just foolish and you are exposing yourself to dangers that are really not necessary. So going out and buying a good safe is your best bet ... and do it ahead of time.

The shops that had the ram bars which are the bars in front of the stores that go three feet down into the ground and stop cars and things like that ... well, that's okay for cars and for everyday occurrences, that's very, very good.

What the gangs were doing was stealing the tractor trailer trucks and filling the trailers full of merchandise. They were parking these trailers on the side streets and taking the Peterbilt tractors and ramming them through concrete walls. So even those bars wouldn't stop them.

There was really very little you could do to keep them from getting into your building, and if you made it difficult for them to get into the building, they would just burn it down.

We have cement lined walk-in vaults. Cinderblock vaults are great because they are good for everyday protection of your merchandise. It would take somebody 15 to 20 minutes with the proper tools to break into the cinderblock vaults.

A 15 to 20 minute delay is normally enough to keep a normal burglar from breaking into your safe. And, if your alarm system is properly working, they aren't going to want to stay there any longer than 2 to 3 minutes.

In the case of the riot, however, the mobs had access to our stores for 8 to 10 hours. That was far more than enough time they needed even when the only tools at their disposal were sledgehammers and/or trucks to ram the walls.

As far as fire goes, they didn't torch our building but had they done so, all I can tell you is that it really depends on how hot the fire would have been and how long it would have burned.

There were three banks nearby that were burned. In one of the banks, all of the safe deposit boxes (because they were metal) superheated and all of the merchandise they contained was damaged to one extent or another. The paper money itself was not kept against the walls but kept in a separate metal container. Because of this, most of it was saved.

I didn't see it for myself, but the merchandise that was melted or destroyed, I would imagine, was made up of watches and coins and things like that. Most of the gold pieces were maybe warped or even melted down because the fires burned very hot due to the incendiary nature of the fire bombs. They also burned for a long time.

A vault, basically, is very good insulation. It acts as a buffer for hot and cold. Vaults tend to be very, very cool on a hot day. As the day warms up, so does the vault. Then, when the hottest part of the day subsides and it begins to cool, the vaults tend to get very warm inside. The same principal would apply on a much more radical level in the event of a fire.

If a person really wanted a fire vault and was determined to build it on his own, asbestos is no longer available for use. So another type of insulation would be necessary. Before a project like this is begun, it would be well to remember that fire retardants are good for only a certain amount of time.

I would discourage their use in favor of placing a secondary safe inside of the walk-in vault for the storage of cash and the most valuable and fire vulnerable merchandise.

With a big walk-in vault, I don't think one would experience total destruction. Any type of safe you get should not be a fire safe and if it is possible to place a smaller safe within the walk-in vault, this would provide enhanced protection in the event of burglary and protection indefinitely in the area of insulating against fire.

If one were to purchase a fire vault from a dealer, even the cement insulation in their vaults are cement and good for only three to five years. After that amount of time, they start to break down and disintegrate because the original concept which makes the fire vault resist the heat are the air bubbles which cause it to be very dense and, therefore, very difficult for the heat to pass through.

These air bubbles that are incorporated in the construction of the vault will, in time, tend to work against themselves and begin a process of breaking down into a sandy substance and finally disintegrating into a fine powder substance.

If you were to open up an old fire safe, you would see exactly what I have described. One of the tell-tale signs of an old fire safe, other than the double-door jobs, is that this powder like substance is often visible around the edges of the doors and the hinges. Double door safes are always fire safes ... but don't take a single door safe to be a burglar proof safe. They make plenty of single door fire safes as well.

Somewhere in the third to fifth year this disintegration process begins and this is why these safes are guaranteed by the manufacturers for only three to five years at the most. Then you have to buy a whole brand new one.

One pawnbroker I heard of had his store completely burned to the ground. He had a double-door fire safe which, luckily, happened to be left intact in the middle of the burned out store. When he opened it, he found that everything that was placed against the walls was pretty much melted, damaged, or destroyed. The items which were placed toward the middle of the safe were, basically, pretty safe. Even the fire safes are not 100 percent guaranteed against all damage to the contents.

With or without a fire safe, you should make sure that you don't keep anything of value against the walls or determine that the things you do keep there will be what you are willing to write off as a loss.

A good TR30-6 safe stored inside Class 2 or Class 3 vault should be excellent protection against nearly everything. A Class 2 and Class 3 vault are concrete, reinforced vaults with a U.L.rating which have been tested by U.L. laboratories against things like burn bars which are very sophisticated and carbide drills.

Most burglars and robbers will not have that type of equipment available to them. Every store that had the Class 2 or Class 3 vaults remained intact. All the rioters did was manipulate the dials. They weren't able to get in or breech the vault doors.

There were other cases where they took cutting torches to some of the jewelers' vault doors. They weren't able to get into the main vaults. They did, however, manage to get into the side vaults where some of the incidental merchandise was kept. But when you are talking about 8 to 10 hours ... that's a lot of time and it is a very odd circumstance. Nevertheless, too much security is always preferable to not enough.

Still, it all depends on where you are opening your pawn shop. We had a half million people rioting here in Los Angeles. In Podunk, Iowa, you aren't going to have such a large group of people and the chances of any riot, much less one of the magnitude we experienced are slim to none.

Yet, I wouldn't want to suggest that the aspiring pawnbroker in Podunk, or any other place similar to Podunk, understate the importance of a good security system. Again, let me stress that you can never have too much security. I have always felt you can never be too safe. I would rather give all the options and then say, "What applies, applies."

For instance, in retrospect, we could clearly see some of the things that could have been taken more into consideration prior to selecting a store site.

If you have a liquor store anywhere within 3 doors of your location ... give it up! Don't even try to stay because the gangs that were rioting loved to throw the molitov cocktails into those stores. The alcohol aided in creating a raging inferno in just minutes!

Every liquor store around here took out four to five of the buildings that stood beside it. Once that fire starts and gets going, there is no way the fire department can put it out. So for the guy in Podunk, he might want to take this into consideration when deciding on a location for his store. Perhaps there are no riots to fear, but fires ignite by accident as well.

Another thing to take into consideration, although not as prevalent as liquor stores, are tire stores and dry cleaning establishments. Tires burn very well and those kind of fires are very difficult to extinguish.

The chemicals from dry cleaning establishments also create devastating results. There was a dry cleaners across the street from our store and on Friday, I witnessed the mobs set it on fire. Within five minutes, the building was totally engulfed in flames. It was a total inferno because of all the cleaning solutions that are stored on the premises.

That's why the fire departments want to know about any combustible chemicals that are located on the premises. They do not want to get caught in a situation where they find themselves trapped in a building like that. They wouldn't even try to attempt to fight that fire.

Normally, in locating a pawn shop I would have said that being located next to a liquor store would be ideal because of the check cashing abilities they have plus a steady stream of customers, especially for the various items that they offer other than liquor – candy counters, magazines, newspapers, fast food items, milk, bread, sodas, and in California, the Lottery ticket sales. But in these past few weeks, the results of the rioting caused me to believe that the minuses far outweigh all of the pluses when disaster such as fire results. After what I saw, it's just not worth it.

Now, if I owned commercial property that I was planning to lease out, I wouldn't even allow liquor stores, dry cleaners, or tire stores to occupy my buildings.

Another idea that came by retrospect is that if you are opening a store in a city that is smaller than Los Angeles, it is a good idea to get a permit to install an actual hydrant and a professional fire hose inside the building.

Among the good reasons for having access to an inside fire hose is that if you find yourself in a situation where you are being mobbed, you will probably fair better by taking the hose on top of the building and warding off the mob with strong jet streams of water rather than shooting into the masses with a firearm. I may want to protect my building, but I'm not so ruthless that I would want to indiscriminately shoot into throngs of human beings.

A fire hose would be an effective means for keeping the rioters back at least far enough to prevent them from throwing a molitov cocktail and even if they did, you have the means to put the fire out.

Also, in the event of any fire that is raging three or four doors down from your store, you would be able to keep your roof and the roofs of the adjacent buildings very, very wet so that the flying embers don't set your building or the adjacent buildings on fire. The further you can keep the fire away from you, the better are your chances of saving your property.

One pawnbroker I know who has a very nice store in a more rural area built his own building. Upon obtaining his building permits, he requested a fire hydrant to be placed in front of his store. It was approved and he thought maybe it would be a good idea to place an extension of that hydrant inside his store. He gained immediate approval and now he has fire fighting abilities equal to the fire department inside his store ... plus, he has the mob-fighting capability should he need it because he can take that hose up to his roof and perch up in that position for as long as the water pressure lasts.

Of course, in a riot situation where so much water is being used by the fire departments to extinguish fires, plus all of the broken water mains, pressure could drop drastically. This is why I say that each situation needs to have separate consideration.

It would be a pretty helpless feeling to be standing on a rooftop with an empty water hose in your hand after you just splattered an angry mob all over creation with it!

The problem with getting such a permit for the installation of such things as sprinkler systems and water hydrants is that the City of Los Angeles wants equal $15,000 to $20,000 just for the permits that would allow for any kind of fire fighting equipment of that magnitude.

Unfortunately, the only people who have these systems are the ones who can afford such luxuries ... the owners of the large malls and highrise structures. This $15,000 to $20,000 figure does not include the construction costs of such a project! But I would encourage anyone who is not restricted by such laws to look into the possibility of a fire hydrant that could be located inside of their store."

* * *

I also interviewed Mike deRoulhac, a pawnbroker who owns Film City Jewelry and Loan. Mike's store is located in the Westwood area and although there was plenty of activity in his location, the number of rioters were not nearly so many.

I found Mike's story unique because a large part of what saved his store from looting and burning had to do with the good rapport he'd been so careful to build with his customers. His honesty, patience, and his sense of fair play served him in good stead and certainly in a most unusual manner; a manner that I'm sure he'd never before dreamed.

* * *

"Wednesday night, the first night of the riot, I was at home. I saw it on television like everybody else. I thought we were pretty safe because we were quite a ways from all the action. Then I heard over the news that Westwood was being looted. I thought, "If they can get to Westwood, they can get to my place!"

When I went down to my store, I met one employee there and then on the next day, Thursday, customers started calling and my wife came down, too. I wanted her to go home, but she insisted on staying with me.

Out of all the customers who called, there were four whom I specifically trusted so I told them that I would appreciate the help. They stayed for three days. Some of them had their own firearms and some I provided with firearms.

There were a total of ten of us. We stationed two guys on the roof with about 555,000 candle spotlights. There were six of us inside and two were guarding the rear.

Thursday night was very eerie. They were starting to loot quite extensively. Fires were cropping up everywhere and the sky was turning black. All of the people in the neighborhood were gathering on the corners and on rooftops. We were trying to make a decision on what kind of strategy to take. One idea was to just not go out at all but stay inside and turn out all the lights. If they came in, they came in and we'd just let them have it.

Another alternative was to just go out and make a show of force.

We decided on making ourselves visible so about an hour and a half before sunset, we stood out there, ten abreast, with about eight feet between us, armed with shotguns and sidearms. We stayed out there for about an hour or so. The people yelled at us and jeered, but they started dispersing, at least the locals in the area did.

We came back inside when it started getting dark to organize a little more. Then we heard glass breaking and an alarm going off in the camera store across the street. So we went out and we hollered at them and they took off down the street and down about a half a block. When they realized that we weren't going to do anything, they all came back, but this time it was roving bands of cars. They wouldn't leave and I figured if they got started, then the whole neighborhood was going to join in with them and everything was going to go. We fired off about ten or twelve warning shots over their heads with our shotguns and they left!

Thursday night, all night long, there were no police. We were standing out there and we were heavily armed. The police would race by in their squad cars with their sirens and their lights going and as they passed by us, they gave us the 'thumbs up' sign. That was all we were going to see of them for a long time.

After they left, the looters started pulling up in front of our place and all the lights were out. They'd come up two and three cars at a time and got out with bars and crowbars and things like that.

Then our guys up on the roof (with whom we were in constant communication) would turn on those big floodlights and all the looters could see was six shotguns pointed at them. They jumped into their cars and took off!

This went on until about four in the morning. Then I got a call from one of my guys on the roof who told me that someone was out there on the street beating up a woman.

I went outside to see what was going on. I had my shotgun slung over my shoulder with a Baretta sidearm. I was doing this kind of thing all night long ... checking out the situation. I could see the girl and she was coming down the street toward me. She was staggering, almost like she was drunk or something. There were two guys following along about forty feet behind her.

I hollered up to one of my men on the roof and asked if that was her and he confirmed it. I could see these two guys. One was Hispanic and one was black.

Just then I saw four unmarked police cars coming down the street. I figured I'd flag them down and let them take care of it. So I began waving my arms and they tore head in straight at me. They all jumped out, about twelve or fourteen of them, and they pointed all of their weapons at me! I dropped my guns and I felt like asking them where the hell they'd been ... I'd been here all night! But I thought better of it. I didn't want to antagonize them.

One cop picked up my shotgun and said that

he didn't think it was legal. He compared his riot gun to mine and my shotgun started to look incredibly short next to his! Then he compared them to the base and mine turned out to be a little bigger than his was.

Finally, I was able to tell him about the situation regarding the girl and the guys who were after her.

The cop said that the next time I had to flag them down not to come out armed. I told him that I was out there earlier and the cops were driving by giving me the thumbs up sign!

He placed my weapons against the gate and told me not to pick them up until they had left.

"What about the girl?" I asked.

He shrugged his shoulders and replied, "We gotta go to a fire."

We never knew what became of the girl.

Then about five in the morning there were a few looters circling the block. We got a call from the guys on the roof and we were just about to get ready for another seige. The looters parked their cars on the side street and got out and headed for our store.

They got up to the door and were about to force the gate when we were going to turn on the lights. Suddenly, some police cars came racing up. They jumped out and they all leveled their guns into the store. Well, we were all in here! So we flipped the lights on and we were waving our arms like crazy!

If the timing was off just a second or two, we would have flicked the lights on and would have been aiming back at the police!

It was such a strange feeling to see the armored personnel carriers and humvies with machine guns mounted on top. It didn't seem like we were still in America.

One awesome sight was a caravan of fire engines from every city and county in the state, practically. There were all different colors going by and it was difficult to tell how many of them passed through, but it took quite awhile for them to go by.

The next day the police department began to make a show of force and I think we counted fifteen or sixteen squad cars tearing past with their sirens going.

I think the reason so many of my customers came to the fore was that we just have good customer relations. There are any number of my customers whom I wouldn't hesitate to call on ... and vice-versa.

I've only been here two and a half years. I purchased his store from another pawnbroker who had very good rapport with his customers. I was lucky in that I could sort of take up where he left off.

The interesting thing about the customers who were here was that they were a real cross section of people. One guy was white who was into heavy metal. Another fellow was oriental. I had a Hispanic and a car salesman. Even after the worst of it when we still didn't know if things were going to flare back up again, people came into the store and told me to call them if I needed them. Every race and every color from all walks of life offered to help in any way they could.

I don't agree with the verdict at all. The media made such an issue of the police refraining from going into the problem areas that a bunch of light bulbs went on and people just figured it was 'free merchandise day!'

From the way things looked to me, between the looters and those who came to the fore to volunteer their time and even their lives ... I saw no evidence of racial distinction!

As far as I can tell, the rioting was made up of opportunists. There were those who saw it as an opportunity to get something for nothing. Then there were the gang bangers who used it as an opportunity to get away with doing what they like to do best ... vandalize and terrorize.

I think the saddest part about the whole thing is that there was a loss of around 10,000 businesses, untold amounts of injuries ... and we had a city government of elected officials and a police department that, for the most part, abandoned us. They pretty much told us that we had to fend for ourselves.

Gates dropped the ball, no doubt about it. In my view, the political officials such as the City Council were afraid to pick it up. I really feel that they were afraid to step in and take action because whatever action they chose might not end up being politically correct.

Here you have the businesses who support the government and pay their salaries, but they went ahead and sacrificed them for votes."

* * *

As you can see, by our pawnbrokers' experience, a good security system is only worth everything you are willing to risk ... and, in many cases, that could be your entire livelihood and maybe your life.

If there is any place to cut the corners, don't do it when it comes to your security. Granted, you certainly won't need a $60,000 Class 3 walk-in vault when you are just starting out. But there are safes that are U.L. TL-30s and hold up to 14 cubic feet that can be purchased brand new for around $3,500. The payment plans on something like this can be as low as $125 per month. It can be written off, just like anything else in your business.

If you are willing to shop around, you might be able to locate such a vault used for as little as $1,000 - $1,500. Or look for something equally as secure but smaller for even less. The smaller versions can be mounted right into the floor.

Many of these burglar-proof safes offer drawers that take two keys to open. This is especially helpful to a businessman who must be away from his store. He can keep the extra cash that might be needed inside the drawer. Two of the most trusted employees are each given a key. This way no *one* employee has free access to the cash or the valuable jewelry.

Without a properly secured store, there is no sense in even thinking of opening a business such as a pawn shop. A pawn shop is like a bank. Without their security system, there would be no bank!

A good security system does not mean you must spend an ungodly amount of money on it. A good security system is a 'common sense' system. Each building you wish to secure must be evaluated with the greatest of care.

The single most important thing to consider is

this: "If I wanted to rob this place, what would I do in order to gain entry?"

Play the devil's advocate until you are sure that every avenue of possible entry has been noted. If you can think of a way to get in, then the potential thief will have thought of it, plus one more way you didn't even consider. You must think like a burglar. What are the most vulnerable areas and what is open, accessible, and worth the risk?

An unbarred building with jewelry and/or guns in view is an open invitation to the common thief. The most elaborate alarm system in the world will not deter a potential thief from the temptation to *smash, grab, and run.* This can happen even when the store is open and doing business. They know that by the time the police are notified and a patrol unit is dispatched, they will have been long gone with their ill-gotten gains.

FIRST RULE: A GOOD VAULT

WHEN YOU CLOSE YOUR STORE, PUT EVERYTHING OF VALUE IN THE VAULTS.

IF YOU CAN'T GET EVERYTHING IN THE VAULTS, THEN HIDE THE ITEMS SOMEWHERE OUT OF SIGHT.

Remember that **TIME** *is the burglar's worst enemy.* The more you make him hunt for the things he's looking for, the better your odds in getting him out of there empty handed.

The whole idea behind a good security system is to slow the burglar down. The longer it takes, the more he will be enticed to move on and look for easier pickings.

Do not leave anything on display that can be seen through your windows when you are closed. Do not tempt the devil! He will take you up on your offer every time and without hestitation.

Iron bars are one of the best barriers around and, although they can be costly, one successful burglary can prove to be much costlier.

The most common *mistake* made with iron bars is to place them outside of the windows and doors. That gives the intruder the entire night to saw through them. All he has to do is stop and hide every time a car passes by.

Set the bars **INSIDE** *where the burglar must trip the alarm by breaking a window BEFORE he begins sawing.*

The further back you can set the bars from the windows and doors, the better. In one of our stores we have the bars set back whenever possible. We use the space between the bars and windows to display large items such as bicycles, large musical instruments, console TVs, etc. If the bars cannot be set back, it is better to have them directly INSIDE the windows.

Many areas will consider the barred windows if the bars can be set back and if the bars blend in so that they do not seem so noticeable. With the bars painted black, it is difficult to see that they are in place.

Many towns have local ordinances against security bars of any kind. They are beginning to come around because they are finding that what is even more unsightly than security bars are boarded up buildings because businesses won't lease buildings that can't be secured.

Security bars on windows and doors are essential! Don't even try to open a pawn shop without them. If they are definitely outlawed where you would like to open, then consider a building that doesn't feature large showcase windows in front. The less windows and doors you have, the less money you are going to spend securing them.

Don't forget to look over your head! Air vents and ducts are a favorite entry for burglars. They can usually go more undetected from the roof than from any window or door.

We had a call at three o'clock one morning that someone had broken into our Azusa store. By the time we got there, the place was surrounded by police officers with guns drawn at the ready.

When they had no luck flushing the character out, they called in the police dog and we gave them the keys to the store. After several dramatic hours, it turned out that the burglar made his escape shortly before the police arrived.

We entered the store and there in our warehouse was a garden hose dangling from the ceiling. We'd overlooked barring the vent.

The potential thief managed to lower himself to the floor but he had the misfortune to put his foot on a console television that we had on pawn. The television had casters and it rolled away, breaking the laser beam alarm.

If the thief had successfully gained entry, it is possible (if he really knew what he was doing) that he could have avoided the alarm laser beams and sprays and done quite a bit of damage.

There were no handguns in the area, but he could have handed up to his accomplice practically every rifle we had in pawn storage.

Needless to say, iron bars were installed over all of the overhead vents as soon as the new day began.

Had we studied the situation a bit more carefully, we would have seen that there was a possibility (no matter how remote) that someone who was up to no good could and would take advantage of a vulnerable spot. I think we considered it but rationalized that the vent was too narrow for a man to crawl through. We didn't even think about a smaller than average man. Now we consider children, dwarfs, women, EVERYONE!

SECOND RULE: IRON SECURITY BARS

SECURE THE INSIDE OF THE
BUILDING WITH
IRON SECURITY BARS!

Another of the latest trends going in the art of breaking and entering is 'tunneling.' Burglars get next to a dark corner of the building and use a sledge hammer to pound through the plaster.

Once the hole is large enough for a person to get easily through, they go in (tripping the spray and/or beam alarms) and grab as much merchandise as they can and make a break for it in a car or on foot.

In order to prevent this kind of entry, keep the color of your building light. Dark colors allow for a good camouflage and the police who are patrolling seldom catch sight of this kind of activity at night.

Security lights that operate on motion detectors and light up the area by movement are another good deterrent. Just don't set them to be so sensitive that they will light up for a passing neighborhood alley cat!

If your building is made of concrete blocks, you shouldn't have to worry about this kind of breaking in. If the building is made of plaster, then it is a good idea to work toward a degree of prevention.

The best deterrent, in cases such as these is ¾" plywood nailed to the walls. The thieves usually break in low, so line the walls from about one foot above the floor line to about four to five feet high.

Line those walls where you keep the most valuable merchandise like guns and guitars. If it is feasible, line the outer walls of the building with the plywood and use cement bolts to hold the plywood in place. Paint the plywood to match the building ... don't forget to use a very light color. Dark colors camouflage thieves.

Even though we are not liable for customer's goods being stolen or destroyed, by means that are beyond our control, it doesn't prevent the unpleasantness of explaining the loss of such merchandise to the customer.

THIRD RULE: BURGLAR ALARMS!

An alarm is essential! The alarm is what limits the intruder's time inside the area and creates enough diversion to where the more time spent in the building enhances the chances of being apprehended.

As with the bars, *the* **MORE** *windows and doors you have to secure, the GREATER THE COST of the system and the* **LESS EFFECTIVE IT WILL BE!!!**

This means, if you have extra doors and windows, you will do much better to remove them permanently, replacing them with a wall.

One of our stores has five doors leading into the building. All but one are permanently sealed with iron bars and padlocks. They can be reopened when necessary but they are never used by normal ingress and egress by the customers or by ourselves. We open and close by the same door the customers use.

Another store has four doors. It was expedient to seal only one door and one window. Bars cover the rest of the windows and doors. The customers use the front door only. The employees use the rear exit to their cars which are parked in the immediate area.

The third store has two doors, one in front and one in the rear. The rear door is lead lined with a double lock and an inside cross bar across the middle.

Sometimes there are many ways around a situation and sometimes you have no alternative but to develop a secondary plan. In any event, consider all the avenues of potential problems and consider alternative solutions until you've arrived at one which makes you feel most at ease.

You can find the perfect location and discover that you are required to keep the property in such a manner that it is not feasible to operate your store in a safe and secure manner. That is the moment when you have to make the decision on whether the location is worth the risk. I can't make that decision for you, but if experience is any judge, location is not a large factor in the ability to run a successful operation. A good location is desirable, of course, but not at the expense of great loss to your property and most certainly, not to your peace of mind.

Pawnbrokers generally keep their pawned, outright buys, and lay-away jewelry in vaults or safes. Many of them purchase additional safes if they don't have a walk-in vault that will accommodate the handguns as well. Handguns are becoming the most popular target (over jewelry) for burglaries and thefts.

Many pawnbrokers are beginning to keep their pawned jewelry in safe deposit boxes at their local banks. This is the only sure-fire method of safeguarding your pawner's merchandise. It is inexpensive as well. But as you can well imagine, it is very time consuming.

Bank vault storage will probably become quite popular here in Southern California since our experience in April-May of 1992. Several pawn shops were cleaned out in South Central L.A.

The method by which they work this kind of storage is to ask the pawner to call the store 24 hours in advance to notify the pawnbroker of his intention to pick up his goods. Many pawnbrokers keep a dedicated telephone line operating for this purpose. The line is manned by a telephone answering machine that announces the pawn shop and asks the customer to leave his name and the pawn ticket number on the message recorder.

The pawnbroker then picks up the messages before he leaves for work the next morning. On his way in, he stops by the bank and selects all of the envelopes that will be picked up that day. If the customer doesn't pick up the item, the pawnbroker holds the items for an additional week and then returns the unredeemed items to the bank.

Many pawnbrokers don't like this method because of the additional time it takes to deposit and redeem the jewelry at the bank.

Another trick of the trade is for the pawnbroker to keep the jewelry in the store safe but to remove all of the drawers and relocate them somewhere else in the back of the store out of sight of the customers. The safe is then relocked and armed.

The first thing a thief will ask the pawnbroker to do in a holdup is to open the safe. The pawnbroker's reaction should be one of compliance, but first he should warn the thief that the safe is empty but agree to open it anyway. As soon as the door swings open, the silent alarm should go off and alert the monitoring company that a holdup is in progress.

DO NOT ARM THE SAFE IN A WAY WHICH SETS OFF WARNING SIRENS. KEEP ANY AND ALL HOLD-UP ALARMS SILENT!

The thief was warned that the vault was empty. You haven't tricked him and your chances of a violent reaction might narrow considerably. The guy is very nervous to begin with. He won't take well to any surprises. Keep as calm as possible. Remember, NO surprises. Be honest and tell him ahead of time what he will find or not find in the vault. If your vault is wired for loud warning devices, tell him that as well. The only thing you don't tell him about is the silent alarm — not before you open the vault and certainly not after!

You might want to store some of your items that are a little too valuable to place right out on shelves but not so valuable that you need to purchase an extra safe that is an expensive one.

We don't have a huge inventory of handguns, but we don't want them sitting out there on a storage shelf either.

We found an old office safe with perfectly placed shelves and drawers for what we needed. We got a good deal on that safe, too.

It is approximately seven feet tall and six feet wide with a set of double inner doors and a set of double outer doors. We got it for $800. Had we been looking for such a safe, we would have paid over $3,000 ... at least! We made the purchase when we had no need for it and then the need was created.

New safes are not cheap. Although they are new and state of the art, bomb-proof, burglar-proof and every other kind of 'proof,' think about what you will be using them for before you place an extra financial burden on yourself that you might not really need now.

A good 6' x 6', or 6' x 8' double door with a working combination lock is a good beginning.

DO NOT PURCHASE A SAFE THAT IS LOCKED WITH NO COMBINATION!

You could double your outlay in locksmith fees alone! As long as the door is OPEN, it is okay not to have the combination. *Any locksmith can set a new combination on an* ***OPEN*** *safe.*

This brings to mind the story of a pawnbroker friend (John) who went to a business sale.

There was a huge safe there and it had no price tag. John asked the proprietor if the safe was for sale.

The man told him that the safe was locked and they didn't have the combination, but if my friend wanted it, the man was willing to sell the thing for $100 just to get rid of it.

John nodded with a furrowed brow because he was familiar with the trivials of a locked safe and (out of sheer curiosity) looked at it a bit closer.

The man walked away to help other customers. John walked around the monster and wondered just how much it would cost to get the safe opened. The temptation to purchase it was great because had it not been locked, its value would have been twenty times a hundred dollars.

To this day, John doesn't know what made him tug on the door handle, but he did. The door swung open! John pushed it shut and called the man over.

"Sir, I believe I'll take you up on that offer of $100, but there is one thing you should know."

The proprietor asked what it was.

"This safe is open."

John got the safe for $100!!!

Moving a safe can be expensive OR YOU CAN USE YOUR HEAD!

We purchased our handgun safe in another town (about ten miles distant). The safe was immense and we had no other experience in safe hauling ... at least not one that heavy. We called a safe-moving company and they quoted a price of $1,300 (the same price we paid for the safe alone). Well, that was for the birds.

We put our heads together and came up with

the idea of calling a towing service. We asked how much it would be to haul the safe over the ten miles. The towing service said they'd never hauled a safe before but figured it would cost around $100.

We hired them and they moved the safe successfully. We were so happy about saving $1,200 that we gave them another $50 for their trouble. The safe was moved and everybody was happy!

At night, you will want to remove the more precious items of jewelry from your showcases and place them in your good vault.

Our rule-of-thumb is all jewelry with a price tag of $200 or more goes into the vault. Smaller items like wedding bands can be displayed in trays that will easily lift out of the showcase into a less secure safe.

All lay-away handguns go into a smaller safe as well.

Every night you will put your paperwork and files in a safe, too. Many pawnbrokers put their backed up computer disks and tapes into their safes, but it is much wiser to take them home.

When our stores were too small to accommodate an extra safe or before we could afford the additional expense, we would lock up our handguns in drawers that were underneath the gun display counters. They can be secured with padlocks. A thief can break in, but if he doesn't know where to look, he's slowed down considerably.

Another security hint. Many pawn shops fill their cash registers with a certain amount of cash and pile the rest of the cash in the safe during the day. Whenever they need extra cash, they just pull open the vault doors. I don't see this as much of a deterrent against loss during a potential holdup.

We've never felt very secure by this method of storing the extra cash. This is why we count out the money that will go in the register and keep a few hundred dollar bills and several stacks of smaller bills in the safe. ***Amounts over $1,500 are distributed in certain designated areas of the storage rooms, bathrooms, etc.***

Place the cash in an unlikely spot somewhere in your storage area. An old recipe box or a tattered brown paper bag can be tucked away under old rags or in a mock trash can with some assorted papers and cans could conceal a large amount of cash.

This way your cash is readily available if you need it but not in the most likely place, your safe. The robber will get what you have in the register or the safe, but you will be able to salvage a great deal of cash with this method. It's also a great way to be creative! At night, when you close, take the cash and tuck it back inside your armed safe.

We've never been held up, but in the event we are, we will give the robber all of the register money and all monies contained within our safe. I'm relatively sure the culprit won't stick around to find out if there is any other money to be had.

Once again, criminals like to work on a 'hit and run' M.O. and they will never stay longer than is immediately necessary. If the robber is not pacified with the register and the safe money, he is probably a nut case and it would be wise to reconsider the situation and possibly give them all they ask for. We can earn the money again, but we only live once ... that I can vouch for anyway.

Many times, customers will ask us if we are insured. We always tell them NO. Their homeowner's or renter's policies cover the theft of their items. Insurance on their property is their responsibility. If they feel uncomfortable with this, then I do not hesitate to invite them NOT to pawn with us. Remember, until the date the title transfers to the pawnbroker, the item remains the *customer's* chattel property. It remains his responsibility to insure.

Since the riots, I understand that this is going to be put to the test in the court systems.

Shoplifting is common. You cannot prevent it entirely. But as in securing the building, there are things you can do to make shoplifting less appealing in your store.

We tend to suspect the grubby man who is in dire need of a good bath and overlook the pretty young lady and her clean-cut gentleman escort.

Our biggest loss was from the pretty lady and her clean-cut boyfriend. We caught it all on video tape, but we never saw it happen.

It was on Christmas Eve and the store was busy. A pretty young woman came in with two well dressed men. One man came toward the clerks behind the counter, looking as if he were waiting his turn to ask a question. The other man stood with the lady at the jewelry showcases. She put her oversize handbag on the showcase and took a brush out and ran it through her hair several times.

She fussed and fixed and then the man at the clerk's station turned around and they all walked out together.

Upon a closer inspection of the video replay, the girl was masking the man next to her by primping and preening innocently. All the while, she was blocking our view from her partner as he was breaking into the showcase that held three gold men's wristwatches.

When I first began in the pawn business, I allowed myself to become easily intimidated by individuals who thought they could manipulate me into lending them more money than I should on an item, or into giving them the lowest prices on purchase items. I even had several encounters with a few law enforcement officers who tried to use their position to make me feel like I should give them better deals. After giving in the first few times, I became determined to not let this kind of thing happen to me again.

I almost lost my resolve the day a huge, burly biker came in and shoved his face into mine, demanding why I didn't want to give him a loan on an item that I normally wouldn't take in anyway.

I just planted my feet and looked him straight in the eye. I kept my gaze level and unflinching.

"I'm sorry. We just don't take in those items any longer. Perhaps you will do better to go down the street."

He responded with, "I still don't see why you won't take this!"

"Well, there are many reasons but the fact remains we just don't take them in anymore. Please don't take it personally. The same rule applies to everyone. Thanks for coming in."

The first time is always the hardest! Believe me when I say it gets easier with practice.

I am courteous all the while remaining unbending. Since I began standing up to these individuals, I haven't lost a bout yet.

At first, it can be difficult to discern the difference between an attitude and a potential security problem.

An ideal barrier to throw up between yourself and intimidating customers is a step-up behind the counters so that the floor where you are standing is about a foot higher than where the customers will stand.

Michael Korda gives some prime examples in his book *Power.* Mr. Korda relates how attorneys and executives use many little tricks to get the upper hand in business deals. How many times have you gone into an attorney's office only to be offered a seat on a low couch or chair?

The attorney sits behind a barrier, his huge desk, and is perched upon an oversized upholstered throne while the client is seated in a crouched or subservient position. These mind games work! Use them. On the other hand, don't get so over-confident that you are caught off guard. Keep alert.

My brother-in-law instructed my cousin (who was working for him in his pawn shop) to get out on the floor with the customers and watch them. He was sick of losing merchandise to shoplifters. My cousin took her job seriously, trailing every single customer who came into the store. One customer became very annoyed at her. He lashed out, "I'm not going to steal anything!"

She replied, "I know."

Remember when 'Grandma' quoted Proverbs? ... *"An ounce of prevention is worth a pound of cure!"*

PROTECT YOURSELF WITH THESE TIPS

1. Keep your banking irregular. Do not go to the bank at any given time. Keep every move unpredictable. The only predictable thing you do is open and close your store at the designated hours.

2. If you opt to use two-way mirrors, most people don't know that they only work effectively when the lighting is correct. The side of the mirror that your customer sees should have lighting directly overhead. The side from where you will be observing should be lit from below!

3. Hide excess cash in places other than your register and safe.

4. Don't give anyone a reason to linger around your store — no public pay phones, no newspaper stands, no vending machines of any kind. All you are doing is giving a thief a reason to be there.

5. Lock all jewelry showcases, placing keys out of customer's reach.

6. Seal all edges of your showcases with epoxy glue. Shoplifters have perfected the art of prying up a glass showcase top in order to remove small items.

7. If jewelry showcases need glass top replacements, replace them with tempered safety glass.

8. Show only one piece of jewelry at a time. There's an art to lifting small items right before your eyes. Groups of two or more and often only one clever thief can use confusion as their cover. They ask to see several pieces at once. You think you have a buyer when, suddenly they must go. You thank them politely and begin replacing the rings in the showcase. That's when you discover you have one empty ring box!

9. Watch out for groups of people who split up and try to distract all of the employees. You can be sure there is an additional person in the group who is left free to go unnoticed.

10. Pick up jewelry and guns at night and store in locked safe.

11. Display the most expensive jewelry and the jewelry trays in the center and toward the front of the showcases, away from reaching hands.

12. Display largest and least expensive sale items nearer the door and the smaller, more expensive items near you and on wall shelves that are behind the counters.

13. Invite friends and relatives to sit behind the counters when they come in to visit. Encourage them to wait on the customers when the store gets busy. This creates confusion as to how many people actually work in the store.

14. Place all stereo and television equipment that has knobs or removable parts back behind the counters. They take the knobs!

15. Some owners keep a small light on in the back with a TV on or a shortwave tuned in to a station (other than police calls) so that a night prowler might think a security guard is inside the store.

PAWNSHOP
TOOLS GUNS
TVS VCR
CAMERAS
WATCHES & JEWELRY
COME IN!!
THANK YOU FOR NOT SMOKING

CHAPTER 6

PAWN SHOP SETUPS

Setting up a pawn shop can be a confusing job at best. Once done, the process of learning by trial and error begins to unfold. Hopefully, this process does not reach too deeply into your pockets. And more hopefully, we will be able to counteract that problem at the outset by the writings contained in this manual.

Where do we begin? Well, let's look at the primary reasons why you might want your store set up in a particular way.

There is the issue of *organization.* With a mind constantly toward security, design your store in the most convenient and complimentary fashion possible. A less aesthetic pawn shop is preferable if it is organized behind the counter.

I have seen some beautiful pawn shops with the most depressing tangle of trash stacked carelessly behind the counters. A well displayed store can't do you much good when you are fumbling around in desperation while making weak excuses to the police officer who has requested records that you can't find. It makes you look like you are stalling for time in an attempt to hide something. Or it looks like you just don't know what you are doing. I don't know which is worse.

You will find your confidence will remain much higher when you feel like you are organized.

There is the issue of *security* which we covered in the preceding chapter. A definite consideration. We always strive for eye-catching displays but not at the expense of losing stock to shoplifting, burglaries and the unthinkable armed robbery.

We have experienced a few break-in attempts, two slightly successful in that the thieves were able to grab several items and run. We had only one major shoplifting incident that caused us a $5,000 retail loss. We have had no armed robbery attempts and I say that with a thankful heart to God.

I truly believe that part of the reason for this is the manner in which we set up our counter displays, our storage procedures and our timing so that other than opening and closing, no particular time can be attached to anything we do.

Our alarm systems are loaded with all of the

whistles and bells and accounterments that are available. *(Read chapter on 'Security Systems'.)*

The following list of *Do's and Don'ts* might offer more in the way of alerting you to possible problems.

1. Do place all counters in such a fashion that there is not easily accessible route to clerical areas. *(See diagrams on 'Shop Setups'.)*

2. Keep all firearms behind you or in the showcase closest to where you normally work.

3. If you decide to sell ammunition, keep it out of sight.

4. Keep the most expensive pieces of jewelry as close to you as possible.

5. Keep larger, less expensive items toward the door and the smaller and most expensive items closer to you.

6. Set up a test station with eight to ten 110 electrical outlets (ideally 220 as well).

7. The ideal test station features a complete stereo component system with speakers. This is in order that a single component the pawner brings in can be tested.

8. Equip test station with cable TV hookup if reception in your area is bad. Generally, stores have fluorescent lighting which interferes with TV reception. You will want the best pictures possible on the TVs you have for sale.

9. Complete the test station with a television that can allow the VCRs to be tested.

10. Keep test VCR tapes on hand.

11. Ideally, there should be drawers under the showcase that features the handguns for easy storage at night.

12. Place security bars *inside* the store.

13. There should be only one entrance to the store.

14. Build as many storage shelves as possible. Look for old warehouse shelving that might be forgotten by the owner. We have had many instances where we found the owners and they were delighted with the extra cash for items they thought to be useless to themselves.

15. Be sure your storage shelving is sturdy and capable of holding up ample items like televisions, electric guitars, tools, and the heavier items you plan to take in.

16. Guitars can be displayed by wrapping twist-tie vegetable wiring around the tuning keys. Make a loop so that the guitar can be hung on a nail. On the electric guitars that feature tuning keys on only one side, you can hang those directly on the nail by the top key with no twist-ties.

17. Many pawnbrokers store and display rifles by hanging them on a nail by the trigger guard. Many times this is hard on the trigger. We overcame this by building a shelf where they can sit on the butts and the barrel fits into notched grooves that are placed into a 2x4 and nailed across the wall.

18. Post "AS IS" signs and "NO CASH REFUND" signs around the store. Post every law and rule you can. You never know when you will need that sign if you are called to court. If the sign

was posted, it is considered fair warning to customers. Make them big and make them legible. Gun laws should always be posted.

19. The best advertising (other than word of mouth) is the human interest story that the local papers will run for nothing. When you join the National Pawnbroker's Association, they will notify the papers you select and a reporter and a photographer will come to your store to do a story on you. Prepare some good human interest material about yourself and what your goals are. Give the reporter information about the 'new image' of pawnshops. The only person available to educate the public in your area is YOU.

* * *

A well thought out floor plan accomplishes many goals for a pawnbroker. The first advantage is that the pawnbroker has given himself convenient work areas where he is able to keep an eye on the rest of his store while waiting on the customers.

Another good reason for spending some additional time and effort in creating an ideally suited setup is security. When showcases are too close to the walls, this allows the merchandise displayed on the shelves behind them to be accessible.

In addition, *wider aisles behind the counters make for more comfortable working conditions,* especially as additional help is required. Nothing is worse than having to step around other people in a cramped work area. It is far more preferable to give the customer less shopping space than to fight cramped quarters behind the counters all day long.

Well equipped testing stations are a blessing to the pawnbroker. With the proper setups, the pawnbroker doesn't need to fool with trying to figure out which connections go where.

With a complete stereo system (including all the components and speakers), there should never be a problem with testing stereo components or speakers. Adding to this, keep a small portable television (preferably hooked up to cable) and a VCR at the ready for testing televisions and VCR recorders.

Keep plenty of cassette tapes, VCR tapes, CDs and a cross section of batteries on hand. You will lose the tapes, CDs and batteries on a regular basis because they will be inadvertently left inside the equipment that was being tested. We chalk those losses up to part of cost of doing business.

For the first several years in our business, one person would test the equipment and another would write up the loan. This method consisted of the person testing calling out the brands, serial and model numbers across the counters to the person who was writing the loans. This proved to be confusing, especially when the store was busy and the commotion was so great that information required repeating several times. We devised another method for eliminating this confusion and thereby creating more accuracy when writing the tickets.

Each testing station is equipped with a stack of small papers on which is printed:

ITEM ______________________________

BRAND______________________________

SERIAL NO.__________________________

MODEL NAME/NO.____________________

LOAN AMOUNT_______________________

This slip of paper is filled out by the person testing the item. Usually *the pawnbroker determines an amount based on IF the item works.* Once the customer agrees to the amount, the item is tested.

Too much time and energy is wasted if the item is tested before a loan value is agreed upon. If the customer doesn't get what he wants, the testing was done for nothing.

The item is then taken over to the testing area and tested. If the item doesn't work as it is supposed to, it is rejected. If it works to the satisfaction of the person testing it, that person then fills out the rest of the paper and transfers the paper to the clerk who is writing the loan.

Even if the pawnbroker is doing everything, he still leaves the item at the testing table and writes his loan from his own notes on the paper. This system is far more convenient than any other we've devised.

Keep your store clean and equip it with plenty of lighting. Lighting can make or break a sale. No one is going to invest five hundred dollars in a diamond they cannot see!

The cash register will be the central area where the pawnbroker and the clerks will be congregating. For this reason, plenty of room will be needed around it for everyone to function.

The next area that sees the most traffic is the safe where the pawned jewelry is stored. If you choose to keep your jewelry centrally located in a safe during business hours, this area as well should be clear for foot traffic. However, I would like to caution you to opt for relocating it each morning and keep your safe locked during business hours. Jewelry is the most frequently pawned and redeemed pawn item so be aware that there will be more activity around that area than the rest of the storage facility.

Some pawnbrokers don't keep jewelry on the premises but opt for safe deposit boxes at the local bank. In that event, customers are required to call 24 hours in advance of redeeming the merchandise. Each morning the pawnbroker makes a trip to his bank and pulls the items for redemption. At night, he deposits the newly pawned items. This makes for a pattern of activity that I don't really recommend.

Whether you charge for storage or not, *the pawn storeroom is the room that will be making the money for you.* Plan to make the most of every square foot of space, even if it isn't full for awhile. It will be.

If you start off with a proper plan, you will find it pays off in the long run. Don't make your aisles so narrow that you are wrestling the merchandise around, knocking other items off the shelves. By the same token, don't waste your precious space by making your aisles too big.

Select a space where you plan to store your larger items and keep that space open. Don't make it too big. If you do, you will encourage a room full of yard tools. Why not take it if you have the room? Consider this. In California, we could be stuck with sitting on five months worth of space that could be housing 20 VCRs rather than 2 old lawnmowers. I can sell 20 VCRs a lot faster than I can sell one leaky power mower.

The lion's share of your loans will be wrapped up in the jewelry and the jewelry will take up the smallest amount of space in your store. Your next largest inventory will be the guns. Handguns don't take much space and you will find that they will comprise the second largest share of the loans.

VCRs, cameras, televisions, stereos and guitars will make up another major portion of the loans.

Lawnmowers, generators, weedeaters, large tool chests and other bulky items generate the least amount of dollars for your store unless your state allows you (and you have a customer who is willing) to pay an exorbitant amount of storage fees. You will want to limit the area to the number of those items you are willing to take in. And *never* lend money on any item that you feel you can't sell.

Once you run out of the space, you might be forced to turn away an item that you would really like to have in pawn. Being forced to turn away nice TVs or VCRs seems criminal. Those are the items that sell fastest and fast sales are what is needed in order to generate more dollars to loan out again.

You are paying your landlord for every square foot you are using, so it would behoove you to use each of those square feet as wisely as possible. Always keep in mind just what items will generate the most dollars for you and create the space for those items to be stored.

Sloppy storerooms are a sign that the pawnbroker is not utilizing his space to his fullest advantage. Sloppy storerooms also make for items that get lost in the confusion. More than one pawnbroker has had to pay a customer for a lost item (he doesn't have to but he should if he wants to keep a good reputation) only to find the item months later.

Aesthetics. Keep the sales area of your store clean and neat. Used merchandise isn't very desirable if it is dusty and is lost in clutter. Because merchandise is used doesn't mean it should be devalued by stacking it up against windows and strewn all about the place. How you treat your merchandise says a lot about how you value it.

Go into a fancy top drawer jewelry store and note how carefully the jeweler handles the merchandise. They never show a customer a piece without carefully wiping it with a soft cloth before and after they show it. The jeweler is wiping off fingerprints while, at the same time, sending a body language message to the customer that the piece is valuable and warrants very special care. It's an old trick but it works!

The idea here is to sell the merchandise as quickly as possible in order that more dollars are generated for loans. If the merchandise sits out forever, this isn't making any money for the pawnbroker.

Image. Sloppy, dark, dusty pawn shops do nothing to dispel the poor image of pawn shops. Pawnbrokers need to work together to make the public realize that pawn shops are not places to be ashamed of.

There is no more shame in borrowing the equity in a diamond ring than there is in borrowing the equity in real estate. It is up to the new pawnbrokers of today to work extra hard to dispel those false notions.

Some pawnbrokers confuse clean, well organized, well lit pawn shops with the necessity to purchase wall-to-wall carpeting and expensive showcases. Because they don't want to make the kind of investment those things require, they do nothing. The only investments they really need to make are a few extra lighting fixtures, some Pledge, some Windex and a whole lot of elbow grease!

In order to save money in our Escondido store, we compromised and built the showcases ourselves. We needed certain dimensions that would have been too costly to purchase. Our first idea was to build them out of rough wood in keeping with a country motif. As we began our project, we kept coming up with more ideas. The tools could be displayed on a kind of wooden platform surrounded by a decorator corral fence or hitching post. This kept it possible to display tools right next to the jewelry.

While working with the cheap 3" tree planting posts, my partner split a piece lengthwise considering what could be done with it. We held it up against the front of an unfinished showcase and viola! We had a unique display case that took on a centralized theme that we carried throughout the store. The rifle display became a calvary fort that housed the showcases which displayed handguns. We had handpainted signs on rough wood made and set them above each display so that the tool area read, 'Wimpey's Tool Shed' and 'The Armory.' A potted plant here and there and the setting was perfect. We planned on beginning with a nicer store than usual. We filled that store with eight large custom showcases plus all the shelving and extra decor for less than three thousand dollars.

If nothing else, a few potted plants here and there work miracles for the shabbiest of pawn shops. If you have a brown thumb, wholesale warehouses feature inexpensive silk plants that need nothing but a semi-annual dusting!

Dress up your store old west style with a few deer heads, some animal pelts, an old scythe and an Indian blanket or two. It is not necessary to go out and purchase these things. Usually, it isn't long before things of that nature begin to find their way into the pawn shop.

Keep your store clean and interesting. Make it a pleasure to shop in your store by making it unique. Some pawn shops carry old books and baseball cards. If they are displayed right, customers love to spend time in the book section just browsing and spending the time.

Another interesting idea is to find an old mannequin (or if you are handy, make a life-size doll) and dress it in period clothing from the pioneer days. Sit it in a chair by the door so it can greet your customers.

You could make a life-size rag doll into an old cowboy or an Indian. A Mexican taking a siesta in his sombrero and serape makes for a unique display. Wooden Indians are fun, too.

In our Escondido store, my partner has created a jewelry showcase sensation with yards of burlap. Gold and diamonds take on a new meaning in elegance when displayed with a backdrop of the coarse brown material. For an extra effect, she kept some of the burlap lettering in part of the display.

Whatever your ideas, direct them toward creating a welcome atmosphere for the customers. When you do this, you will be surprised at how quickly the word of mouth spreads and you will attract many curiosity seekers who just want to drop in and look around. This is a marvelous way to introduce yourself and your new business to the town. They care about how the pawn shops look ... show them you do, too.

* * *

First and foremost, be sure your inventory is clean. Clean merchandise is more critical than the displaying of it. Too many pawnbrokers don't like to take the time to even clean out a dirty microwave. Then they can't figure out why no one is interested in buying the nasty thing. The price is not always the most desirable motivation for buyers.

Use plenty of Windex and Pledge. Shine the stereos, VCRs, and TVs in order to make them most desirable. Apply a little elbow grease to even the most insignificant items like a Walk-Man, a camera or a small figurine. Clean up the tools you sell. It makes a difference.

Use polishing cloths to clean up the gold jewelry. Steam cleaners are great for blowing out all of the dirt and grime that collects underneath precious stones. Be careful not to blow out the small stones.

Even if you have no extra cash and no decorating skills whatsoever, you can still keep your showcases free of dust and fingerprints even if it is a cut up bed sheet. Keep the material you use in your showcases clean and stain free. I went into a pawn shop in Las Vegas and when I peered into the jewelry display, cockroaches were socializing among the various rings and neck chains. Other roaches were lying around in altered states of cockroach decomposition with their little legs up in the air. It was very effective. I left.

Change your displays around every two or three months so you don't get the reputation of having the same old stuff out for sale. New merchandise can be added to old displays and no one will notice. Change an old display and your customers will swear the items weren't there before. The eye gets trained to the same layout, then it won't pick up that unique piece that has been lurking in the corner for months.

You can even change prices, up or down. With a new display it's rarely noticed. When I become tired of looking at the same item that doesn't sell, I rearrange things and change a color scheme. I then raise the price, say from $19.95 to some odd figure like $27.50 and it never fails to sell. It's not unusual to sell it to the same customer who rejected it many times before. If an old customer happened to notice the price went up, I tell them that I'd since discovered that the value was actually a little higher, but since they saw it at the old price, I'd go ahead and let it go for that. I think I get a bigger kick out of turning a piece of merchandise like that than I do on those four figure sales. It's the challenge.

Take the same old merchandise and change it around and watch the sales pick up once again. It works every single time.

Take pride in your displays. It seems very time consuming to keep resetting your displays, but when you see your sales double after making those changes, the time spent seems well worth the effort.

Another good reason for making the changes is for security reasons. It is best to keep your especially large and costly jewelry pieces shuffled around from time to time. Some shoplifters set their eye on a particular piece. They will usually return several times to case the location, sometimes even loosening the top of a display a little bit each time. If the piece has been moved several times, it will be more difficult for the would-be thief to score.

Send off for velvet ring boxes, velvet thumbs, bracelet and necklace displays and boxes. Ring trays are useful if you don't load them with the expensive things. It's too easy for a thief to grab the tray and run. We use the trays for the lighter weight rings which you will find are more common.

Stock up on some gift boxes in order to offer your customers a nice little box with their purchase. (See the chapter on *'Initial Inventory'* for a list of vendors.)

Price your items for a twenty percent mark down in order to make that particularly difficult sale. Often times, when I think a buyer is about ready to walk, I suggest a twenty percent drop in price if they are willing to pay cash for the item and not utilize the lay-away option. If there was any hestitation before, the twenty percent discount offer usually sways them into deciding to go ahead with the purchase.

Keep mirrors around the jewelry displays. Ladies love to try things on to see how they look.

It's always nice to keep one or two stools near the jewelry displays so the customers can make themselves comfortable while making their selections.

If you allow smoking in your store, well-placed ashtrays on the showcase counters will keep customers browsing while they enjoy their cigarettes.

Keep a jar full of small candies on the counter. Customers always like to find a treat. The candies also help quiet their children while the parents are conducting their business.

Don't be shy about decorating your store for the holidays. Use every holiday to create festive and cheerful new displays that will be interesting to the customers.

Easter is a time when colored candy eggs and plenty of colorful basket filling can be used for jewelry displays. Find a stuffed bunny rabbit and let it peek out from behind the guitars.

Halloween is a fun time to hang cardboard witches and friendly ghosts by light fishing line around the store. In Escondido, we sponsor a Halloween costume contest and we are in charge of the local pumpkin bash. Play a tape of spooky background noises. Most important, have fun! If you aren't having a good time, no one else will.

Don't forget holidays like Independence Day, Veteran's Day, and Memorial Day. Decorate your store with red, white and blue streamers and American flags. Try some helium filled balloons to give to the customer's kids. Use your imagination.

Christmas always finds our stores lit up with Christmas lights and plenty of garlands. Don't forget to add the Star of David. This is the time of year when it is *everybody's* holiday. Even if there is nothing to celebrate for some, it creates a sense of pending joy that is experienced by everyone. Christmas is the time of year when smiles are always a little brighter and tempers less quick to flare.

Christmas music on the stereo always adds a cheerful note for holiday shoppers. Remember, if the large shopping malls are doing it, it is probably working! Stores like May Company, Bullocks, Broadway among others have spent massive fortunes hiring the finest experts in the world just to research what compels the average shopper to spend their money. The research is finished and the results are in. And the data is yours for free! You can copy everything they do. It makes sense that a person will do well to emulate those successful entrepreneurs. Be wise and spend their money instead of yours.

* * *

Be sure your store displays all of the signs that are needed for the customer's information. You cannot enforce a store policy if you don't bother to let your customers know what the policies are.

If you don't want to give cash refunds, display a proper sign that informs the customers of this. State your case in writing. A store policy is worth nothing if it isn't displayed clearly and conspicuously.

Our store policy is all clearly displayed as follows:

- NO CASH REFUNDS
- NO CHECKS
- LAY-AWAY AVAILABLE
- ALL MERCHANDISE SOLD AS IS
- AVOID EXTRA CHARGES, REDEEM LOANS WITHIN 90 DAYS
- YOUR LOAN DEPENDS ON YOUR ATTITUDE
- SHIRTS AND SHOES REQUIRED
- NO CURSING
- PRICES SUBJECT TO CHANGE ACCORDING TO CUSTOMER'S ATTITUDE
- PRICES SUBJECT TO CHANGE ACCORDING TO PAWNBROKER'S ATTITUDE – ACT ACCORDINGLY

Many of our signs are intended for humor, but there is a grain of truth to all of them!

* * *

I would like to interject a word here about customer relations. One of our signs that reads YOUR LOAN DEPENDS UPON YOUR ATTITUDE is true. Customers who come in with sour attitudes seldom return for their merchandise with a much better attitude than the one they originally brought in with them. We are very reluctant to do business with someone who dislikes and distrusts us from the outset. Often times, we find it is best to turn the loan away.

But what needs to be said here is that attitude is a two-way street. Many pawnbrokers don't think they need to worry about their attitude. After all, the store belongs to them and they can do business with whomever they choose. This is the absolute truth.

Bad news travels fast. Pawnbrokers with poor attitudes get poor reputations in a twinkling of an eye. Many pawnbrokers will tell you they don't care, but if they saw the business they actually lose by the negative word-of-mouth advertising, they would soon change their thinking. They, however, don't see the damage they do to themselves so they go on making the same mistakes.

Many of you reading this have heard that the very best advertising a business can have is word-of-mouth advertising. Any of the world's largest public relations firms will attest to this as absolute fact. There again ... another monumental fortune that was spent on hiring legions of experts to research this data. This means that you not only can believe it, you can take it to the bank! Negative word of mouth is the worst thing that can happen to any business. This is free gratis research. Use it. Copy the large corporate structures that spent the money.

I don't mean that a pawnbroker should take any guff from an irritable pawner. There are ways of dealing with this problem.

I tell pawners who cop an attitude that if they want to go ahead and do business in our store, they must act in a polite and mannerly fashion. I tell them that it has been historically true that people who come in and pawn with poor attitudes give us the most trouble when they return for their merchandise. I ask them to present themselves in a more pleasing manner and I make them promise that they will return in a better frame of mind. Otherwise, I will be forced to ask them to take their business elsewhere. Weigh this with all of the politeness you can muster. If you are an honest and fair pawnbroker, they won't want to do business anywhere else. They are there in the first place because they trust you.

When a customer is approached in this manner, they seem to calm down and become more reasonable. Once they know that no one owes them a loan, it becomes clear to them that poor attitudes don't gain them a single thing.

Your store can be everything you've ever dreamed it could be. There is a great joy to be found in helping people to get through the rough times. It's neat to watch customer find special buys that they wouldn't normally have been able to afford. But pawnbrokers who approach their customers with a negative attitude lose out on all of the positive experiences that are available for the taking, not to mention the extra sales that could have been made in place of alienating customers.

If you believe that you can derive joy in giving, then the pawn shop is the business for you!

If you can't enjoy what you are doing, it is better to get out and leave such a business for those who will do it justice and glean the joy from the true meaning of giving.

On a final note, take a deep and personal interest in your store. Pride of ownership is what makes good residential neighborhoods. The same pride of ownership will create more positive feelings toward collateral lenders.

Don't allow your store to deteriorate into a junk shop. This is one of the things that most communities object to. Once the town sees that you are operating a business that is an asset to the community, then you will see less and less resistance toward pawn shops.

* * *

Many pawnbrokers don't care what the community thinks about their store. The more negative the feelings toward his store, the happier he is because he knows there will be more resistance to any more new pawn shops being allowed into the community. This is very wrong thinking. Fear of competition is unworthy of any good businessman.

If competition was a thing to be afraid of, then why is there more than one shoe store in a shopping mall? People won't frequent a mall that offers only one of each kind of store. People like to have plenty to choose from.

All truly successful pawnbrokers love competition. I know of several who wanted competition so badly that when none moved into their neighborhood, they opened up another pawn shop right across the street and became their own competition. And don't be afraid to set your store up directly across the street from a competitor. It will make you and your competition better pawnbrokers!

There's nothing wrong with comparison shopping and, personally, it's the competition that keeps me on my toes!

NC Attorney General
Thornburg

President of NC
Pawnbroker's Association
Stewart Auten

CHAPTER 7

BUREAUCRATS AND HOW TO DEAL WITH THEM

... or, as per Matthew Lesko,
The Care and Feeding of Bureaucrats

One of the biggest headaches in opening any business is obtaining the required licenses and permits. The red tape can seem endless because no *one* person and no *one* institution customarily provides information on all the rules, regulations and guidelines that must be followed by individual businesses. Pawn shops are no exception.

There are many agencies which set up guidelines for different segments of the pawn business. Your job will be to identify these agencies and learn about all of the requirements that are set forth by them. This means that your first job is to identify all of the items that you will be dealing in that come under separate agencies and follow the procedures that they lay out for you.

BUREAUCRATS AND THE LAW

Ignorance is no excuse for breaking the law. This is why your initial step must be ***education.*** You must learn to educate yourself ... because, unless you are acquainted with an unusually cooperative pawnbroker, no pawnbroker in your town (and for that matter, any other) will be willing to part with any worthwhile information. In other words, don't take someone else's word for it ... *go to the source* and find out for yourself.

The *wrong* way to gain your education is from those few pawnbrokers who do share – even if the pawnbroker is your favorite Uncle Harry who would never steer you wrong.

Most of them are from the old school and they are still running their stores in the old ways. Chances are that they were taught by a pawnbroker from the generation prior to theirs. This would be somewhat analogous to learning the techniques of auto repair or brain surgery from a person who had all of their training back in 1952.

The idea of teaching the new pawnbrokers the correct and up-to-date legal methods for running their stores is just now getting off the ground.

The pawnbrokers who are not active members of their state associations are ignorant of new legislation. The only changes in the laws that these old-timers learn of are the changes in the firearm laws. Sometimes the local police departments will impart some information. They don't always know. When they do, they share it only if they *feel* a change is important to them ... like the size of the police reports or which color of the NCR form they want to receive.

The law in California says that the reports are to be submitted to the police department on a *daily* basis. But if the department is backed up on paperwork, they aren't going to make an issue of it ... that is until the Department of Justice comes down on them. Then guess who the fall guy is going to be? And they will hang you from the highest limb when that happens! They certainly aren't going to take the flack for not insisting you turn in your police reports every day.

And don't fool yourself! Just because *Uncle Harry* has been turning in his reports once a week for twenty years and nothing has happened to him ... your luck might not be as good as Uncle Harry's. And, if by chance your luck does run cold, will Uncle Harry bail *you* out of the slammer?

Hopefully, you will be convinced that the smartest thing you can do is to join your state and national associations and take an active interest in the associations. Part of what the state associations do is monitor their members, making sure they are operating within the prescribed laws.

The state associations keep their members posted on all of the seminars regarding legislation, new techniques for more efficient operation, and even for teaching new tricks of the trade ... like gem identification, the best gold smelting prices, new technology in security systems, etc.

If pawnbrokers expect to be viewed as professionals, then they must *act* like professionals and follow up on all of the current information that applies to their trade.

A good example is *medical doctors who are responsible for their own efforts in keeping themselves current* on new discoveries and techniques in the world of medicine.

Not unlike the Pawnbroker's Associations, the function of the American Medical Association is to monitor their members to be sure they are operating under the guidelines of the prescribed laws. They also notify their members of upcoming seminars, on laws, medical procedures, and which learning seminars are available to the members. It is not their function to mandate that the physicians keep themselves current on the things that concern them. But it is their function to concern themselves with violations of the laws.

It is not the responsibility of the American Medical Association, the State Bar Association, the Realtor's Association, nor is it the responsibility of the State and National Pawnbroker's Association to babysit their members. It is their assumption that their members are professionals. Being a professional means that we accept the responsibility to constantly update our education and it means that we will conduct ourselves accordingly.

It is scary to think of what it would be like if our own family physicians conducted themselves in the same manner as many of the pawnbrokers do. "But," you say, "that's not the same thing. Doctors are risking the lives of others."

This is true. But that is assuming that all doctors are humanitarians. Unfortunately, there are those who are out for the almighty dollar. And that has to be okay, too. There is no law against immoral motivations. But if the doctor is negligent of the law (knowing or unknowing), and whatever his motivations (noble or devious), the cost will be his license, his livelihood, all that he has accumulated throughout the years. Beyond all that, it is likely that his personal relationships will falter as well. The loss of family is usually even more devastating than a sentence of several years in jail.

Pawnbrokers can be prosecuted in the same manner for cheating customers (whether he is aware or not and whether his motivations were noble or devious). Often, the unlucky pawnbroker is convicted of charging usurious interest rates when his charges were really far less than the pawnbroker who was working within the law!

A pawnbroker who is writing his loans properly must charge state-mandated interest rates but he is sometimes allowed by law to tack on other charges such as storage, origination fees, gun fees, and inflated late fees.

Consequently, he stands to make much more money on each loan than the pawnbroker who is just charging interest rates that are a little too high.

Not fair? It's the law! The usual sentence is to repay every customer since the inception of his business all of the monies charged over and above the legal interest rate. Sometimes the sentence includes some very serious jail time as well.

The enlightened pawnbroker understands that he and the brain surgeon can share the same destiny as neighbors. It can go either way. There is the option of luxurious living in view homes on Nob Hill or adjoining cells in the state penitentiary. Personally, I prefer Nob Hill!

Your education is *your* responsibility. If you neglect it, it is the bureaucrats who will see to your undoing.

The state associations and the National Pawnbroker's Association cannot make it mandatory for the pawnbrokers to join or to attend the meetings after they've joined. If you think saving yourself a few hundred bucks is worth the risk, all I have to say is, "God bless you, because nobody else will!"

Many old-time pawnbrokers don't like to join the associations because they feel like their private affairs are none of anyone's business.

If a pawnbroker who is a member is found to be infringing on the laws, he will get a call from his association. They are very polite when they call because nine times out of ten, it is only a misunderstanding on the pawnbroker's part regarding certain points of the law.

I had a call myself not long ago from the president of our association. As it turned out, in an effort to help a customer get a small break on storage charges, my clerk wrote in an earlier date other than the contract specified. The customer misunderstood and called another pawnbroker and that pawnbroker directed him to our association (as he rightfully should).

I am grateful to that pawnbroker because I would rather hear from my association than from a cop with an arrest warrant for altering a contract! That other pawnbroker understood that he could not help the customer and that he would be doing a colleague a great disservice by directing the customer to the Department of Justice. The legal entities don't fool around. They arrest now and ask questions later.

It is true that many of the new laws are very restrictive. But pawnbrokers have been freed up in a multitude of areas. Not only are they able to collect additional charges, but they have certain rights regarding the confiscation of pawned items that are suspected of being stolen goods.

In California, there was a time not long ago when the police could walk into any pawn shop and inform the pawnbroker he had possession of a suspected stolen item. On the strength of that statement, the officer could remove the item from the store and never have an obligation to contact the pawnbroker regarding the validity of his suspicion.

It was common for an officer to come into the pawn shop with a person who only *claimed* that the merchandise was his. On the basis of that claim alone, the officer would remove the merchandise from the store and hand it to the claimant. No proof. No trial. And, no thief for a suspect. Needless to say, the relationship between the police and the pawnbrokers were on pretty shaky ground. They were calling us fences and we were calling them thieves.

Things were pretty rough in those days! Our California association dues are $350 per year. Before that particular legislation, we lost the equivalent of the annual dues around two to three times every month!

There are a few dishonest cops out there who *still* take advantage of some of the old-timers who refuse to join the associations. That's why it is so important to stay informed. Dishonesty knows no professional distinction!

The California association banned together and hired lobbyists to fight for our rights and now there are strict laws that govern confiscation of pawned merchandise.

What you need to know is inside these pages. If I don't provide the information, I will tell you where to find it.

About one hundred percent of the energy needed to run your new pawn shop will be just about half enough of what you will need in order to get started! So let's move on.

BUREAUCRATS AND POLITICS

Getting down to business, the first thing you need to know is if the community you have selected for the site of your business will tolerate a pawn shop ... or *one more* pawn shop if there are others.

Many towns declare moratoriums on certain businesses if those businesses become too high in density for the population. A good example of those high density businesses was the beginning of the video rental stores. It wasn't long before we were seeing one on nearly every corner. Many towns found that they were forced to place moratoriums on them which meant that the owners could keep the stores they had but no more could be built without variances.

You can request a variance, but it is usually a waste of time. In the first place, a variance is difficult to get. It means that the moratorium is lifted for the new business and then reset into place again. People in existing businesses or people who were turned down for the same request can get very upset when a variance is issued. It tends to become very political.

There are other reasons for moratoriums. Pawn shops are a good example because they are a high priority due to the *mistaken notion* that pawnbrokers are nothing more than legal thieves. We know better and we understand that our image is a poor one. Creating a good image is the goal for our associations. If you don't care about creating a good image, the associations won't want much to do with you.

We have learned that by following all of the rules (even if we don't always agree with them), our image has vastly improved and the state legislatures are kinder to us when it comes to making laws that might restrict us in any manner. It takes years to make our image better. It takes one stupid person to drag us back down to the bottom overnight.

Once a town is soured on pawn shops, attempting to educate them otherwise is a virtual waste of time. Look someplace else and **DON'T FIGHT CITY HALL.** It's not fair but few things seldom are. You are going to lose the battle and even if you win, it won't be without spending needless time, money, and energy. Move on. Don't waste your time.

Finding out whether a pawn shop is allowed in the community is a matter of checking with your local code enforcement officer. They will be able to tell you if pawn shops are allowed and if so, what areas you should consider for location. Zoning ordinances are very strict and pawn shops are usually placed in the same areas as stores that deal in secondhand merchandise.

THE BUREAUCRATIC POLICE

The next step is to check with the local police department. If there are other pawn shops in the town, they will be familiar with the pawning procedures.

If other pawn shops exist, often you will find that the local police have formed a special unit called a *pawn detail.* Ask to speak with an officer from the pawn detail and let him/her know what you plan to do.

Inquire about the specific problems with which they are most confronted. Then ask them to outline several ideas that will enable you to work more efficiently with them. If you look like you will be an asset to them, you will pave a smoother road for yourself in the future.

If a community has no history of pawn businesses,chances are you will probably have to educate the law enforcement officers.

This is what takes place in the local police department when there are no other pawn shops in the community.

Whenever a pawn shop opens in a town, the local police must create another arena within their system. Unless the watch commander or the chief of police has been made familiar with pawn shops sometime in the recent past, the police department is initially unaware of the procedures.

If the local law *is* familiar with pawn shop procedures but there are no other pawn shops in the area, they will resist your efforts to open one because they know all about the extra work it is going to put them through. They are on a budget and spending extra money does **NOT** make them happy.

If they do resist, then it is up to you to use tact and diplomacy. *Do **NOT** make enemies of them.* You will need to be on a good rapport level with the local law enforcement. They can make your job easy or they can make it as tough as they want to make it.

If the local authorities know nothing about how a pawn shop operates, don't come off as a know-it-all by telling them too much until you get your doors open. You'll only make them angry, defensive, and leery of the extra efforts that will be required of them. Answer their questions and let the sleeping dogs continue to doze in the shade.

If there is any resistance at ANY point, even after you open, assure the authorities that you are a member in good standing of the *National Pawnbroker's Association* and also a member of your state organization that represents pawn shops.

Let the police know that you are not only willing but anxious to work with them. Inform them that you do understand the state laws governing pawn shops and that you are seeking their assistance in helping you to learn about all the local city ordinances as well. Tell them that whenever they hear of any legislation that affects you, you would like for them to let you know.

There are even computer programs designed for pawn shops that are connected via modem into the local police departments. This system saves the departments large chunks of time. Rather than feed in every police report you submit into their system, the information is being sent to them the moment you feed it into your computer. All the departments need to do is to feed in the stolen property descriptions and the suspect's description. The pawn shop computer flags the transaction and everything from halting the loan process to summoning the police via silent alarm can be made to happen. I will address these systems in my chapter on *Computerizing Your Pawn Shop.*

It helps to carry in a newsletter or magazine from the NPA or your local organization. Any data you can get your hands on that tells of how pawn shops are not fabled 'Shylocks' of yesteryear is helpful.

What NOT TO DO is to 'bogart' your way in and make it seem like you know more about the laws than they do, even if you think you do.

Once you open your doors, the police are required to comply with the state laws by screening all of the police reports of who you are dealing with and what items you have taken in.

This is about the time they realize that they probably should have discouraged you in the beginning. If they are already processing these reports (IN CALIFORNIA THEY ARE CALLED THE JUS 123 forms), then they will be less likely to frown on another pawn shop.

The only thing the authorities are interested in is keeping law and order and not having to face an irate Mayor and/or City Council because they didn't do their job properly.

Every time you deal with the local law enforcement, you are dealing with your own destiny. It is important to bear this in mind!

Once you have assured the police that you are, indeed, cooperating with the Department of Justice and show them proof of all your paperwork where you made all your applications for your licenses and permits, they will begin to leave you alone ... calling on you less and less with suspicious inquiries. Be patient, be polite. Answer all their questions. Remember, if you are not breaking the law, the law will work FOR you.

It is imperative that you establish yourself with the local law enforcement as a law abiding citizen with the sole intent of earning an honest living.

Anyone who ever got pulled over for a traffic violation and got out of a ticket knows that only a good and humble attitude helped them out of trouble. Wise off to a cop and you can expect anything but good to come of it. They deal with ignorance all day, every day. They can only assume that you are just one more problem to contend with. The fun part is to watch their attitude change when they realize that you are no threat and can even assist them in accomplishing their jobs.

The Collateral Loan and Secondhand Dealers Association of California (C.L.S.D.A.) set up several forms that are not legal but can be incorporated within a pawn shop business as 'company policy' in any state.

The police like *company policy* because bureaucrats always understand policies. They might not know what the policies are for, but they sure know how important it is to follow them!

One of our policies is that *we 'ask,'* NOT REQUIRE, *a seizing police officer to sign a form stating that the property they are confiscating is being removed from our premises without our express consent ... that the officer is taking it upon himself to remove the property and he agrees to make himself answerable to the disbursement and/or disposal of like property.* (See forms at the end of this chapter.)

This form is valuable because it places the burden of the officer's decision to remove items from the premises solely upon the officer. It is merely an acknowledgement of the fact that we do not willfully give up the property and we do not acknowledge the property has been stolen.

This form also protects the pawnbroker in a court of law because the officer agrees (on the form) that the pawnbroker was ignorant of taking in stolen goods.

All precautions of avoiding self-incrimination have been taken. Sometimes, allowing an act to take place can turn out to be incriminating.

Allowing an officer to remove allegedly stolen property is almost an admission, in some courts of law, that you were aware of the property being stolen or illegal in some manner.

It was *this* form that gave me the idea of what to tell people who asked to redeem an item that was pawned by someone other than themselves (especially if the signature on the redemption receipt is questionable). I simply say, "I would be happy to release the merchandise to you if you can find a police officer who will be willing to sign off on the pawn ticket."

Few officers want to take on such a responsibility. I get to be the good guy and I might even get another good customer. The bearer of bad tidings usually doesn't win any popularity contests and the cops are used to being the villains.

Additional forms we use include a customer's release form that clears the pawnbroker of any accidental injuries or deaths involving a firearm that was purchased from the pawnbroker.

All of these forms are pretty much self-explanatory. They, as well, are included at the end of this chapter.

Joining the National Pawnbroker's Association and your State Association (even when you are not yet in the business) presents the picture that you are very interested in running a legal and ethical store. It is important that they know you are a member in good standing.

You should invite them to send one or several representatives to the conventions. Invite them to speak, addressing particular problems the police are confronted with regarding pawn shops.

NITTY GRITTY BUREAUCRATS

Bureaucracy generally consists of thousands of agencies and sub agencies. These agencies are for the express purpose of creating guidelines and policies that govern each aspect of every nature of business. Because you are opening a pawn shop, you must get very specific on exactly what items you plan to deal in.

There are several agencies for firearms, sometimes more, depending on if you choose to carry ammunition or not. There is one for dealing in secondhand items which you will need and then another for dealing in secondhand items that are upholstered. There's one for clothing and there's one for cigarettes if you decide to carry them.

Your responsibility lies in identifying the agencies and sub agencies that set the laws and policies out so you can carefully follow their procedures. Although the bureaucracies are a complicated snarl that must be sorted out inch by inch, ignorance is still no excuse for disobeying the law. Henceforth, it is your job to identify those agencies and take the necessary steps toward meeting all of the requirements and criteria set forth by them.

Let's say there are no laws against pawn shops, no moratoriums are in force, and you have found a location that is suitable for your purpose.

You now have an address and you can apply for your *Business License from City Hall.*

Your next bureaucratic step is to obtain a *State Seller's Permit.* In California, they are commonly referred to as a State Resale License. You *may* not need one if your state charges no sales tax. Be sure to verify this with the state.

In California, there are local agencies that can help you to apply for your resale license number. Look in your local telephone directory under State Agencies.

One of the things the agency will ask of you is how much you think you will generate in monthly sales. **DO NOT** give them the figure of the sales you *hope* to generate. Give them a *low ball* figure. When we open a new store, we stipulate only $1,000 per month. It is possible that we won't even make as many sales as that during the first few months.

State agencies have a way of expecting you to pay taxes on your most optimistic estimate and they inquire if you don't tally up close to your predictions.

You can always take your figures up, but it is very difficult to run them down and expect the State to accept any explanation.

In the state of California, pawn shops must apply for yet another license from another sector of our bureaucracy. This is called a *Secondhand Dealer's License.* Outside of a firearms license, this license is the most crucial and difficult to come by.

The Secondhand Dealer's License allows for the sale of all secondhand merchandise with the exception of clothing and upholstered items, the bureaucratic sub agencies I spoke of earlier.

Many would-be pawnbrokers discount the possibility of dealing in these items but they eventually find that there is a tidy profit to be made in dealing with leather, motorcycle, and bomber jackets. If you choose to deal in the leather jackets, call your State offices and ask them to tell you, or mail to you, a detailed outline on the requirements and regulations concerning clothing and upholstered items.

Applications for the Secondhand Dealer's License can be obtained from the local police department or from the California Department of Justice. If pawn shops already exist in town, the police will have the paperwork for you. If not, you may have to deal directly with the State.

When you receive your application, fill it out and then make an appointment with the police department to be fingerprinted.

Fingerprinting costs around $10 to $20 per set. The application fees can be as low as nothing or as high as the State and local police department want them to be.

We opened 3 stores in Southern California. They were in three different counties and located approximately 100 miles apart from one another.

In our first store we paid nothing for the first ten years. Recently, we paid $32 for 2 sets of fingerprints for the two of us. The stores in the other two counties came to $235 each. Application fees were requested, as well as fingerprints. Don't argue. Just pay.

In all other states there is some form of regulation. If you cannot find the information you seek, call the National Pawnbroker's Association. Their toll free number is 1 (800) 235-5400. They will be happy to forward any information you might need regarding your State laws and where to go for licensing and information. They can also assist you with gun law information.

Most local libraries carry the State Financial Codes. There will be so many volumes that the mind will boggle ... the secret is to find the latest edition, leaf to the very back of the latest book and stapled inside are (usually) the most current State Financial Laws.

The next step is to *file for your DBA.* A DBA is a notice to the public that you are going to be Doing Business As... and whatever the name of your business will be. In order to do this, you must fill out a form at your local newspaper office and it must be publicly posted for a set amount of time (according to your state laws).

Next, you must *open a Business Account* with your local bank (or the bank of your choice).

If you plan on carrying firearms, you must deal with the Federal bureaucracy's sub agency of the Bureau of Alcohol, Tobacco, and Firearms for your gun seller's permit or your gun license. They will issue an application for a gun license. Get it filled out and returned to the proper authorities as soon as possible because you could wind up open but not able to deal in your firearms at all.

We were open for business, but we couldn't deal in guns. We couldn't buy guns, sell guns or loan on guns. We built our gun display and put the guns out that we intended to sell. This helped to spark customer interest even though we couldn't even show the weapons. When our license did arrive, we had built-in customers for them.

If you have any felonies, drug charges or a history of mental problems where a court adjudicated you to be a danger to others at any time, you will probably not be able to obtain the gun license.

I have known of cases where gun dealers put the permits into their wive's names, although I have trouble condoning such methods.

I believe it is better to try and get a person's name legally cleared rather than going about dealing in weaponry in any kind of underhanded manner or what could be construed by a judicial system as anything but completely above board.

The Federal Agency that handles Alcohol, Tobacco and Firearms Control requires you to obtain a gun license. They also require what is known as a 4473 form to be filled out by the customer and the dealer on each firearm that is removed from the premises. THIS APPLIES TO PAWNED GUNS AS WELL AS SOLD GUNS.

This also requires that an up-to-the-moment gun LOG BOOK be kept current at all times. The Federal Agents can (and will) come in to check your records without prior notice.

BUILDING CODE BUREAUCRATS

If you are planning on building your store or on making renovations on a building you are leasing, you will need certain permits.

The mere change of putting up one partition might require permits and subsequent inspections. It turns into a domino effect. Knock the first one over and they all tumble down. Before you begin, be sure that you are ready to pick up every one of them and reset them up in a different, more expensive, and more complicated pattern.

The fire department will inspect your building. The planning department will approve (or disapprove you). Want a neon sign? A painted sign? A canned lit sign? You take what the City tells you to take. It will be the size, shape, and color that they dictate. It sometimes seems hard to believe we are free citizens in a free country when it comes to opening any new business.

City permits are always needed and you must not argue, but follow them without complaint. If you are located on a state highway, you will need additional permits and approval from the state.

Want to lower a curb so that cars can park in the paved lot you lease or own next door? You need a permit. Does your city require certain landscaping or lighting? Again, permits and inspections.

Remember, usually any changes that you make

that would cause the property to be changed and/or improved might trigger a list of other requirements as long as your arm.

It is common to hear about businessmen who simply wanted to partition part of an office for the sake of convenience and were told this kind of improvement cannot be made without upgrading the electrical wiring, renovating the front of his building and repaving his existing parking lot to include lighting, landscaping, automatic sprinkler systems, and hosts of other demands.

This is why you can sometimes see businesses in certain areas needing a serious coat of paint. Paint's cheap, you think? Yes. But if that owner paints his building, he might also be required to lower his roof by ten feet to meet up with stricter earthquake codes!

Lease or purchase your property on a contingency that you will be able to successfully open up your pawn shop. This gives you the right to back out of the deal with a full refund of your deposits if it becomes impossible to open your store.

Arrange it so that your escrow won't close or your lease won't go into force until the day before you open your doors. This gives you time to set your store up for business. This is not an unreasonable request and most leasing companies and landlords will readily comply with those terms. Usually, the new business is given between two weeks and one month to set up. An escrow can be designed in the same manner.

Also, if you are purchasing your building, decide before you make your offer on what things you will want to change and check with code enforcement and planning regarding which items will need permits and what other mandatory improvements will be triggered so you will know if you will want to take the time and money to make them.

If the owner wants an immediate deposit, make the contract stipulate (in time increments) as to how you will progress in obtaining information and permits. For instance, give yourself the first week in which to find out if you can have the pawn shop in that particular building, figure out what changes you will need to make, and learn about all of the requirements needed to make those changes.

The second week can be devoted to submitting your plans for approval and allows for you to obtain bids from contracting agencies in order to comply with the city ordinances, if any.

At any one of these sectors, you can be turned down or find it too costly to pursue your business in that particular location.

Many business people look for buildings that will most suit their purposes with little to no improvements.

Most pawn shops partition off the front of their store from the rear ... the front being for sales and the rear portion saved for the storage of pawned items. We found several times that we could get away with partitioning *without* a permit if the partition stopped *ten inches* from the ceiling.

The strictness of these ordinances usually vary with the size, the prosperity, and the popularity of the community. For instance, here in California a pawnbroker requesting a permit to open a pawn shop in communities like Brentwood, Solvang or Carmel would probably be considered to be a raving lunatic and laughed out of town ... or committed ... or he could run the risk of being tarred and feathered and run out of town on a rail simply for having the gall to make such an idiotic request!

If a permit is requested in a city like San Diego or San Jose or Oceanside, the aspiring pawnbroker is handed a sizable and depressing list of restrictions that pertain to zoning, signs, parking, lighting, window displays, and landscaping. All this, according to the latest whim or fancy that sounded impressive and authoritative and went with the mood of the Mayor and his council at any given time. You will find that it is sometimes difficult to reason out the why of these ordinances. It doesn't matter. Do it or look elsewhere! The system is not designed for you to win.

Then there are other outlying areas that are poor in industry and commerce who would welcome any sort of tax base revenue. I won't mention them because we all know them when we see them. They aren't too difficult to recognize. Those are the little towns where pawn shops would be greeted with open arms. In fact, they probably wouldn't care if the pawn shop was painted green and purple and it offered a tattoo parlor in the back room as an additional customer service!

In fact, the community would be fairly ecstatic because the request for a business license wasn't for opening a palm reading room or an adult video store. Even questionable massage parlors are grudgingly accepted!

BUREAUCRATS AND THE TELEPHONE

The telephone is a great time saver when seeking information. But it must be used *effectively*. The normal first encounter is with a grumpy old maid or a nineteen year old co-ed who is snapping her gum in your ear. Either way, they both have the same attitude ... you are interrupting their day.

For the sake of illustration, I will use the co-ed who is manning the telephones while on vacation from the local community college. My luck usually runs that way, so I can relate better.

You are now caught up in a telephone maze that leads you around to the most amazing intricacy of civic positions. I never knew cities had job positions with titles like *Second Yardman In Charge of Pigeon Doo!* Absolutely unbelievable!

The odds are something like ninety-five to one that this little telephone tour will stop at nine different locations, eventually winding up right back with the gum chomper. Normally, this is about the time you get wild-eyed and consider jumping into your car, careening down the street toward City Hall, with an embellishing fantasy of jerking up Miss Double Bubble by her braces, paper clipping her to one of your wire rims and taking her for a spin or two around the parking lot ... if not to shake her out of her vagueness ... then merely as a public service.

My advice? Don't.

Although you are frustrated beyond redemption, grit your teeth and smile brightly as you speak. Make yourself sound like you just dialed the telephone and you are delighted with whoever answers.

Too many times that little teeny-bopper or the grumpy old sow are just the ones you need to charm in order to get past them to where you really need to go. They can help you or they can put your entire life on hold. They will have you begging for mercy!

Many of the people in these positions have no other power in their lives. But in this job, they are god divine ... and you ... you are but a lowly peasant. They can take kindly to you and bestow upon you the great blessing of cutting through miles of red tape ... if you are humble and gracious and you make them feel good about themselves. Cross them and they can (no – they will!) make your life a veritable hell – a life so full of misery that it is just not worth living.

Verily, verily, I say unto you. Offer up, with great reverence and humility, the power and the authority they earnestly desire and great blessings will pour forth upon you. And lo, you will be blessed with the proper person to answer all of your questions! Maybe.

Shed your pride like a dirty coat. Drop to your knees in submission. They can make you do it! And they won't get fired! You won't win. You can't win. The system is not designed for you to win – not unless you are the president of the United States, and he doesn't always get to win (although I'm willing to bet he didn't have much trouble with getting permits to rebuild his house in Kennebunkport after the hurricane).

*In **Lesko's Info Power**, Matthew Lesko writes:*

There is no magic in how you treat experts. Simply remember to treat them the way you want to be treated. But this is easy to forget when the bureaucratic runaround triggers instant frustration. While making your seven phone calls to find your expert — beware. These are common reactions:

- *You get put on hold for what seems like hours.*
- *Everyone you talk with cannot understand your question and thinks you are off your rocker.*
- *After getting transferred and trying other numbers, you wind up talking with the same person twice.*

What's important is not to lose your composure. Keep in mind that it will take an average of seven phone calls to find the person who can help. Otherwise, by the time you reach the expert, you'll be angry and frustrated and that attitude will usually cause this information provider to end the conversation immediately. Remember that the expert wants to help you — if you give them a chance.

Information on where to send for the forms and for the Federal Firearm Regulations is incorporated at the close of this chapter.

* Join the National Pawnbroker's Association and your state Collateral Loan and Secondhand Dealers Association. These are the very best ways to find out about all of the laws you will need to start up your pawn shop. By spending the little bit of extra money ($100 for the National Association and approximately $200 to $400 for your State Association), you will save yourself not hours and days, but weeks and months worth of legwork and paper mazes.

NO GOODS SHOWN UNTIL PAID FOR

Sunrise Pawnbrokers, Inc.
3043 N. FEDERAL HIGHWAY (U. S. 1)
FORT LAUDERDALE, FLORIDA 33306
Phone: 563-3147

Nº 47357

RECEIVED OF ____________________

FOLLOWING DESCRIBED PROPERTY ____________________

____

____

____

The said property having been pledged with the undersigned as security for a loan made this day to be returned to said pledgor only upon the surrender of this receipt and the payment of $__________ with interest thereon, and in default of such payment said property to be disposed of without reserve or notice.

CHARGES $__________ FIRST MONTH (INCLUDES STORAGE / APPRAISAL FEE WHERE APPLICABLE). $__________ PER MONTH NEXT FIVE MONTHS. CHARGES 3% PER MONTH. 36% PER YEAR.

ALL LOANS GOOD FOR SIX MONTHS

This receipt MUST be PRESENTED when claiming goods

NO CHECKS ACCEPTED

AMOUNT LOANED ____________________

ARTICLE

AAAA - FOUR ACES
PAWNBROKERS. INC.
1984 A FLASTBUSH AVENUE
BROOKLYN, N. Y. 11234

AGREEMENT

I am the owner of the above mentioned pledge and have the legal right to pawn the same and I do hereby agree to all terms and conditions of this loan and pledge, as contained on both sides of the pawnticket delivered to same.

I hereby request and authorized you to give special service and extra care to the above mentioned pledge and to protect the same against damage or breakage, for all of which I agree to pay. ____________________

Date ____________________

Time ☐ A. M. ☐ P. M.

Name ____________________

Address ____________________

Telephone ____________________

CONTRACT AND DISCLOSURE STATEMENT

ANY PERSONAL PROPERTY PLEDGED TO A PAWNBROKER WITHIN THIS STATE IS SUBJECT TO SALE OR DISPOSAL WHEN THERE HAS BEEN NO PAYMENT MADE ON THE ACCOUNT FOR A PERIOD OF 60 DAYS PAST MATURITY DATE OF THE ORIGINAL CONTRACT. NO FURTHER NOTICE IS NECESSARY. THE PLEDGOR OF THIS ITEM ATTESTS THAT IT IS NOT STOLEN, HAS NO LIENS OR ENCUMBRANCES, AND IS THE PLEDGOR'S TO SELL OR PAWN. THE ITEM PAWNED IS REDEEMABLE ONLY BY THE BEARER OF THIS TICKET OR BY IDENTIFICATION OF THE PERSON MAKING THE PAWN.

SUMMARY OF TRANSACTION

LOAN by LENDER to BORROWER is secured by a PLEDGE or pawn of property described herein. LENDER retains a Security interest in said Collateral, pursuant to the North Carolina Uniform Commercial Code, until this secured loan is fully paid according to terms herein. The interest and pawnbroker's fee are deemed earned on the date of the loan. You will not be entitled to a refund of any portion of these charges. This contract is renewable for periods of 30 days each if agreed upon by both parties, as outlined by Chapter 91A of the general statutes of N.C. Agreed upon "stated value" between pledgor and pawnbroker in case of loss or destruction of pledged item shall be the same as the loan value unless otherwise noted.

ACKNOWLEDGEMENTS OF RECEIPT OF DISCLOSURES

The undersigned BORROWER does herewith acknowledge receipt of the DISCLOSURES contained herein and in the LOAN CONTRACT. They, further, acknowledge that at the time they received a copy of this Statement and executed said LOAN CONTRACT, such forms were completed and filled in, and that all blanks in such forms were filled in prior to their executing the same. BORROWER also consents to the sale or disposal of this property according to the terms set forth herein.

LOAN BY: ____________________

____

Signature of Borrower: ____________________

PAYMENT Date	PAYMENT Amount	LENDER	PAYMENT Date	PAYMENT Amount	DATE	TIME
		***Ray's* PAWN SHOP, INC.**				
		2937 Shamrock Drive Charlotte, NC 28205			LOAN [illegible]	
		Telephone 568-5832				

FINANCE CHARGES	
Stated Value and Amount Paid Borrower Amount Financed	$
Service, Storage & Monthly Fees	$
Total Loan Interest	$
Total Payments: 24% Annual Percentage Rate or 2% Monthly	$
TOTAL OF PAYMENTS DUE ON __________, 19 ______, IN FULL	

BORROWER:
NAME ____________________
STREET ____________________
CITY ____________ STATE ____________ ZIP ____________
PHONE

☐ M ☐ W ☐ F ☐ B ☐ I ☐ O

WT ____________
HT ____________
DATE OF BIRTH ____________

ID NUMBER

LOAN AMOUNT
$

ID SOURCE
1 ☐ Driver's License
2 ☐ Social Security
3 ☐ Credit Card
4 ☐ Draft Card
5 ☐ ____________

Article 1.	Article 2.	Article 3.	Article 4.	Article 5.
MANUFACTURER	MANUFACTURER	MANUFACTURER	MANUFACTURER	MANUFACTURER
MODEL	MODEL	MODEL	MODEL	MODEL
ARTICLE SER. NO.	ARTICLE SER. NO.	ARTICLE SER. NO.	ARTICLE SER. NO.	ARTICLE SER. NO.
DESCRIPTION OF ARTICLE	DESCRIPTION OF ARTICLE	DESCRIPTION OF ARTICLE	DESCRIPTION OF ARTICLE	DESCRIPTION OF ARTICLE

Original - White / Policy Copy - Canary / Customer's Copy - Pink
Duplicate - Goldenrod

CHAPTER 8

THE PAWN TICKET

Attempting to include within these pages the lending laws governing every state in the union would be a ponderous task at best, not to mention the postage factor!

Because our stores are governed by California law, I will use our laws for the sake of illustration only.

California's lending laws are some of the most restrictive in the Union. Chances are you will find the laws that govern your state far more lenient and much more to your liking.

Some states have laws that pertain to collateral lending and other laws that allow for 30 day buy back stores. In the event that this is so in your state, you will need to determine which kind of store you wish to operate.

If a state has created legislation for collateral lending and for buy back stores, then it is up to the local governments to determine whether they will accept one, both, or none at all in their communities.

Be very careful about which name you choose to operate under. If you are a pawn shop, then the collateral lending laws apply to you. You fall under the guidelines of a lender and are subject to strict usury laws.

If you determine to call yourself a buy back store, you are subject to the laws that govern buy back stores.

Some states require proof of $150,000 liquid assets before issuing such a license. Some require nothing more than a Secondhand Dealer's license for a small fee.

Whichever is the case in your state, much information included in this chapter can and will concern you. Reporting all of your transactions is just as important no matter which laws you are operating under. The only difference is that the contracts do not read the same and the time elements change to one degree or another.

Reporting your transactions is important and you don't want to be put out of business because you didn't follow through with the proper reporting.

To find out what laws affect you and how you go about finding the correct reporting forms, call your State Association.

If your state has not yet formed its association, call the National Pawnbroker's Association for assistance on who to contact within your state.

You might also pick up the state laws regarding pawn shops and buy back stores through your local police department and/or the Department of Justice that governs your state.

While it is wise to check with your State Association and to send off for the state financial codes that pertain to your state regulations on collateral lending, the aspiring pawnbroker must check with the local municipalities where he is considering the placement of his pawn shop location.

Often times, certain communities create laws that add to the requirements set forth by state mandate. Some local municipalities require additional time limitations or restrictions. What often happens is that the potential pawnbroker does all of his state legislation homework only to find out when he is ready to get started that the locality where he would like to operate has outlawed pawn shops and buy backs completely. (See Chapter 6.)

State law *only* comes into play once it is established that the local powers that be authorize such operations.

The basic restrictions that pertain to pawn tickets and buy back options are *state mandated,* therefore it is necessary to understand what kinds of legislation you will be contending with when you are operating as either a collateral lender or as a buy back store.

Unless the complicated legislation is converted into layman's terms, it is difficult for the average person like myself to grasp them with any real understanding. I strongly advise this chapter be incorporated into your studies, whether or not these laws apply to your particular state.

The rule of thumb is that ***the most restrictive law applies.*** Some communities have no provisions for pawn shop laws or buy back stores.

Because the local municipalities are ignorant of the laws regulating pawnbrokers does not mean that the pawnbroker may operate willy-nilly, ignoring the state regulations regarding pawnbrokers.

THE BUY BACK STORE

Buy back stores are just what they sound like. The operator of the store actually buys the merchandise from the customer and extends the customer the option to buy the items back at a pre-agreed upon price at the end of a pre-arranged time lapse.

The time lapse is often 30 days. This gives the police and the state the time to investigate for stolen merchandise. After the time lapse, the customer may return to exercise his option and buy back his merchandise ... or the store owner might allow the customer to pay an extension fee which renews his option for another 30 days for a set amount of money (usually 10% of the original sale). After the initial mandatory 30 day wait, if the customer extends his option, it is not necessary to wait for another 30 days. Because the goods have already gone through the initial investigation, the customer may return at any time. Options are usually extended in increments of 30 days for as long as the customer wishes.

The buy back store can be an advantage to the pawnbroker because his money can be turned over much faster. Also, many customers extend their options ... some for even years at a stretch!

The drawbacks to buy back stores are several. First, buy back stores usually contend with more competition. Secondly, customers tend to be a bit leery of them because of some unscrupulous (and unwise) pawnbrokers who sometimes offer no grace period. They pull the customer's merchandise out of stock for sale on the day after the option was due.

A good buy back store operator will give up to a 90 day grace period. They will wait 60 days past the next extension date that is due before they pull the merchandise. If the customer shows up within that framework of time, all that is required is that he pay for each 30 day increment in which the pawnbroker held his option.

A fair policy is to even grant 3 days into the 30 day increment before charging that extra extension fee. The customer saves a few bucks and he feels fairly treated.

The buy back store may NOT charge any other fees except state-mandated gun fees and a lost ticket charge. No interest and no storage can be charged.

THE COLLATERAL LENDER

The difference between the buy back and the collateral lender are the charges, the time frames and the title of ownership. A buy back store actually *buys* the merchandise with a bill of sale that includes the option to buy back. The collateral lender *lends* cash for collateral and, instead of a bill of sale, a lending contract is signed between the parties.

The contract must stipulate the time frame of the loan, a state-mandated redemption period, and the Truth In Lending Act which allows for the borrower to know the exact amount of annual interest he is being charged.

Remember, the time frame of the loan is one thing and the time frame for the allowable interest is another. It is easy to confuse the times with the interest charges. Both time and interest are state regulated, but not coinciding. Because the time elements and the allowable interest are not in tune with one another, the laws become difficult to interpret.

THE TIME ELEMENTS PERTAINING TO LOANS

1. **THE LOAN PERIOD.** In California, the loan period is by agreement between the borrower and the lender. It could be a 30, 60 or 90 day loan or it could be a 1 day loan. Traditionally, California pawnbrokers extend a 20 day loan.

2. **THE REDEMPTION PERIOD.** When the loan period ends, the redemption period begins. This redemption period is mandated by the state. In California, the law requires a 4 month redemption period, so this means that the borrower has the traditional 20 day loan, plus he has 4 months *after* that 20 days to redeem his merchandise.

3. **THE 30 DAY WINDOW.** When the loan

redemption period lapses, there is an increment of time that is known as *the 30 day window*. This is a window of time that opens up to the lender in which he is required to mail a *10 day notice* of foreclosure to the borrower.

4. **THE TEN DAY NOTICE.** The ten day notice tells the borrower that as of the date of the mailing, the borrower has 10 more days to retrieve his goods or legal title to said goods will be transferred to the pledgee (the pawnbroker). **If the pawnbroker fails to send the 10 day notice of foreclosure *inside* of that 30 day window, the law says that the pawnbroker may *never* claim legal title to the goods. In other words, the pawnbroker may never sell, nor may he dispose of, *in any manner,* the pledged merchandise. He must keep it on his premises permanently.** If the borrower returns for his merchandise in ten years, the pawnbroker may collect only for that which he might have charged during the normal course of the loan originally agreed upon.

THE TIME ELEMENTS PERTAINING TO INTEREST

Interest rates in California are set according to loan amounts. The smaller the loan, the higher the interest rates.

1. 30 day interest loans are only for those loans which are $14 or less. The interest is limited to $1 per month for the first 90 days and then a 2½% interest charge is added for each of the two months left on the loan (until the end of the redemption period).

2. On loans of $15 or more, there is a flat 90 day interest rate where the borrower must pay back the set interest whether he's had the loan for 1 day or 90 days. After the initial 90 days, the pawnbroker adds 2½% interest charges for each of the two months left on the loan (until the end of the redemption period).

TIME ELEMENTS PERTAINING TO STORAGE FEES

Storage fees are flat rates that are charged for the entire loan time, whether 1 day or until the customer returns with a ten day notice.

STORAGE FEES

1. $ 3 for any item that cannot be contained within 1 cubic foot.
2. $ 9 for any item that cannot be contained within 3 cubic feet.
3. $18 for any item that cannot be contained within 6 cubic feet.
4. $ 1 for each cubic foot in excess of 6 cubic feet.

GUN FEES

$4 for each firearm pawned.

LOAN FEES

$2 for each pawn ticket written.

THE LOST TICKET FEE

The pawnbroker may charge up to $10 to the borrower if he/she returns without their copy of the contract.

HOW BUY BACK STORES CAME ABOUT IN THE STATE OF CALIFORNIA AND WHY THEY WERE FINALLY OUTLAWED

In early America there was only one place to

procure a loan and that was through a reputable pawnbroker. The reputable pawnbrokers were the ones who had fine business establishments that were not necessarily slum bound. Pawn shops were simply a way of life.

The disreputable pawnbrokers had no stores. They did business right out of their pockets.

Those pawnbrokers could usually be found in local seaport towns. Every wharfside tavern catered to the pawnbrokers and insurance agents because they brought in much of their business.

Shipping companies did their business with the insurance agents, purchasing insurance on loads of cargo that were to be shipped overseas.

The sailors borrowed the money they needed on their gold hoop earrings.

The sailor's earring wasn't a fashion statement. Rather it was their savings account ... a nest egg (so to speak), placed safely into the lobe of their ears where thieving crewmates couldn't take it from them while they slept.

It was a common practice for the shipping companies to pay their men only after they left their home port for the next voyage. This is the way the shipping companies could be assured they would have a full and experienced crew when they were ready to set sail once again.

The sailors spent most of their wages in foreign ports and often, their earring was all they had when they returned. As soon as they came ashore, they found a pawnbroker to borrow the money they needed while they were ashore. It took several months for the ship to be refitted, loaded with the new cargo and made ready to set sail once again. During that time, the sailors went home to their families (if they had one), and they found work ashore to earn enough money so that they might help out with their families and redeem their earrings. Off again they went, on another voyage. It was just a way of life.

Eventually, the savings and loan institutions became popular and a few of the wealthiest uptown pawnbrokers remained solvently in business. The majority of the pawnbrokers were pushed to the seedier sides of town where they became the lending agents for the lower class and poor.

Strict legislation was introduced, time after time, which made it nearly impossible for pawn shops to operate with any real success.

Those who weren't run out of business could barely make ends meet and their living conditions were a bit less deplorable than those who utilized their services. Still, a few hung on ... most likely by cheating the customers whenever possible.

Because pawnbrokers had no representation in the legislature, the archaic laws remained on the books and the pawnbrokers were forced to abide by them. Two of the most crippling pieces of outdated legislation included interest rates that were outdated shortly after the depression and the requirement by law that, upon the subsequent sale of all forfeited pledges, the pawnbroker was bound to hand over a lion's share of the proceeds to the person who failed to redeem his goods.

This created mountains of paperwork for pawnbrokers. They had to keep numerous and exacting check lists of every single item. Forfeiture and subsequent sale of the item didn't end the paper trail.

A strict inventory had to be maintained at all times on these items that were presented for sale to the public.

Between a bit of negligent paperwork, a misplaced code bearing tag, and an occasional shoplifter, the task had to be unbelievable, especially when we consider that back then the only computer available to pawnbrokers was blank paper and a drawer full of pencils!

This meant the pawnbroker had to risk trouble by selling the items in his store. Consequently, in order to avoid such discrepancies, most of the forfeited pledges were sent to public auctions.

Often, the merchandise sold for drastically low prices and the auction house drew ten percent of the gross sales right off the top for their services.

After the sale, the pawnbroker took out his interest and the small percentage of his allowable profit, if any. The balance had to be refunded to the original borrower. Half the time these borrowers were transient and locating them was costly, if not impossible. This meant that the pawnbroker was obliged to hold that part of the sale back for a predetermined length of time that amounted to years, rather than weeks or months.

The pawnbrokers who risked reselling the items in their stores for a higher profit had even a more troublesome time locating the original owners. Some merchandise can sit on a shelf for several years before it is recognized as a treasure for some lucky shopper.

In those days, the pawn ticket was anything that suited the pawnbroker's needs to accomplish his job.

Eventually, pawnbrokers got wise to the lending laws and tried to figure a way around them so that they could legally realize profits that would be more to their liking.

It didn't take long for pawnbrokers to notice that the laws which pertained to them were *lending laws. So, they stopped lending and began buying!* They purchased the customer's merchandise instead, giving the customer the option to buy the items back at a predetermined price.

It is easy to see why buy back stores rapidly caught on with the pawnbrokers who were old-timers in the business. It was a way of getting around calling the loan *a loan.* If he was buying and not loaning, he wasn't under the jurisdiction of the state financial codes pertaining to collateral lending.

There was nothing in the law that precluded a person from buying an item and agreeing to allow the seller the option to repurchase the item at a predetermined price on a predetermined date.

Pawnbrokers converted their loans to buy back options simply to survive and remain in business for themselves.

The vast majority of pawnbrokers didn't like to treat their customers poorly. The pawnbrokers, who might have done so, restrained themselves when they realized that they were in jeopardy of losing customers to the fair pawnbrokers.

Amazingly, without an association and without any communications, the buy back stores were establishing policies that were fair to the customers and were amazingly similar, one store with another.

Ample grace periods were set for those customers who returned past the agreed upon time limits to exercise their options. Lending on items became rather uniform and the option charges settled into a standard rate of 10% for 30 days and 10% to extend the option for additional 30 day periods. Grace periods standardized themselves at 90 days and if customers lost their receipts, they were not severely penalized.

With a proper amount of good competition, the water was seeking its own level.

Many states simply adopted the standards that were set by the buy back stores rather than try to impose laws on an area of lending that the legislators didn't clearly understand. Now many states accept buy back stores as a fair trade and they are regulated accordingly.

Unfortunately, California is one of the states where the legislative body refused to allow the competitive water to seek its own level. Rather, they publicized pawn shops in a light which did not reflect reality. Hollywood came out with the infamous *Pawnbroker,* indelibly tarnishing the pawn industry.

This gave the politicians just the ammunition they needed. They pointed their fingers at the pawn shops and declared the unfortunate pawnbrokers as the sole reason for crime! Their platform was that there wouldn't be thieves if it wasn't for pawn shops. Pawnbrokers had a license to steal. Their customers were the prostitutes and the drug dealers. If pawn shops were eliminated, their constituents would be residing in Utopia.

Well, everything they wanted to do has been done. The rigid laws are in place and all is right with the world ... isn't it?

Giving the devil his dues, a large part of the reason for the decline in the image of pawn shops must be attributed to those less-than-honest pawnbrokers who treated their customers with disrespect and continually cheated them out of their goods.

The worst of the thieving culprits made it mandatory for their customers to return on exactly the 30th day. They wouldn't allow the customer to come in one day before nor one day after. Those pawnbrokers never stayed in business for very long.

Unfortunately, their poor reputations didn't leave town with them. Consequently, the buy back stores who did survive because they were treating their customers fairly were left with the tainted reputation of those unscrupulous *carpetbaggers.*

Word of mouth is a powerful source of information, especially in the more impoverished urban cities and in some rural communities. Many of these people are not sophisticated enough or they simply have no real desire for keeping up with currcnt cvcnts. Thcy arc too busy carning their living, some of them barely getting by. They get their news from telephone calls and chats over backyard fences.

It isn't long before dishonest pawnbrokers find themselves running short on customers. When there is no repeat business, there is **NO** business. There are only so many people in a community and only so many of those are acquainted with conducting business in pawn shops.

Statistics have shown that a satisfied customer might tell two or three of his friends about the good service he received. But a dissatisfied customer will repeat his negative experience to an average of 20 to 30 people. The more he feels insulted or cheated, the more he will verbalize his disdain for being treated disrespectfully and/or unfairly.

Had new legislation been put into place that regulated buy back stores in their inception, proper monitoring and reporting procedures would have been firmly established. When everyone is singing from the same sheet of music, it is not difficult to glean out the sour notes.

THE CALIFORNIA PAWN TICKET

In the state of California, the term 'pawn ticket' is a bit misleading. In reality, there are no actual pawn tickets. Instead, there are two separate pieces ... the 'contract' and the 'police report.'

The pawn 'ticket' is divided in two parts. The upper portion is the actual *contract* between the pawnbroker and the customer.

The contract explains all of the terms, costs and conditions of the agreement. In the state of California, the California Financial Code as it applies to collateral loans is printed on the contract. The customer retains the pink copy of the contract and submits it back to the pawnbroker upon redemption.

The bottom portion is the *police report* which bears all of the information regarding the customer and the merchandise that is being held by the pawnbroker as collateral. By law, the pawnbroker must retain a copy of the police report in his files for a period of not less than three years.

FILLING OUT THE CONTRACT

The contract is filled out ONLY when loaning on collateral. If the pawnbroker is making an outright purchase and the customer has no intention of returning to redeem the item, do NOT fill out the contract. The customer gets NO contract. *The contract is only in the event of a loan.*

In the upper lefthand corner of the contract is a box that allows for the pawnbroker to insert the amount of the initial loan. This does not include interest, fees or additional charges.

The box below the amount loaned is where the finance charge is added. The finance charges are incorporated in the reverse side of the contract.

Find the 90 day interest charge on the back of the contract example and enter that figure in the finance charge box (i.e. A $50 loan = $7.50 in interest). The principal and interest for 90 days is $57.50.

Many pawnbrokers don't offer the figures for the annual interest rates. This is against the law. Every loan must show the annual rate in order to be in compliance with truth in lending. I have included an annual percentage chart that quotes the annual interest rates of $1 to $170. *** If the store is computerized, the computers automatically figure the annual percentage rate.

If there are storage fees, enter them on the upper right side of the contract where it says storage fees. If a firearm is being pawned, there is an automatic $4 per weapon (one firearm to each ticket). No storage fees on firearms.

In California, the time specified for a loan is twenty days. Enter 'Today's Date' for the loan date. Count twenty days from 'Today's Date' and enter that date (i.e. LOAN DATE 07-01-90 DUE DATE 07-21-90). The redemption period begins on 07-22-90 and the clock begins ticking for a full four months (120 days). After the clock runs out on the 120 days, the pawnbroker is given a 'window' of 30 days in which to notify the pawner that his loan has expired. The notice must be in writing and sent by Certificate of Mailing.

This letter gives the pawner ten days to redeem his merchandise. The ten day count begins from the date the Certificate of Mailing is posted. The notice must be sent inside the thirty-day window which would begin on the loan expiration date and end thirty days after the redemption period ends. Under the old ruling, when a pawnbroker failed to give notice of the ten day grace period within thirty days after the redemption period ended, he could not perfect title to the property. This was called the "window of perfection". If the pawnbroker did not perfect title during the thirty day period, title went out the window.

Under the new amendment, if the pawnbroker fails to send the notice within the thirty day period, he is not able to receive interest after the thirty day period but he will, however, obtain title ten days after he mails the "ten day grace notice" regardless of how late the notice is mailed. **(The Post Office provides the Certificate of Mailing books.)**

Next, the amount of the loan is spelled out and then written in numerals just as a check is written in a checkbook.

Under the **DESCRIPTION OF ARTICLES** (PLEDGED PROPERTY), a basic description of the property is noted. If it is a piece of jewelry, for instance, write 'diamond ring,' or 'stereo' with model number and serial number or 'gun' with the serial number. I put a model and/or a serial number for accurate identification, but I don't include much of a description just in case the pawner lost his ticket and another person was trying to redeem the merchandise.

If I suspect the person redeeming is not who they say they are, I have an edge, other than identification (that could have been with the pawn ticket in a wallet).

If the gun is a rifle and the person redeeming it tells me it is a handgun, I won't make the mistake of releasing the weapon to anyone other than the person who pawned the gun.

If an entire description, complete with serial numbers, is contained on the contract, someone else could identify the merchandise as theirs. Notice the customer's copy doesn't even bear his name. The customer must show ID or at least be able to give the first letter of the pawner's surname in order for the pawnbroker to find the police report copy.

It is not a unique event for someone to find or come by a pledge contract and try to figure out how to redeem the merchandise. We are able to put a stop to this by not placing the customer's name and their property description on the contract.

The person redeeming the merchandise is supposed to be the same person who pawned it. If this is not the case, they must show (to the pawnbroker's satisfaction) that they are entitled to redeem the merchandise.

One of our stores had a lot of trouble with people who were incarcerated. They were bartering for desired items with their pledge contracts as currency. There were so many people coming in with endorsed pledge contracts that it was getting out of hand. We are not handwriting experts and we ARE liable if we release goods to the wrong party. Rather than take that risk, we made the decision to not release property to *anyone* other than who pawned the merchandise.

It was during that time span that we heard of a case (by attending a California Collateral and Secondhand Dealer's Association convention) where the signature was forged and the pawnbroker released the merchandise. The pawnbroker was held liable because (as the cross-examining attorney pleaded) the pawnbroker was not a handwriting expert. In that case, it was the other guy's lesson that was good enough for us.

We keep the store policy strict and simple. Whoever pawns, picks up. True, we do make exceptions, but we do it when we are completely convinced of the accuracy of the extenuating circumstances.

We make our customers believe that our rules are totally unbending. Post the rules where they can read them while they are waiting for their loan to be written up.

These are our rules: THESE ARE THE CIRCUMSTANCES IN WHICH YOU MAY REDEEM THE PLEDGED PROPERTY OF ANY OTHER PERSON.

1. The party redeeming the merchandise has an original Power of Attorney from the pledgor.
2. The party redeeming the merchandise can prove they are the next of kin and they are able to present an original Death Certificate for our inspection.
3. A very convincing handwritten letter that is signed by the pledgor giving specific permission for a specific person to redeem their goods. This letter must be accompanied by a photostatic copy of the driver's license or state ID the pledgor used to pawn the merchandise.
4. The party redeeming the merchandise to be accompanied by a local governing peace officer who is willing to accept responsibility in the event that a mistake is made.
5. If you are a member of our immediate family, you could possibly warrant a moment of consideration before you are turned down.

* * *

One time we released a wedding set to the husband after the wife pawned it several weeks earlier. It was not uncommon for the same couple to pawn and redeem each other's goods. They'd been dealing with us in the same manner for several years. On this particular occasion, we came to find out that the couple had separated and the man picked up his wife's wedding rings to spite her. This kind of thing leaves the pawnbroker open to lawsuits.

It is very tempting to do special favors for good customers. I (like most people) do not enjoy giving a "no" answer, especially if that answer is going to create hard feelings between myself and a good customer. But the outcome of saying "yes" can sometimes reverse itself and the favor granted becomes the proverbial millstone around our own necks. Besides, ALL LOANS ARE CONFIDENTIAL! This even applies between spouses, parents and children (the children being of age, of course).

Our new computer tickets have been altered to advise holders of pledge contracts that our contracts are *not transferable.*

It was with this strict rule I learned the reason for the old saying,

"Rules are made to be broken!"

One secret I learned a long time ago, make strict policies and then put on a great big white hat when you make your exceptions. The customers will *love* you for it! There's no better advertising!

When you do make exceptions, know in your own mind that everything is on the up and up. Once you do, you can turn your strict policy around and make it really work for you.

This is what I call good customer relations.

The dialogue goes something like this...

"Now you know, Mr. Jones, it is our policy not to release someone's pledge to anyone else. But, Mr. Jones, being as it's you, I'll go ahead and release this to you. Now, mind you, this is an exception for just this one time."

For some reason, the customer feels so privileged when I say, "Being as it's you..." It makes them feel like they are my very special customer and they walk out glowing with praise for our store.

Whenever you make any exception, do it with color and flair so they don't forget it any time soon.

I have shamed them with it, too. If they try to get to me, I remind them of how I went out of my way to treat them with special favor and now here they are trying to get to me. I tell them they should be ashamed and they are!

"Mr. Jones, now you know that I've always done right by you, don't you?" Mr. Jones nods his head and looks humble.

Women can really get away with scolding. I don't mean nagging ... just a good old-fashioned schoolmarm scolding. I know men can do it, too. You get your point across and you keep a customer!

WHAT HAPPENS TO THE CONTRACT AND THE COPIES

If the pawnbroker is purchasing the item, a separate bill of sale is written up. The upper portion of the police report is a loan contract and cannot be used in place of a bill of sale. Contracts are only written in the event of a LOAN. Do not confuse the contracts with police reports. A police report must be written on every single item bought, pawned, consigned, or traded (with the exception of wholesale dealers).

The contracts usually consist of three NCR forms. The original is white, the first copy – the 'BORROWER'S COPY' is pink – and the 'STORE COPY' is yellow.

The pawnbroker keeps the original white 'OFFICE COPY' and the yellow 'STORE COPY.' The customer retains the pink 'BORROWER COPY.'

The yellow copy, the 'STORE COPY,' is taped to the merchandise or placed inside the envelope with the jewelry so that it may be readily available for the customer to sign upon redemption of the item should he/she forget to bring in their copy.

The original contracts are filed only according to date on double spindle file boards. As the pawns are redeemed or forfeited, they are pulled from the spindle file boards and placed face down, first contract on the bottom and last contract on the top. This is done for the protection of the pawnbroker. It is always good to have the original contract on hand for awhile ... just in case some problem arises. The same thing applies with the bills of sale.

We keep ours for at least three years. When the pile gets high enough, we bundle them with rubber bands and store them away. They get tossed after a few years. My motto is save as much as you can for as long as you can. That *ism* has helped me more than a few times and it hasn't yet hurt me, except for a little inconvenience in finding storage space. One of our stores has some great attic space over the bathrooms.

PAWN TICKETS AND CONTRACTS

Every item taken in by a pawnbroker (whether he is a collateral lender or a buy back store) must be reported to the police. In California, it is required that these reports are turned in on a daily basis.

Today, there are state requirements pertaining to what kind of police reports and contracts the pawnbroker must use. They are regulated by law as to the written agreements on the contracts and by the information that must be included on *every* police report.

The regulations include the size of the police report and how it is set up. The states want all of those reports to look exactly the same. This saves time hunting around each report for driver's license numbers, personal identification and items pledged or purchased.

In 1980, California law changed the holding period for buying merchandise over the counter from 10 days to 30 days. The police needed more time to check out all of the pawnbroker's police reports for stolen merchandise.

Before last year, there was a 20% law in California that allowed dealers who did 20% or less of their business in over-the-counter buying from unlicensed persons to buy such items without reporting them.

Today, *every* dealer (this includes jewelry stores, coin shops, baseball card stores, antique stores, etc.) is required by law to report these transactions even if they only do one in a year!

More and more stolen merchandise is now being tracked to stores that take trade-ins or buy over-the-counter items for resale. Most local police departments don't know about this law and the ones who do don't have the time or the necessary manpower to enforce it.

In the past, these laws were seldom enforced, even in the pawn shops. When they were, it was only when a complaint was filed and a follow-up of the complaint would gain some credit for the law enforcement or some votes for a local politician. Or sometimes it only had to do with bad blood between the pawnbroker and the police department or the District Attorney's office.

It was not unheard of for a person to go to the local police and claim that an item in the pawnbroker's store was lost or stolen from them even years ago. Without the privilege of his constitutional rights, the officer became the judge and jury, forcing the pawnbroker to hand the items over to the complainant or be faced with arrest.

The courts seldom looked favorably on the pawnbroker and many times they still don't today.

Laws were enforced against the offending pawnbroker whenever the governing body chose to pursue the issue. Often, the governing bodies would be ambivalent because pawn shops were not currently a hot issue. During these times, pawnbrokers were left to their own devices and many of them took advantage of the situation, conducting their business in a less than seemly manner.

Pawn tickets vary from state to state and municipality to municipality. If your local law enforcement seems unconcerned with the laws governing a pawn shop, then you must comply with your state ordinances.

The pawn ticket varies from state to state. Usually the Department of Justice presiding in each state has a regulation copy of the kind of pawn tickets they will accept.

Some states require thumbprinting (as the State of California does). The easiest way to find out about the rules and regulations that pertain to your state is to contact the National Pawnbroker's Association.

National Pawnbroker's Association
600 S. Federal Street, Suite 400
Chicago, Illinois 60605
(312) 922-3100 (800) 235-5400
(312) 922-3374 FAX

Your State Association should be listed with the NPA. The NPA puts out a seasonal news magazine that gives tips and information on the pawn business.

My experience in pawnbroking is limited to California, so I am able to cite only those laws and requirements that apply in my state. If you reside in any other state, the above 800 number of the NPA should guide you to the proper authorities who will give you the guidelines for your municipal and state financial codes.

* * *

HOW TO FILL OUT THE POLICE REPORTS

Police reports are required whether you are loaning or working a buy back store. This portion applies to everyone.

The police reports must be filled out accurately. If handwritten, they must be legibly printed in blue or black ink.

Ask the customer for his valid driver's license or state ID.

Remember, when you void a ticket, be sure to write the reason on it and send it in with all of your pawn tickets to the police department at night. They will want to know what that missing number is.

THUMBPRINTS

Thumbprinting is now mandatory in California. If the pawn ticket does not provide a place for the thumbprint on the front, then the print should be placed on the back of the ticket and the print tag initialed by the clerk who is writing the customer's ticket.

GOLD TEST KIT
CAUTION

CHAPTER 9

HOW TO PAWN GOLD

Gold is weighed by the pennyweight or by the gram. Generally, pawnbrokers use the pennyweight system because it is easier and quicker to figure. There are 20 pennyweights to an ounce as opposed to 31.1 grams to an ounce ... clearly, you can see why the pennyweight system is preferable.

Gold is divided in 24 parts which equal 100 percent. The chart below should help you develop a clear understanding of how gold content is measured. Bear in mind – **the alloy is worthless.**

24 karat = 24 parts gold and 0 parts alloy
22 karat = 22 parts gold and 2 parts alloy
18 karat = 18 parts gold and 6 parts alloy
14 karat = 14 parts gold and 10 parts alloy
10 karat = 10 parts gold and 14 parts alloy
8 karat = 8 parts gold and 16 parts alloy

The karat weight of gold is the *content* of gold. It is vital that you understand the concept of karat weight as opposed to the weight a piece comes to on a pennyweight scale.

For the past ten years, the gold market has fluctuated from around $250 per ounce to as much as $800 per ounce. These are the extremes. The market has pretty much established itself (at this writing) around $360 per ounce for the past several years ... 1988, 1989 and 1990. *When the price of gold is quoted over the stock exchange, the quote you are hearing is for 24 karat only.*

For the sake of argument (and for the sake of simple math), let's assume that the gold market for today is at $360. You have a customer who brought in a 14 karat yellow gold nugget ring.

** NOTE there is NO DIFFERENCE in the value of yellow gold and white gold!*

You've placed the ring on your scale and it is a nice heavy piece weighing in at 12 pennyweights. Now you know three things. You know that the gold market is at $360 per ounce.

You have tested and you determine the gold content to be 14 karat.

Weigh the ring (for our purposes, we will say 12 pennyweights).

The price you will pay will be determined in this manner:

Divide 24 karats into $360 (our hypothetical price for the current gold market) in order to

determine how much 24 karat gold is going per pennyweight).

$360 divided by 24 equals $15 per pennyweight.

The ring is 14 karat gold, so you will multiply 14 by $15 which equals the going market value for 14 karat gold. 14 times $15 equals $210 per ounce.

There are 20 pennyweights to an ounce. Divide $210 by 20. This equals $10.50 per pennyweight. This figure, less around 50 to 75 cents is smelter's price when you sell it to a dealer. In bulk, you can expect around $9.75 to $10 per pennyweight for 14 karat gold. This is roughly the price you will be able to expect at a $360 per ounce market.

But you do not want to loan or buy at today's market. You want to **buy at half the market.** If you buy or loan at today's market, you are gambling that gold prices will not drop in the next several months.

The length of time you must keep the gold can become a major factor in the daily price quotes. A piece of gold could be pawned when the market is at $700 and if it is not redeemed, gold prices could drop in the meantime.

Cover all your bases. The risk ratio is high. There is a risk of stolen property. The item might have to be returned to the rightful owner without compensation. This is not the norm and we will cover this problem and how to overcome it in another chapter.

The pawnbroker's price to buy/pawn gold is leveled out at half the market or around **$5 per pennyweight on 14 karat** (market $360 per ounce). Hence, the 14 karat gold nugget ring weighing 12 pennyweights will be worth $60 (buy or loan) to the pawnbroker ... $5 times 12 pennyweights.

At $360 per ounce, the price for **10 karat gold is $3 per pennyweight. 18 karat gold = $7 per pennyweight, and 22 karat would be at $9 per pennyweight.**

You will find yourself to be very competitive at those prices when the market is under $400. If it slips to $300, you will want to drop your prices accordingly. The 14 karat nugget ring was purchased by the pawnbroker at $5 per pennyweight. In this case, the pawnbroker purchased the ring for $60. If he were to turn it over to a smelter, he would make at least double on his money.

But let's say that the ring is one that is quite popular and would probably sell easily.

A good buy on such a ring in a pawn shop would probably be somewhere around $20 per pennyweight. The ring should retail in your showcase for about $240.

If the ring is a custom one-of-a-kind that would be highly desirable, it is likely the pawnbroker would tack on another $50 to the price ... bringing the total retail price to $290.

The same ring would, quite probably, sell for

somewhere in the neighborhood of $50 to $65 per pennyweight in a jewelry store ... depending on the location of the store and the type of clientele it attracts. People pay as much as $780 for such a piece when they shop at quality stores. $290 is a wonderful bargain!

Beware, though! ***Don't get greedy.*** Some pawnbrokers will price themselves right out of the market. If Zales can get $780, why not price it at $500? The reason why not is, people expect to get BETTER THAN GOOD DEALS in a pawn shop. They expect to get *excellent* or *better than excellent* deals ... and you (the pawnbroker) are in a wonderful position to give them just that. And the beauty of it is that the return is mighty handsome as well.

HOW DO WE KNOW IF IT'S GOLD?

Gold testing kits are available through several jeweler's wholesale companies. They offer everything a jeweler might need to run a jewelry store. (See the chapter on *Vendors.*)

Most items are "frills" for the pawnbroker, but there are some things that you just cannot do without. One of these items is a **gold testing kit.** This kit comes with acid and an acid neutralizer. It has a small whetstone and a set of gold sample needles. The kit comes with full instructions for its use.

You will be surprised at how easy it is to identify gold and the karat weight of each piece. Electronic gold testers are also available and are becoming more and more foolproof as they are perfected. I would suggest the testing kit because it is much more affordable.

When testing a piece for gold content, rub the gold piece on the stone until it leaves a clear mark. I usually take a sample from several areas of the item to be sure the karat weight is the same throughout. (Sometimes a 14k ring will have a 10k shank.) This procedure takes only a minute sample of the gold and will not harm the jewelry. Select the karat weight that matches the weight of the jewelry from your gold sample needles and make a mark alongside the others. Place a drop of acid (that you mixed according to the kit instructions) on the gold marks from the jewelry and the sample needle.

Now compare the results. If the marks from the 14k jewelry are the same color as the mark from the 14k sample needle, then you can be pretty sure that the jewelry is actually 14k. If the sample needle shows a steady yellow while the jewelry mark fades to red, make the same test again using the 10k sample needle. When you match the marks, you have a karat weight reading.

Be sure to ***keep your acid bottles and the rags you will use to wipe the whetstone well away from all electronic equipment such as calculators, electronic diamond testers and computers.*** The acid is capable of rusting metals from as far as three to four feet in diameter of where it is being utilized. The fumes can play havoc on your equipment and don't forget, it can be very harmful to the metal on guns as well.

If you spill acid on your skin, bathe the area with clear water as soon as possible. Sometimes, you won't know the acid has touched you until you become aware of a tingling sensation on your skin. If your fingernail beds turn yellow, it isn't mustard. You got acid on them. In a few days, the yellow will peel off like sunburned skin as it heals.

I can't warn you too much about allowing children to play near your gold testing area.

We had a horrifying experience in our family which resulted in a two-year-old being permanently scarred on his chest and arm. It took *weeks* for the acid to stop working its way into the child's tender skin and there was nothing the doctors could do to neutralize the acid once it worked its way deep into the soft flesh. We had to wait for the acid to neutralize itself on its own.

Sometimes, you need to pour acid directly on the jewelry because you might not trust the whetstone. If the piece is not gold, it will sizzle and turn green. If it is gold, the acid won't harm it.

There are the exceptions which follow:

Remember to *ALWAYS RINSE OFF THE PIECE IN WATER BEFORE RETURNING IT TO THE CUSTOMER!* Imagine the damage the acid could do if the customer replaced the jewelry on his finger or neck. And imagine the lawsuit in which you could become entangled.

As in all things of the universe, there are exceptions to the acid test as well. Two very important exceptions are the two metals that can sometimes fool the pawnbroker.

The first is silver. Silver will leave a creamy trace on the whetstone that could mislead a person to believe the metal is white gold.

As a general rule, diamonds are not mounted in silver and turquoise is seldom mounted in gold. Many items in silver tend to look a bit coarse and 'unfinished.'

If you purchase silver at gold prices, you will have made a great error. *Gold markets at $350 per ounce and silver markets somewhere around $5 per ounce,* according to today's (2nd quarter 1990) market – a substantial difference in prices.

The second exception is copper.

I will share another anecdote that cost sixty dollars to learn and has literally saved hundreds (perhaps thousands) in poor investments. The sixty dollar lesson proved to be quite valuable in the long run.

One day, a woman came into one of our stores and offered to sell a nice looking gold bracelet. The bracelet looked gold and it tested gold. Still, there was something about it that seemed as if it consisted of some metal other than gold. The trinket was tested and retested. Everytime it came up gold on the whetstone. The broker even dug a little niche into the metal to see if the acid would react to an inner part of the bracelet. Still, the test showed positive. With great trepidation, the broker purchased the bracelet from the woman. Later, the broker discovered the bracelet was heavily plated copper. Copper will show positive on the acid test.

This mistake taught two lessons to the broker. Number one – some ***copper tests positive with nitric acid.***

(A more thorough test done with the alternate acids and neutralizers would have told the broker he was testing copper ... follow *ALL* the instructions in your acid testing kit.)

Number two – *Copper smells like copper!* Smell the piece in question after acid is applied directly on the metal. Sometimes a scent of copper can be clearly detected without the acid. **Copper has a distinct odor.** Compare the smell to the scent of a jar of pennies.

Most importantly, trust your own instincts on any items in question. *If there is doubt, pass!* Most errors are made when the store is busy and the broker is concerned about getting to each individual effectively.

Especially after some experience in gold testing, the broker tends to be lulled into a false sense of security and when he/she feels hurried, it is very tempting to shortcut the procedures required for accuracy.

You can pick up a lot of valuable information by subscribing to magazines like the international magazine, *Today's Pawnbroker* and the national association's *National Pawnbroker,* the two most informative publications in the collateral lending industry.

Many interesting bits and pieces of information can be obtained through your state Collateral Loan and Secondhand Dealer's Association and/or the National Pawnbroker's Association.

Both state and national conventions are held regularly and vendors are invited to display and demonstrate new developments in a wide variety of fields, including all precious metals.

You would be surprised at the wide range of gadgets and computers that are made available to the pawnbroker. Allow the vendors to demonstrate their wares and don't be afraid of high pressure tactics. Ask lots of questions! Soon, you will be able to discern what is right for you. The proper tools are crucial in order to do your job effectively, especially in the area of precious metals. Some fun things won't be worth the investment while other items are really necessities that you shouldn't be without. The choice is yours ... but whatever you choose, it is all available at wholesale convention prices. The smelting companies are always well represented at these conventions and you can pick up a wealth of information just by introducing yourself to their friendly and helpful representatives.

Precious metals dealers aren't only interested in smelting scrap gold, platinum, and silver. There are dealers who deal in specifics such as silver flatware. Several deal in nothing but silverplated items and they are particularly interested in the design of the plated flatware because it is their business to cater to people who want to replace missing pieces of various antique settings.

Other precious metals dealers are interested in bulk purchases of gold plate and gold-filled items. Some deals are struck on entire barrels of gold plate and filled pieces.

Indeed, the business of precious metals is most lucrative and very intriguing.

GOLD PAYMENT CHART (Marked Gold)

New York Close	10K Per DWT	14K Per DWT	Dental Per DWT	18K Per DWT
250	4.50	6.60	7.50	8.50
260	4.68	6.86	7.80	8.84
270	4.86	7.12	8.18	9.18
280	5.04	7.38	8.40	9.52
290	5.22	7.54	8.70	9.86
300	5.40	7.80	9.00	10.20
310	5.58	8.06	9.30	10.54
320	5.76	8.32	9.60	10.88
330	5.94	8.58	9.90	11.22
340	6.12	8.84	10.20	11.56
350	6.30	9.10	10.50	11.90
360	6.48	9.36	10.80	12.24
370	6.66	9.62	11.10	12.58
380	6.84	9.88	11.40	12.92
390	7.02	10.14	11.70	13.26
400	7.20	10.40	12.00	13.60
410	7.38	10.66	12.30	13.94
420	7.56	10.92	12.60	14.28
430	7.74	11.18	12.90	14.62
440	7.92	11.44	13.20	14.96
450	8.10	11.70	13.50	15.30
460	8.28	11.96	13.80	15.64
470	8.46	12.22	14.10	15.98
480	8.64	12.48	14.40	16.32
490	8.82	12.74	14.70	16.66
500	9.00	13.00	15.00	17.00
510	9.18	13.26	15.30	17.34
520	9.36	13.52	15.60	17.68
530	9.54	13.78	15.90	18.02
540	9.72	14.04	16.20	18.36
550	9.90	14.30	16.50	18.70
560	10.08	14.56	16.80	19.04
570	10.26	14.82	17.10	19.38
580	10.44	15.08	17.40	19.72
590	10.62	15.34	17.70	20.06
600	10.80	15.60	18.00	20.40
610	10.98	15.86	18.30	20.74
620	11.15	15.12	18.60	21.08
630	11.34	16.38	18.90	21.42
640	11.52	16.64	19.20	21.76
650	11.70	16.90	19.50	22.10
660	11.88	17.16	19.80	22.44
670	12.06	17.42	20.10	22.78
680	12.24	17.68	20.40	23.12
690	12.42	17.94	20.70	23.46
700	12.60	18.20	21.00	23.80
710	12.78	18.46	21.30	24.14
720	12.96	18.72	21.60	24.48
730	13.14	18.98	21.90	24.82
740	13.32	19.24	22.20	25.15
750	13.50	19.50	22.50	25.50 *

FINENESS OF GOLD KARATS

KARAT	FINENESS
10K	.41666
13K	.54166
13½K	.56250
14K	.58333
18K	.75000
22K	.91666
24K	1.00000

WEIGHT EQUIVALENTS

1 Avoirdupois lb.	= 14,583 Troy oz.
1 Avoirdupois lb.	= 16 Avoirdupois ozs.
1 Kilogram	= 32.15076 Troy oz.
1 Troy oz.	= 31.10348 Grams
1 Gram	= .03215 Troy oz.
1 Troy oz.	= 20 Pennyweights
1 Pennyweight	= 24 Grains
1 Pennyweight	= .05 Troy oz.
1000 Grams	= 1 Kilogram
1 Kilogram	= 2.2046 lbs.
1 Avoirdupois oz.	= .9115 Troy oz.
1.55517 Grams	= 1 Pennyweight
1 Gram	= .643 Pennyweights

GOLD TESTING KITS and pricing charts can be obtained through various merchandisers who can be found in the advertiser's section of this book and the specialty publications such as *Today's Pawnbroker*, the international magazine and *The National Pawnbroker*, the national association's magazine.

* Note the charted gold prices vary by 18 cents per ten dollars on the 10 karat, 26 cents per ten dollars on the 14 karat, 30 cents per ten dollars on the dental gold and 34 cents per dollar on the 18 karat.

If you keep your buying prices at half the smelter's prices and your retail prices at double the smelter's prices, you should be very competitive in the buying and retail selling of gold.

CHAPTER 10

SILVER

There is only one secret to determining if metal is silver. The word *Sterling* (and/or .925) will be stamped on the back or the bottom of the piece in question. Many times the word *Sterling* is accompanied by the number .925 which means 92.5 percent pure silver. Some pieces only carry the numbering. The number .925/100 is only another form of .925. There are a few exceptions but, for the most part, ALL true Sterling Silver pieces are marked in this manner.

In other words, ***IF IT ISN'T MARKED, IT ISN'T!*** Usually, if you can't find the magic word *Sterling* and/or the 925 number stamped on the piece, you can be sure it is only silver-plated.

Silver is weighed in *troy ounces.* Twenty pennyweights are in a troy ounce. If you are weighing by the avoirdupois ounce (which is highly unusual), then one troy ounce is equal to 31.103 grams or 2.753 grams heavier than the troy ounce.

Like gold, silver is a soft metal and must be mixed with another alloy in order to allow the piece to maintain its intended shape. Actually, sterling is not pure silver. It is 92.5 percent silver and 7.5 percent alloy or a metal that hardens the piece. Copper is commonly used as the alternated hardening alloy.

An average Sterling Silver teaspoon weighs approximately one troy ounce.

For the most part, there are two types of silver that the pawnbroker is likely to deal in. There is the flatware or the table settings that are made of Sterling Silver. Then there is the hollowware (derived from the term hollow ware) that is comprised of pitchers, bowls, trays, candle holders, etc. Large serving spoons and ladles are categorized in the area of flatware.

Ladles, trays and pitchers will render the nearest melt value. Books can be obtained on patterns if the dealer has an interest in values other than melt. Most pawnbrokers don't specialize, therefore quoting only melt value to parties interested in selling their silver pieces.

There are exceptions to determining weights

which the pawnbroker should make clear to the person who is selling.

Knives are made of stainless steel and the handles are weighted with cement which is used to affix the handle to the blade. These knives usually can be estimated to be close to a half ounce in weight (or ten pennyweights). Most candle-stick holders are weighted and in so being make it difficult to judge an accurate weight.

If your intention is to purchse Sterling Silver for scrap purposes only, then at today's prices, flatware priced individually is nearly worthless to the buyer.

If the market is at five dollars and fifty cents per troy ounce, a Sterling Silver teaspoon that weighs one ounce (.925 of spot, less the refiner's cut) will command four dollars at the very most. This means that a table knife commands two dollars at the local pawn shop.

If an accurate weight can be obtained, a good rule of thumb is to figure .85 times the market.

Based on a $5.50 market, a dealer can expect to realize $4.67 for his scrap Silver. Of course, he would want to make a reasonable profit and this justifies a $4.00 price the dealer offers the customer.

Be aware that the market (like any other market) is subject to daily changes. Many times, the pawnbroker insures his loan with only half of what he would purchase the pieces for ... or $2.00 per troy ounce on a loan. This justifies any market changes that might occur over the long haul providing the owner chooses not to redeem the merchandise.

I know people who deal exclusively in Silver. Personally, we have found that (unless we are going to deal in it by the pound) there is really not much payoff.

Many people got rich overnight in 1980 when the Hunt brothers drove up the market by their wild spending spree. They also went to jail! Considering what happened to the Hunt brothers, I doubt if there are too many people left with the means and the moxie to defy the law, risking millions of dollars to do it.

The Hunt brothers drove the Silver market right through the sky and silver soared from $3 per ounce to $65 per ounce. Everybody jumped in with their dollars in order to get on the bandwagon.

The first ones in and the first ones out made the big dollars. Everyone else got caught by getting in too late at inflated prices and lagging behind hoping for another surge. But by then, the market was tumbling downward and it stopped almost right where it started. It has hovered around $3.00 to $4.50 an ounce now for years.

Because we don't do much dealing in Silver, my best advice would be to visit someone who deals in fine metals and who specializes in silver metals. (See chapter on *Vendors* for dealers.)

CHAPTER 11

DIAMOND OR FAKE?

Diamonds are a girl's best friend, but they can put the pawnbroker out of business in a hurry if he isn't careful!

HOW CAN I TELL IF IT'S A DIAMOND?

The most common way that pawnbrokers test diamonds is with an electronic diamond probe. This is the most inexpensive and practical aid in helping to identify diamonds. It is also the most reliable and nearly foolproof for the inexperienced layman. There are several methods of testing diamonds and the apprentice pawnbroker would be wise to utilize several of these techniques in order to confirm positive identification.

One of the unique properties of natural diamonds is their ability to conduct heat even more rapidly than copper or aluminum. No diamond simulant can match this high thermal conductivity. Glass, for example, is a very poor conductor of heat.

The electronic diamond probe has been designed to assist jewelers and gemologists who can identify the older, more unsophisticated diamond simulants, but who may have some difficulty in identifying CZ gems, particularly the smaller set stones.

When the tip of the diamond probe is placed perpendicular in the center of the table facet of the stone in question, the stone's thermal conductivity is measured and the probe will give a specific reading as to the validity of the diamond.

The indicator will either read *imitation* or *true* diamond. This method has been the most successful in detecting even the most sophisticated fakes in the business. The diamond probe is well worth the investment, approximately two hundred dollars. Some of the finer models allow for recalibration.

Instructions come with the diamond probe which are simple to follow.

After charging up the probe for the specified period of time written in the instructions, turn the probe on and place the metal point directly on the table facet (as mentioned above). Sometimes a test can be difficult if the stone has been layered with lotion or oil or is not at room temperature.

Often, people will inadvertently heat up the stone by holding the tip of the probe on it too long or by re-testing the stone several times in a row. The stone *must* be at room temperature.

For the most accurate test, be sure the stone is

clean of all soapy or oily film, it is completely dry, and that the stone is no warmer or cooler than room temperature.

DO NOT ALLOW THE METAL TIP OF THE PROBE TO TOUCH THE METAL PRONGS ON THE STONE SETTING. AND, VERY IMPORTANT, KEEP YOUR GOLD TESTING ACID COMPLETELY CLEAR OF THE DIAMOND TESTER. *Nitric acid will destroy the inner workings of a diamond probe in a matter of days!*

When I question my electronic diamond tester (which I seldom do), I use the tried and true stagecoach method as an alternative. That would be a ***diamond scratcher*** which is simply a metal pen with a carbide tip.

The diamond is rated at the highest number 10. Ten (10) is the hardest substance in the world. The carbide tester will scratch anything but a natural diamond.

Take the carbide tip of the pen and bear down on the center of the stone you wish to test. If it gouges the stone, it is not a diamond (probably a cubic zirconium). If you cannot make a mark on the diamond, then you can be sure what you are contemplating to buy or pawn is the real thing.

If you intend to utilize the scratcher pen, do not forget to warn your customer that if their stone is not a real diamond, it will be permanently marked with a scratch across the table.

If the customer is trying to put one over on you, they will back up on the testing. In that case, lend strictly on the gold content (completely discounting the stone).

Once you have the customer's permission, be sure to bear down on the stone to make certain that the scratcher pen isn't sliding over an oily area. You will be amazed at how easily the scratcher works. When just starting out, a $5 scratcher pen looks a lot more sensible than a $200 electronic tester.

The above items and more are available through many of the specialty merchandisers. (See the chapter on *Stocking Your Store.)*

There are other methods of telling a real diamond from a fake. The most obvious is ***visual*** which requires some expertise in the field of grading diamonds.

There is a quality about diamonds that is unique from all other stones. This particular peculiarity of well cut diamonds is called *foreshortening* by the experts.

To examine for foreshortening, the back of the facet edges must be inspected while looking through the table or the uppermost flat surface under a good light. Foreshortening makes the stone appear shallower than it actually is. This is the nature of an optical illusion, caused by the play of light.

Another form of visual inspection is the *tilt test.* In this test, the diamond is held close to the eye with the table in an upward position. Slowly, tilt the table away from your eye. If the stone is genuine, the brilliance and sparkle will remain even as it is observed through the table, even as the angle is exaggerated. If the stone begins to lose some of its fire as the table is tilted away, it is probably a fake.

Some diamond dealers use the *breath test* whereupon they breathe on the stone in question while (at the same time) breathe on a known diamond. If the coating of moisture clears from both at the same time, this is an indication that the stone in question is a diamond. If it clears noticeably sooner from the diamond, the subject-stone can be presumed to be made from a mineral other than diamond.

The *magnetic test.* Diamonds have a magnetic quality that seems to magnetize water! For this test, the table of stone must be perfectly clean. A drop of water is placed on the table. If it begins to spread about, it is probably not a diamond. A diamond has the ability to keep water magnetized, holding it firmly in place on the table.

The *heat test.* Diamonds also have a powerful heat conductivity. A simple temperature test can help determine the genuineness of a stone. Take a known simulated cubic zircon and expose it with the stone in question to either heat or cold. Immediately place each stone against your lips. The diamond is the one that has retained the heat or cold while the CZ loses the thermal conductivity rapidly.

HOW CAN I TELL THE SIZE OF A DIAMOND?

Unless you remove the stone from this mounting and weigh it, you can only take an educated guess of the size. There are a myriad of tools available to jewelers. Among them are diamond estimators. These consist of a set of metal disks. Each disk is made up of holes that measure the circumference of the stone and gives an estimated carat weight. Many merchandisers offer these for sale at very low prices.

The stone is placed up against the back of the disk holes, moving it up and down the scale until the hole that shows the diamond in its entirety, without any space between the stone and the hole, is found. The reading on the side of the hole is the approximate diamond size.

A one carat diamond consists of one hundred points ... or one hundred parts — one hundred slices of a pie, if you will. A diamond that shows .50 or ½ ct. on the measuring device is 50 points or ½ carat. A twenty-five point diamond is .25 or ¼ carat.

The math is as easy as dollars and cents! If a pawnbroker is paying $2 per point on average stones, he will pay $50 on a ¼ carat diamond. That same ¼ carat diamond can sell for as much as $250 (or $10 per point) if it is a decent stone. (That price does not take the gold weight into consideration!)

When dealing in very large stones of two carats or better, the scale tends to exaggerate itself. A good quality two carat diamond can sell easily in a pawn shop for at least $6,000. I sold a two carat diamond to a gentleman for his wife. I asked $7,500 for the stone because of the unusually clean and clear quality. He had it appraised later for $17,500. I purchased the diamond for $2,000 from a customer.

The larger the diamond and the better the quality, the rarer the find it is. I have heard it said that it takes one million tons of earth to uncover a one carat stone. That should give one a slight idea to the rarity of any diamond of quality over one carat in size.

HOW DO I TELL THE QUALITY OF A DIAMOND?

The basic rule of thumb regarding diamond

grading is, *what you see is what you get.* i.e.:

THE FIVE FATAL FLAWS:

1. Chipped, cracked or broken;
2. Milky or foggy;
3. Black specks visible to the naked eye;
4. White feathery streaks;
5. Lacking sparkle and fire exclusive only to diamonds.

If, after you are sure the stone is clean and free of all lotions and oils, any one of these factors is a good reason to pay nothing (or next to nothing) for the stone. IF THE DIAMOND IS CHIPPED OR BROKEN, DON'T COUNT IT AT ALL! You can still make your pawn or purchase measuring the gold weight of the jewelry, giving little or no value to the diamond.

CLARITY CHARACTERISTICS:

(Taken from the 1983 Official Price Guide to Antique Jewelry by Guy Kaplan. Published by The House of Collectibles, Inc., Orlando, FL.)

Clarity characteristics of diamonds are really defect characteristics. It is important to note that *blemishes* are marks or other characteristics on the surface of a stone. *Inclusions* are trapped or imbedded within the diamond.

The more commonly encountered BLEMISHES are:

ABRASION: Chip on the facet edge, nearly always caused by two diamonds coming into contact with each other. Sometimes called papermarks.

EXTRA FACET: An additional facet or plane surface,beyond the number required in shaping. This generally occurs through accident in the cutting process.

NATURAL: An overlying portion of the crystal covering or skin. Found, if at all, near or at the girdle.

PIT: Small nick or cavity. Also known as a CHIP.

SCRATCH MARK, WHEEL MARK: Scratches on diamonds may result from contact with other diamonds or defects in the polishing wheel.

SURFACE GRAIN LINE: Evidence (at the surface) of irregular crystal development.

COMMON INCLUSIONS:

CLOUD: An area within a diamond that is not perfectly clear but appears opaque.

FEATHER: Break in structure of diamond.

FEATHERED GIRDLE: Networks of very fine feathery lines radiating outward from the girdle into the stone's interior.

INCLUDED CRYSTAL: A second crystal within the first or main crystal. It may be clear or colored. When the included crystal is colored or has the appearance of black, it is called a "dark included crystal."

INTERNAL GRAIN LINE: Internal grain marks of abnormal crystal development.

KNOT: Included crystal (second diamond crystal) which has broken through the surface.

LAZAR FILL HOLE: Tiny hole caused by drilling with a laser beam in an effort to launder the stone.

THE DIAMOND CUT

Grading diamonds for cut is rather difficult for an inexperienced person such as the average pawnbroker. The ability to distinguish between good and bad cuts lies in the amount of time acquired by handling and inspection of many diamonds.

Some diamonds are intentionally out of proportion for the sake of saving carat weight.

The difference between good and bad may be so slight as to be virtually indistinguishable to the naked eye. We have a pawnbroker in the family who likes to quip, "I grade diamonds three ways ... good, bad and ugly. I accept only the good ones!"

That is just about how much diamond knowledge most successful pawnbrokers obtain!

DIAMOND SHAPES

"There are six traditional or popular shapes in which diamonds are cut: *Round, Marquis, Emerald, Heart, Oval and Pear.*

Many variations in shaping and/or faceting of these shapes are possible and will be encountered on the market. You will also find diamonds of other shapes ... usually referred to as *fancy* or miscellaneous shapes.

Diamonds with shapes other than these six are normally not invariably European Cuts and many are antique. For example, the *Mazarin Cut,* named after Cardinal Mazarin (17th century), is a French version of today's Round Brilliant. It is almost but not perfectly circular.

ROUND: Also known as *Round Brilliant.* "This has come to be the most popular cut. The name is self-explanatory."

This cut affords the greatest sparkle. The most desirable of the brilliant cuts are the newer cuts with a larger table (top of the diamond). This larger table allows for the brilliance of the facets to show up through the middle of the stone and refracts the greatest amount of light.

Round diamonds that are cut up high from the girdle (the edge of the stone) to the top of the table with a small area left for the table are old and not considered to be of much value. Generally, they are very hard to sell unless they happen to be set in antique or unique settings.

"An early forerunner of the Round Brilliant was the *European or English Square Cut,* which was not truly square but featured bowed sides.

Through experimentation and evolution, the sides became more bowed and gradually the shape was altered from roughly square to roughly circular, until the point was reached of shaping the stone perfectly circular.

The so-called *Old Single Cut* was an intermediate step between square and round. It was rounded but squared off into an octagon, either with a large table and short crown or virtually no table at all and a high crown.

The *Rounded Single Cut,* now also obsolete, was similar but with a more rounded girdle. Single facets only were cut into the crowns of these stones. They were attractive but the single faceting did not make full use of a diamond's ability to refract light. These cuts were admired in their time because buyers were not exposed to anything better. None are being produced today except in limited quantities of reproductions of antique jewelry."

Round cuts generally have 48 facets cut into them. There is no way to count them without being an expert. But the round diamonds that have less facets (usually 24) are easily spotted because they are generally smaller and placed around larger stones for effect.

A 24 faceted round is easy to spot if you use a 10 power loop and look straight down into the table. Instead of a multi-faceted reflection, you will see something like 'pie wedges.' Even though these test out to be genuine, they are single cut diamonds and not worth counting in the setting.

Beware of *Philippine diamonds.* They are generally off color (light yellow) and/or full of inclusions and black carbon markings. Philippine ring settings are usually mounted on tall prongs and sit high above the finger.

MARQUISE: "The *Marquise* is a variation of the brilliant cut in which the stone is oval shaped and comes to a point at either end. It may be cut into the classic Marquise, featuring a long table squared at either end and bowing out slightly into a semi-triangle at the sides, or the less common *Navette Marquise* which has a star pattern. The Navette has not been popular in the U.S."

There are two fatal flaws in the Marquise that would make a pawnbroker turn a marquise away or bid extremely low. The first is a broken tip. Diamonds are the hardest substance in the world but they are also very brittle. Marquise cuts create weaknesses in the stone and the points are often snapped off. If this is the case, discount the stone to zero.

The second fatal flaw is inclusions. For some reason, marquise's seem to be the most susceptible to inclusions. These inclusions probably take place during the time the jeweler set it in the mounting. If not done correctly, the diamond can become overheated, causing milky infractions or a shattering. Take a close look to be sure what you see is actual faceting and not shattered fractures within the stone.

PEAR: "The *Pear Cut* is also sometimes referred to as Teardrop. It is actually egg-shaped, coming to a point at the small end. The table is roughly rectangular, intersected with both straight and curving cuts."

Look for the same weaknesses in those as you would the marquise.

EMERALD: "This is what the name suggests, a shape following that into which emeralds are normally cut. It is rectangular with the corners removed and features a very large rectangular table, also with the corners removed."

The facets are fewer on the emerald cut and, although the stone is usually quite elegant, they still don't have the same fire and refraction capability of a brilliant. Most people will admire the Emerald Cut but they will put their cash down for the Round Cut nine times out of ten!

HEART: "*Heart* shapes were at first rated among the novelty cuts. There are several variations of faceting but all stones have the diamond itself cut into a heart shape."

The *Heart Cut* is rather like the Emerald Cut, quite exquisite but, again, the Round Cut is usually preferable.

OVAL: "The *Oval* shape is just what the name

implies. The table is of modest size and all cuts are curved." Ovals are a particular favorite of mine. They sell well but not like the Round Cuts.

OLD MINE CUT: "The *Old Mine Cut* is generally found in jewelry made before 1900. This is a crudely cut round shape. Proportions are very inaccurate. They are frequently found in fine pieces of antique jewelry. Some people mistakenly believe that there is an antique value to these Mine Cuts, but this is not the case.

"Though a modern well-executed Round Brilliant is valued from 300% to 500% of an Old Mine Cut of the same size on today's market, a re-cut is usually avoided to preserve the historical significance and overall workmanship of the piece of jewelry. The term Old Mine Cut originated from the belief that in the 1800's, diamonds were cut at the mines before wholesaling. This was seldom the case. These cuts simply reflected the standards and state-of-the-art of diamond cutting prior to the development of the Modern Round Brilliant Cut."

BAGUETTE: A diamond cut that is becoming very popular as a mounting to show off larger stones is the *Baguette Cut*. This is a stone that is cut in a tubular shape which is usually wider on one end and more pointed on the other. When mounted in groups, they resemble fiery slivers of light that compliment the main stone. Any stone (be it diamond or any colored stone) will sell well if it is accentuated nicely with baguettes.

RADIANT BRILLIANT: This is a new cut on the market that is very rare but I'm sure we will be seeing a lot more of them in the years to come. The uniqueness of this cut is that it is Emerald Cut on the top side and Round Brilliant Cut on the bottom side. This allows for the maximum reflection of the fully faceted Round Cut to radiate up through the maximum area possible on the large Emerald Cut table. I've only come upon several in the last few years.

Diamonds can be cut in all shapes imaginable. There are *Triangle Cuts, Flower Cuts, Butterfly Cuts,* and once I even saw a very special diamond which was about 6 to 8 carats in size that was cut in the shape of a horse's head!

Please be aware that you are not getting gemologist training in this manual. Diamond experts would probably flinch at most of this advice. They are into grading diamonds according to size, cut, clarity and quality. You will hear things from them like "This diamond is a J-VVSI," which will mean nothing to you and it means very little to me.

Sometimes a little education can go quite a long way. In this case, I would urge the reader to go to the local library and check out several books on diamond cutting, color charting and grading.

As a successful pawnbroker, I must rely on my eye and what education I've been able to muster along the way. From past experience and self-tutoring, I have learned enough to keep me competitive. Now, instead of that Louis Lamour or Agatha Christie paperback, I settle down at night with a good book on gemstones, cameras, tools ... any piece of informative literature which will help me to make better judgements on things I pawn and buy. Learn whatever you can whenever you can!

By doing a little extra reading one evening, I found out that diamonds are color coded from the alphabet beginning at the letter D and going all the way through the letter Z+!

Just for fun (and the information is quite interesting but not totally necessary for pawnbrokers to learn), I will give the reader a bit of 'thumbnail' information so that in the event the conversation arises (and it is inevitable sooner or later), the reader won't be left totally in the dark when a "diamond snob" tries an intimidation maneuver in order to get a better price. I don't need to paint a picture of a "diamond snob" ... you will recognize one the moment he/she begins a conversation with you.

Diamond grading goes something like this:

DETERMINE THE COLOR OF A DIAMOND:

"Reaching correct or reliable conclusions about the color of a diamond is somewhat more challenging than grading for clarity, as a number of variables enter the picture."

It is not only a matter of differences in the human eye to perceive color, but interference from color reflection of other objects. This is an extremely delicate operation. If conditions are not ideal, the results obtained are likely to be unreliable and will be challenged when the stone is subsequently examined by a person using more sophisticated techniques.

"It should also be pointed out that color grading is not an absolute science and that many stones of both high and low ranking could easily be placed into different grades by persons of equal expertise."

Sophisticated equipment is now available on the market for use in determining diamond color ... but pawnbrokers rarely get into this kind of stone grading.

"The most common technique of color grading is "comparison grading," used by the G.I.A. You must use what the industry refers to as a "master set of diamonds." These are stones that have been graded by the G.I.A. into specific color categories. They are placed in a row under correct lighting and the stone of undetermined color is compared to each until the closest match is found."

COLOR CHART
From the 1983 Jewelry 2nd Edition, KAPLAN:

The chart begins with **D**, which refers to the best color (completely colorless) quality of a brilliant blue-white diamond (the most desirable color for investment diamonds). There is no **A, B** or **C** in the scale. The letters toward the beginning of the alphabet represent the more desirable colors; toward the end the less desirable.

D, E, F: These represent the most attractive investments, assuming their other qualities are comparable.

G =	Nearly colorless, fine white
H =	Nearly colorless, white
I =	Nearly colorless, commercial white
J =	Nearly colorless, top silver cape
K =	Slightly tinted, ranging from top silver cape (better) to silver cape (not quite desirable.)
L =	Slightly tinted, silver cape
M =	Slightly tinted, light cape
N =	Slightly tinted, light cape, but not as high as grade M
O =	Pale Yellow, cape
P =	Pale Yellow, cape, lower grade
Q =	Pale Yellow, cape, third lowest grade of this classification
R =	Light Yellow (stronger yellow than above), cape
S =	Light Yellow, dark cape

T =	Light Yellow, dark cape, more heavily colored
U =	Yellow, dark cape
V =	Yellow, dark cape, strong coloration, very little light refraction, not a gem quality stone
X, Y, Z =	Very heavily colored
Z+ =	Extremely heavily colored. Called Fancies. Rare. Considered the most valuable of diamonds, more so than say a "D" flawless.

TERMINOLOGY AND DETERMINATION OF DIAMOND CLARITY: The most complicated terminology refers to gem clarity. This is a series of grades ranging from Flawless — expressed as FL — down to badly defective or "1-3."

(NOTE: 10X magnification is the standard maximum limit for inspecting and grading diamonds throughout the world.)

FL — Flawless — the highest grade

It is presumed by beginners or uninformed persons that to qualify as FL, a diamond must be so crystal clear that no degree of magnification reveals even the slightest blemish or imperfection.

This is not true. Minor deviations from perfection exist; it is an extremely rare stone which magnified to 10X exhibits no flaws whatsoever. There may be slight imperfections that are visible only with a magnification greater than 10X, nevertheless, if an imperfection or a blemish is not visible at 10X, for evaluation purposes it is insignificant.

GRADING SCALE

IF — Internally Flawless - slight surface imperfections but internally the stone is as perfect as an FL;

VVS — Very Very Slight Imperfections - faults slightly easier to observe with 10X magnification. VVS stones are blemished;

VVS-1 — has very tiny inclusions which can be distinguished with extreme difficulty under 10X magnification;

VVS-2 — Like VVS-1 but inclusions a bit easier to see;

VS — Very Slight Imperfection - slightly more pronounced degree than the VVS - may show small colorless crystals or groupings of pinpoints. The VS stone is, despite its lengthy catalogue of possible shortcomings, an extremely worthy speciman. Its faults, while many, are all of minor variety and cannot be observed without a 10X magnification;

VS-1 — Minor Inclusions more pronounced but difficult to see;

VS-2 — Minor Inclusions more noticeable than VS-1 ... fairly easy to see with 10X magnification;

SI — Slight Imperfection - blemishes relatively easy to see with 10X magnification. One or more crystals that are pinpoints or dark in color. As diamonds become more scarce, even Sis should become investment worthy;

SI-I and SI-2 — Inclusions can be seen directly with 10X magnification;

SI-2 reveals some inclusions with naked eye;

I-1 — Imperfect First Degree - all artificial aids abandoned and diamond viewed with 20/20 vision at close range ... inclusions very apparent with 10X magnification;

I-2 — Imperfect Second Degree - blemishes even more pronounced;

I-3 — Imperfect Third Degree - large dark spots, cloudiness, surface scratches, feathering below table, large pieces of carbon clearly visible. Generally, this stone should never have been cut into a finished stone.

*   *   *

This is where a furthered gemology education draws its distinct line and, unless one is willing to become educated extensively in this particular field, it is best to remain very conservative in this area of diamond dealing.

The reason for extreme conservatism is this. There is a vast difference between a natural *fancy* and a *fancy* that has been colored by man. Yes, there is a method that will make a natural diamond change its color. Gemologists use a laser technique that can change the color of a stone. It can make a diamond that has a slight color tendency toward the pale yellow shades deepen into a darker yellow.

The highly prized yellow *fancy* is called a *Canary Diamond.* If the colored diamond is natural, it is worth quite a bit of money. If it has been laser processed, it is worth no more than if it hadn't been treated at all.

Personally, I cannot tell the difference between the two. When called upon to issue a loan or to make an offer to buy, I lend or buy for what I would have paid for an ordinary and unremarkable stone.

If I happen to desire a *fancy,* I have a diamond broker who I can trust and who will deal with me on such an item within reason. Diamond brokers will find their way into your store. There is no need to go out searching. The diamond broker is not there to make the pawnbroker rich; his services can be utilized by a pawnbroker who needs to liquidate some inventory overflow. Sometimes, they profit nicely off the pawnbroker's ignorance. This is fair game!

In the pawnbroking business, it is desirable for a customer to make a good profit from us. This includes the diamond broker. This is what pawnbroking is all about. One should never begrudge giving another person a fantastic deal as long as there was a satisfactory profit at the time of the sale.

WHAT DO I PAY FOR A DIAMOND?

Pay little to nothing for a singly mounted diamond that is less than 5 points. When they are mounted in clusters, you can add up all the points and pay for the total carat weight.

I tend to pay only $1 per point on the small, more common clusters because the stones are usually of a slight milky quality and they are used primarily on cluster rings of that nature. They are intended for people who desire larger diamonds but find them to be unaffordable.

The average pawnbroker pays between $1 and $2 per point. When the stone is over a half carat and it is a particularly beautiful stone that is set in an attractive and desirable setting, $3 and up per point is offered to the customer.

Until you get a feel for your local market, your best bet is to stay in the range of $1 and $2 per point. Your store may not generate much jewelry activity ... although I don't know of many pawn shops that don't. All the same, it is best to remain conservative about the items you know least until you feel more secure with your market.

The good news is that you don't have to be a diamond expert in order to deal in them. If you are conservative, use a good 10X loop*, check for all the above listed fatal flaws, and keep firm on your $2 per point price, you will have no trouble in dealing successfully in the diamond market. If you stick to your guns on being conservative, you will learn much about the diamond trade and never suffer any losses on your investments.

Too good to be true? Not really! Every single subject in the world has its complicated areas, but most all of those same topics have a simplistic side that can be comprehended by most intelligent laymen. Diamonds are no different.

WHAT ABOUT COLORED STONES ... EMERALDS, RUBIES, SAPPHIRES, OPALS, TOPAZ', AMETHYSTS, AQUAMARINE, GARNETS, PEARLS, AND ALL THE MYRIAD OF GEMS AVAILABLE?

The answer to that is **NOTHING!** That's right!

Pawnbrokers are not gemologists and they do not profess to be! That is what we tell the customers. If the piece is very pretty and quite saleable, a pawnbroker might add $10 to $50 for the stone (if it is of any size), depending on the chance he wants to take.

If a large amethyst ring comes in that is particularly nice and it is set in 14 karat gold, weigh the ring and pay gold weight for the entire ring, amethyst and all. Do this when you don't intend to scrap the ring. If you can readily sell a piece, why not go a bit more on it?

When buyers are looking to make a purchase and ask for a guarantee, most pawnbrokers only guarantee a diamond. Whatever the colored stone is, they are probably getting it for free.

Generally, if a piece comes in that looks like it is genuine ruby or emerald, we take it to a jeweler before we set it out with a sale price on it. It is at that time the genuineness may be backed by the pawnbroker.

Don't forget to write *red stone* or *blue stone* on pawn tickets and sales receipts so that the customer cannot come back and claim that he left a genuine gem quality stone with you. Many times, we write *clear stone* for a diamond when we are a bit suspicious of the pawner's honesty regarding bait and switch possibilities.

Be conservative!!! Do not allow the pawner to control the situation. Many times they will say, "You got to be out of your mind! I paid over five hundred dollars for this and you are only offering fifty?"

The answer is simple. "I don't blame you. I wouldn't sell it either if it were mine. Fifty is the price for a sale or a loan. If you don't want to sell it, I would suggest you opt for the loan and you won't lose your merchandise."

When it is explained in those terms, they usually calm down and make their decision on whether or not they want a loan.

Sometimes when the customer gets huffy and leaves, it is not unusual for them to think it over and return to take the loan that was originally offered. Many times this takes place after they check around at other pawn shops only to find that you have given them the best offer.

Always agree that the merchandise is worth far

more than you are offering. That's how pawn shops work. If they want top dollar, it will be neccessary to find a private party to whom they can sell their goods. (See the chapter on *Dealing With Objections.)*

BIRTHSTONE LIST

January	Garnet
February	Amethyst
March	Aquamarine, Bloodstone
April	Diamond, Rose Zircon
May	Emerald
June	Moonstone Pearl, Alexandrite
July	Ruby
August	Peridot, Sardonyx
September	Sapphire
October	Tourmaline, Opal
November	Topaz, Citrine
December	Blue Zircon, Turquoise

** Quotes taken from The Official 1983 Price Guide To Antique Jewelry by Guy Kaplan, House of Collectibles, Inc.*

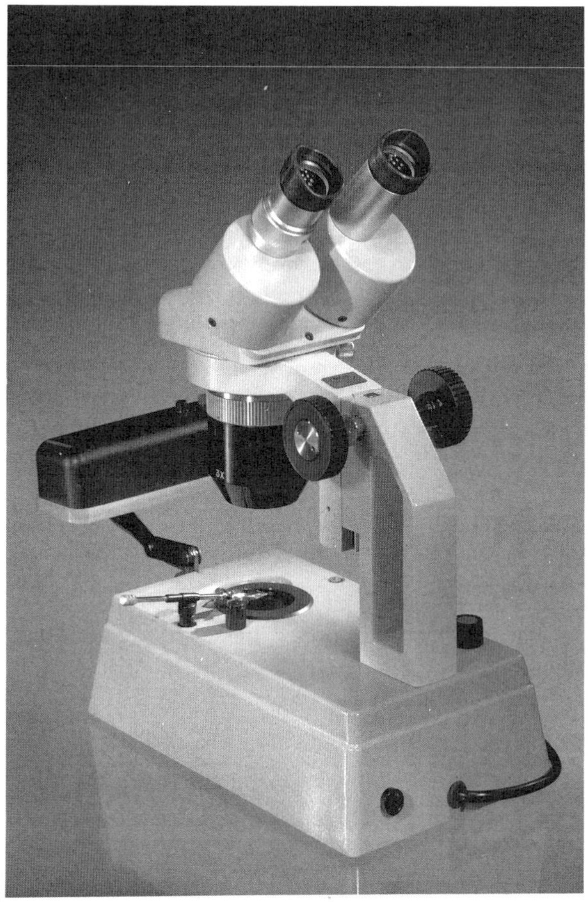

CHAPTER 12

WATCHES (WRIST AND POCKET)

Watches can be good items to pawn and to buy. Watches are also one of the trickiest items to deal in.

The first rule of pawning (buying watches) is to play it conservative!

There are many counterfeits on the market when it comes to wrist watches. The most popular are the Rolex wrist watches.

There are several ways to tell a Rolex from the fakes, but some of the counterfeits are so close to the real thing that it is best to shy away from these items unless you really know your merchandise.

The basic rule of thumb is that if a pawner is presenting what looks to be the real thing but there is a doubt in your mind ... and if the watch really looks good, go ahead and loan or buy ... but do it so that (just in case) you will be able to turn it over *AS A COPY* and at least double your money on the watch.

For awhile, people who dealt in counterfeits were getting into a lot of hot water over the selling of counterfeits as the real thing.

There is a very fine line here. IF the pawnbroker thinks he is making a purchase of the 'real McCoy,' then he is not in violation. Playing it conservative is just 'smart.' If you think the Rolex is a counterfeit, then you wouldn't want it anyway.

A good looking Rolex copy could sell for as much as $100. There are many people who don't mind investing that much rather than the thousands of dollars it would take for the genuine article. So going out on a limb for $50 if the watch looks resalable is not out of line ... especially if it turns out to be the real thing.

Note: For the sake of conversation only, a genuine Rolex differs from most copies in more obvious ways. One sure give-away is the secondhand sweeps smoothly on the Rolex while cheap copies have a secondhand that jumps from second to second.

Another obvious difference is that a Rolex offers a different sort of ticking. If you have a stethoscope handy and you have access to a genuine Rolex, then hold the stethoscope to the face of each watch and you will hear the difference.

A Rolex has sort of a pinging that accompanies the ticks. (Where does one come across a stethoscope? ... we got ours in the pawn shop! Sooner or later, everything seems to cross our threshold!)

There are, however, copies in existence that are just impossible for the layman to tell apart from the genuine article. So buy low and lend conservatively.

The usual rule is to buy gold wrist watches (including the band) for their weight in gold.

If you are buying your gold right (½ the smelter's price), you don't even have to deduct for the workings. Even if the wrist watch doesn't work, the money is in the band.

If the band is not gold but the watch casing is, then a man's large wrist watch usually will get around $20 to $50 if it is working. If the watch is broken, then offer to buy but not pawn. The reason for this is that you will want to take the watch apart and weigh only the gold. If the customer wants to keep the broken watch by just pawning it, then make a very low loan ... $10 is fine.

It is difficult to deal in wrist watches because many of them are battery powered and there is no way to sell a watch that doesn't work.

If a very nice Seiko, Citizens, or Bill Blass, etc. comes in, lend or buy for $10 to $15. You will be able to turn over only the very best of these wrist watches for around $40 to $100. Every once in awhile, you can get up to $200.

Good diving watches and the newer styles are good items to carry. These same wrist watches sell new for up to $600 and more.

Wrist watches that are corroded, dirty, battered and ill-used won't make a dime. Stay away from digital wrist watches as well.

Ladies wrist watches are even more difficult to sell unless you are taking in only the newest models. Remember that a lady's gold watch is usually much smaller than a man's, so be very careful when lending or buying for the gold.

The older ladies wrist watches that are covered with diamonds were once the rage. Today, it is difficult to give one of those away! We had a diamond wrist watch for sale that once cost someone well over $5,000. We pawned it for $300 and we couldn't sell it for $500.

It was too beautiful to dismantle, so it wound up in our family and it appears on a feminine wrist every once in awhile around the holidays and the more formal occasions. It gets heaps of complimentary attention lavished upon it, but those ladies who most truly admire it just get sick when we tell them what we are selling it for. Usually, they groan that their husbands bought them one similar at ten times the amount we are asking.

One lady in particular says (every time she sees it), "If I didn't have one just like it, I'd buy it in a heartbeat." All in all, that still doesn't pay the rent. So if you aren't looking for one of those diamond encrusted wonders to have for your very own, be very careful about your lending.

Perhaps had we been more conservative on the loan (like $100 instead of $300), the pawner would have returned for the wrist watch. But then there would be a few Fletcher ladies without the privilege of donning such a luxury.

Pocket watches are even more difficult. The number of jewels are important, but on some of the antiques, the number of jewels are not so important. The pocket watches are very collectable and many people aspire to own rare collections. There are as many kinds of pocket watches as there are pockets to keep them in.

There are also as many counterfeits and copies. For instance, the old Railroad pocket watches are highly prized. There are also many that aren't. Usually, the bigger, heavy pocket watches are desirable.

If they don't run, offer $10 and don't be afraid to let the customer walk out the door. I usually tell them that it's only a loan and they can retrieve it if they wish.

The gold filled and the gold pocket watches that are the most prized usually have engraving marks on the inside of the casings where the watchmakers who made or worked on the watch at any given time, made their marks. They look sort of like hieroglyphics or shorthand of a kind.

Of course, the pocket watches that are of genuine gold are far more valuable than the ones that are gold filled. Gold filled watches can be pawned for $10 to $25 while the genuine gold pocket watches can be weighed out without the workings.

Happy Sumpter of Sumpter's Jewelry and Pawn, Charlotte, NC says, "watches are a girls best friend."

Becoming an expert on wrist and pocket watches is almost a lifetime achievement. Like any other craft or hobby, it takes almost an obsession on the part of the craftsman or hobbyist in order to earn even a modest living out of the trade.

I say these things here so that you might know not to expect more of yourself than is possible. No one man can know everything and it is the successful pawnbroker who knows that more than anyone.

SALE!

CHAPTER 13

FIREARMS
(FEDERAL AND STATE)

THE 4473 FORM:

THIS FORM IS FEDERAL LAW AND APPLIES TO ANYONE WHO DEALS IN FIREARMS IN THE UNITED STATES AND THE TERRITORIES OF THE UNITED STATES!

The 4473 is a Federal Form **which is divided into two parts. The top portion is for customer information. The customer fills out the form, answers all of the questions, then signs it. No person may carry a firearm out of a licensed dealer's business without completing this form. This includes pawned as well as newly purchased guns.**

Many pawners who borrow money on their guns get upset when they return for their merchandise because they don't realize that the law is clear in that **they must fill out a 4473 form each and every time a transaction is completed and the weapon leaves the premises.**

Every single weapon that goes OUT the door has a 4473 form filled out for it. There are only two exceptions.

1. The holder of the gun license may transport the weapons to another location.
2. When local, State or Federal officers come in to pick up the weapon and request the forms with the weapon.

The forms are filed according to date,the first form going on the bottom of the pile, face down ... the next forms to follow are done the same way. The completed forms are to remain in the care of the gun licensee ***FOREVER!*** You will soon find that if you deal heavily in guns, you will be binding up stacks of completed 4473 forms, filling up every conceivable area you can think of and still looking for more places to stash them.

Do not confuse this 4473 procedure with the

DROS (Dealer's Record of Sale) which is addressed under California law. If the title of a weapon has not transferred to the store (as would be the case in a loan where the weapon is only being held as collateral), then the customer maintains legal title and no transfer has been made. Therefore, no DROS form is necessary.

I will refer to the 4473 form in conjunction with the Gun Log Book because by doing so, you will realize that there is a certain routine which can be implemented so that the 4473 form is always completed on every gun that leaves your store.

FILLING OUT THE 4473 FORM:

THE CUSTOMER: The top half of the 4473 form must be filled out by the customer. He/she must fill out ALL of the blank spaces, making sure that he/she answers the questions completely. The address must include apartment numbers and zip codes. The place of birth must include a city as well as the state or province and country. Every question must be answered with a NO answer or you may not release the firearm to the customer. The customer must sign and date the 4473 form.

THE STORE: The lower half is for the store (or the clerk) to complete. First, at the upper right hand corner of the 4473 form (under Transferor's Transaction Serial Number), the page and assigned number of the weapon must be entered. Moving on down past the customer's signature, everything must be filled out. X the appropriate box then move to Section 9. The type of ID used is entered and in Section 10, enter the ID number. Sections 11, 12, 13, 14 and 15 must be filled out. If there are more than two firearms, turn the form over and continue listing them on the reverse side of the form.

Section 16 is for the store name and address. Most stores stamp these ahead of time. Section 17 is for the store gun license number which is also usually stamped ahead of time by the clerks. Section 18 is for the signature of the person who is handling the transaction (usually a clerk). Section 19 is for entering the transferor's title (clerk, manager or owner). Section 20 must be filled out with the date the form is being filled out ... the same day the firearm is leaving the store.

THE FOLLOWING FEDERAL LAWS ARE APPLICABLE IN ALL STATES:

For a more in-depth look at the Federal laws, I would suggest you obtain a copy of the book regarding firearm laws from the Alcohol, Tobacco and Firearms (ATF) Bureau of the United States.

GUN LOG BOOK

The Federal Government wants a complete record of every firearm that comes ***IN*** the door. A notation in the log book must be made when the same firearm goes ***OUT*** the door.

Every weapon is assigned a special number and entered into a gun log. Our gun logs are spiral notebooks that we maintain by hand. The computer can do this job for us ... and it does. But when a police officer wants to review our gun books, we can sit them down in a chair and hand them all our gun logs and this keeps our computer free for us to continue conducting business as usual.

The gun log is divided into two sides. When the gun log book is laid flat in an open position, the facing pages (the page on the left and the page on the right) have the same page number. This is because it is impossible to place all of the information regarding every firearm in a smaller area and still maintain the space to handwritc the information.

The left side of the open notebook is the beginning of the information regarding each gun. Following along the same lines over to the opposite (right page) will tell everything about the gun from the day it comes into the store until the day it leaves the store.

Beginning on the left page, there are seven columns. Each column is assigned three rows of horizontal lines. Each set of three lines is one firearm and holds all of the information on that firearm.

The first column of the seven on the left page is dedicated to the make of gun and what kind of gun it is. For instance, the make is the brand name like a Colt or a Marlin. Under the make of gun is entered what type of gun it is. There are 3 types of guns that are available in this category. They are: **HANDGUNS – RIFLES – SHOTGUNS.**

The next column to the right is for the model of gun. Most guns carry a model name or number. There are a few exception, though. In those cases, write NMN or no model number.

Moving on again, the heading is serial number. With very few exceptions, almost every gun carries a serial number. The ones that don't are usually old relics and most dealers don't like them because it is a rare case where some old relic (even if it is a hundred years old) is worth very much.

Some old guns have 2 different serial numbers ... one on the bolt and one on the gun. This means that someone lost the original bolt and replaced it with a bolt off of some other old gun. If the serial numbers don't match, enter both, indicating which number goes on the gun and which on the bolt. (Hint: A rare collectible gun can drastically drop its value when serial numbers don't match. This means that all of the parts are not original.)

EXAMPLE: First Half of GUN LOG

PAGE: 1 ***LEFT SIDE ... 1st 1/2 of 2 pages facing one another make up 1 whole page of Gun Log.***

MAKE & TYPE	MODL	SERIAL NUMBER	ACT	CAL	NAME AND ADDRESS BORROWER OR SELLER OF GUN	DATE IN
Raven	P-25	1XX22#330	Semi	.25	William R. Smith	07/01/89
Handgun					432 Main Street	
					Happy Valley, CA 00076	
Colt	Python	X88V789	Rev	.357	Harry Jones	07/02/89
Handgun					555 Walnut	
					Goodway Cove, CA 00567	
Marlin	60	88XXXX90	Semi	.22	Grover Schultz	07/05/89
Rifle					0321 Mockingbird Hill	
					Beautiful Acres, CA 00055	
Mossberg	12	33XX567	Pmp	12g	Harriet Hoover	07/14/89
Shotgun					555 Willow Way	
					Cherry Hill, CA 00045	
Sm & Wes	Lady	00XXX567	Rev	.357	Purity Chandler	07/25/89
Handgun					888 4th Ave.	
					Sunshineville, CA 00011	
Ruger	Blkhwk	XXX0078	Rev	.22	Billy Bumper	08/04/89
Handgun					0342 Wigwam Way	
					Indian Hills, CA 00099	
Lorcin	L-25	000XXX56	Semi	.25	RSR Wholesalers	08/08/89
Handgun					Texas	
Lorcin	L-25	000XXX57	Semi	.25	RSR Wholesalers	08/08/89
Handgun					Texas	
Lorcin	L-25	000XXX58	Semi	.25	RSR Wholesalers	08/08/89
Handgun					Texas	
Winchestr	70	XX0098	Semi	30.06	Reginald Q. Winchester	08/11/89
Rifle					22 Snob Hill	
					Uppity Creek, CA 00059	

EXAMPLE: Second Half of GUN LOG

RIGHT SIDE ... 2nd 1/2 of 2 pages facing one another. Both facing pages assigned same page no.

DATE of PICK UP	DATE STS DATE SOLD	REDEEMED BY: OR SOLD TO: NAME AND ADDRESS	ID PAWNER or SELLER REDEEMER or BUYER	GUN NO 4443 Y/N
Redeems only	*STS 12/11/89*	*John Doe* *DOE bought gun that William Smith forfeited*	*CA DL #1234* *ID of SMITH*	*001* *Day gun IN*
	Wasn't redeemed	*12 Wrong Way Drive* *Info only when gun OUT door*	*ID above gun IN-ID below gun OUT*	*4473 DAY OUT*
	SOLD 1/3/90	*Unlikely, CA 00034* *Remember 4473 or no gun*	*CA ID #4321* *ID of new owner DOE*	*4473* *or no gun*
	STS 08/03/89	*Nothing entered in this column until gun is bought & out the door.*	*MIL ID #123456* *Day gun IN*	*002*
	Must hold for 30 days			*No. day IN*
			ID of new owner day gun OUT door	*#4473 day OUT*
08/02/89		*RECOVERED BY OWNER*	*CA DL #00000001*	*003*
Day gun redeemed		*(Schultz picks up his own gun.)*	*CA DL#00000001*	
		A #4473 form must be pawner or buyer before gun can go OUT door	*(Pawner/Redeemer SAME)*	*4473*
			CA DL #12345	*004*
			Still on pawn	
09/23/89		*RECOVERED BY OWNER*	*MIL ID #000002*	*005*
				4473
	01/04/90	*Quincey Kaddiddlehopper*	*CA ID #77777777777*	*006*
		444 4th Street		
	01/27/90	*Fortunemaker, CA 00009*	*CA DL #88888888888*	*4473*
	08/08/89		*Licensed Gun Dealer*	*007*
	No 30 day wait for			
	guns from lic dlrs			
	08/08/89	*Shelly Schickenschelster*	*Licensed Gun Dealer*	*008*
		555 Shadyoaks Place		
	10/12/89	*Shelbyville, CA 00002*	*CA CL #44400000044*	*4473*
	08/08/89			*009*
	09/12/89	*Suzy Q. Commonpeasant*	*CA DL #000000001*	*010*
		123 Main Street		
	11/16/89	*Plainsville, CA 00001*	*CA ID #10000000000*	*4473*

Next is a small column that is headed by action. The kind of action is placed here. Choose your symbols and have everyone follow the same procedure when logging guns. A semi-automatic can be listed as semi, SA, Auto or A. A revolver can be listed as R, RR or rev. A pump can be listed as pump, pm or P. Bolt actions are bolt, BA, blt or B. Black powder guns are BP, BkP, blk and bpwdr.

No matter how you choose to make your entries, be sure that they are consistent. If you choose B for bolt and your employee decides to use B for black powder, it causes confusion.

Moving on, we come to caliber. This speaks for itself. Be specific. There is a difference between a .22, a .22LR and a .22L/S. Many times, a 30.06 sloppily entered can be mistaken for a 30.30. Many clerks have just entered 30, because they don't understand guns and/or they don't have the concern over the feds dropping in without notice to go over your Federal forms and your Gun Log Book. It's YOUR gun license. YOU make sure the paperwork is done properly.

Next is the name and address of the person who brought the gun into the store. It doesn't matter if they borrowed on the gun or whether they sold it to you. All the authorities want to know is WHO. *They don't care WHY!*

The last column on the left side is the date in column. The date the gun came IN to the store is entered. You be sure and enter each transaction AS IT COMES IN. This is not paperwork that can be placed on the back burner until *you get the time* to do it.

Your time is up the minute those Federal authorities, the State authorities, or even the local police walk through your front door and demand to see your Gun Log Books. If the last gun to come into the store is not entered, then you had better be hunkered down over your Gun Log Book with your pen moving on the pages when they first lay eyes on you!

The entire right side of the Gun Log Book is not devoted to what happens later on with the gun. You must still move over to the right and make some additional entries before the gun is properly recorded.

While entering an incoming firearm on the left side of the book, move over to the right side where you will see five additional columns with these headings:

1. DATE OF PICK UP
2. DATE STS - DATE SOLD
3. REDEEMED BY: OR SOLD TO: NAME AND ADDRESS
4. ID PAWNER or SELLER – REDEEMER or BUYER
5. GUN NO. - 4473 Y/N

Move over to column 4 where it says ID PAWNER or SELLER. On the top line, write in the pawner or seller's ID. Enter the kind of ID which would be a State ID card, a State Driver's License, a Military ID, a Passport, or a Green Card. Then enter the ID number.

The bottom line of that column is reserved for the ID of the person who removes the firearm from the premises, either by a sale or by the original owner on a redemption.

(Be sure you understand what constitutes valid identification in your state. Also, be aware that some gun transactions are limited to buying and not loaning. In California, if a person presents a driver's license from a state that is not California or a state that does not border California, the dealer may not release the gun back to that person. The only people who can take a gun OUT of a gun dealer's place of business are people who live within the restricted area. The one exception is military personnel.)

While still entering the information on the incoming gun, move over to the last column on the right page. This is where you will assign the gun a number. I number my log books in advance to be sure I don't skip a number in error. The bottom line of the last column is reserved for when a customer removes the gun from the premises.

Now that you have successfully made the first incoming gun entry, you must note on your copy of the pawn ticket the page and assigned number of the gun. That way, when you pull the pawn ticket out of your system, you will know exactly where to look in the log book. If there is no number on a gun pawn ticket, that means you forgot to make your entry. It's kind of a double check system.

So the code number that is assigned to that particular gun which came from that particular person will be Page 1 No. 0001. You begin to realize you are a true gun dealer when your numbers reach something like BK 12 PG 156 NO. 5691.

This gun code number will follow along with the gun for the entire time you keep the weapon in the store. Even the back of your sales tags will have the gun number. When you sell the gun (even if you've had it in your showcase for years), you will know exactly where to go to find the information regarding that gun.

Now, we will follow up on the rest of the columns on the right hand page. Column 1 is the date the gun was picked up. This column is dedicated ONLY to people who borrowed on their guns. If a date is entered in this column, it means the gun was recovered by the original owner. If there is a date entered in the first date column, there can be no date entered in the second date column. This column is headed by two date possibilities. The first is the date the gun was sold to stock or STS. When a person sells a gun to a dealer in California, he reports it like he reports any other sale or pawn.

The difference is the dealer must wait for 30 days to allow the police to run the serial numbers through their systems. If the gun is not reported stolen or lost, you won't hear from the police and you are free to go get the weapon out of the storage area where you keep the things you buy on the 30 day holds. (All bought items must be held 30 days in California.)

NEVER display pawned items and **NEVER** display outright buy items that are waiting out the pending 30 days.

The day the gun is sold to stock (STS) is the day it is brought out for sale. The entry is made because the gun was either lost to pawn or because it finished out its 30 day waiting period.

Enter the date in that column and then tag the gun for sale, using the assigned book, page and gun numbers. You will need to refer to them one more time when the gun is sold.

The next column is the **redeemed by** or *sold to name and address* column. If the gun was recovered out of pawn by the original owner, write *Recovered By Owner* or *RBO* in that column.

An RBO or Recovered By Owner will have the date of redemption (pick up) entered in the far left date column and no other date will appear on that page. There is a date the customer came in with the gun and the date that the customer left OUT THE DOOR with the gun.

Now, if the gun was Sold To Stock (STS), it will be out for sale. When you find a buyer for the gun, you will follow all of the procedures required by the state. You will apply for the investigation if required and wait for the required length of time. Sometimes the customers don't return for their weapons for 30 days or more because they made a deal with you on lay-away.

Remember, Federal law wants to know only the basics. They want to know WHEN the gun came in and WHEN the gun went out. They want to know WHO brought it in and WHO took it out. They want to know WHAT kind of gun it was. And they want to know exactly WHERE the gun is located in your store. Is it in your back room or is it out for sale? They don't much care why or how.

Even if the gun has cleared the state regulations, *even* if the gun is completely paid for, *even* if everything is done, but the gun is still inside your store ... *enter nothing else* in your Gun Log Book until the gun is wrapped, given to the customer and he takes the gun **OUT THE DOOR.**

REMEMBER ...
NEVER LET ANY GUN OUT THE DOOR
WITHOUT A *COMPLETED*
4473 FEDERAL FORM!

The customer has filled out and signed the 4473 form. You wrapped his gun so it is concealed. You have your money. The customer is happy. And NOW the customer goes OUT THE DOOR.

NOW, you return to your Gun Log Book. Look the gun up by the BK PG and NO and make entries in 4 columns.

First, in the second column on the right page under DATE STS and DATE SOLD, you will enter TODAY'S DATE directly under the date you previously entered when you sold the gun to stock (you placed it from your storage area to the display section of your store).

Your Gun Log Book now tells you **WHEN** the gun came IN THE DOOR, **WHEN** you put it out for sale (which also indicates WHERE the gun is, in storage or on display) and **WHEN** the gun went OUT THE DOOR.

Next, in the third column under *Redeemed By or Sold To,* you will enter the NAME and ADDRESS of the customer (if not the same one who brought the gun in) who took it out the door. Now you have added two more pieces of information. You entered into your Gun Log **WHO and WHERE** the gun came from and **WHO and WHERE** the gun went.

Move one more column to your right and on the bottom of the three rows under *ID Pawner/Seller Redeemer/Buyer,* enter the type of ID and the number. Now you have the ID of WHO brought the gun in and WHO took the gun out. Recovered by owner means the same person redeemed it so a second entry is unnecessary.

Now there is one more entry to make. This last

entry indicates that you did, indeed, have the 4473 form filled out and filed face down in the 4473 drawer. Write under the assigned gun number *4473*.

The easiest way to remember the 4473 is to make it a habit when a person comes in to redeem a gun or to pick one up out of lay-away, as soon as you know it is a gun and before you take their money, grab a 4473 form and place it in front of them with a pen. The customer is supposed to fill out his information on the top portion of the form.

While you take the money and find the gun, the customer will fill out the form.

DO NOT HAND THE GUN OVER TO THE CUSTOMER UNTIL YOU GET THE 4473 BACK FROM HIM, CHECKING TO SEE THAT EVERYTHING IS FILLED OUT CORRECTLY.

Now that you have learned about the Gun Record Book, let's go over the 4473 form one more time.

Remember, the country or state where the customer was born is not sufficient. There must be a city and a state. If they were born outside the U.S., then they must include the city, the state or province and the country of their birth.

Make sure *every* box is X'd and all of the spaces must be **NO** or you cannot release the firearm.

The form must be dated and signed and their ID and number entered in Section 9 and 10.

The box in the upper right hand corner of the 4473 form where it says Transferor's Transaction Serial Number must be filled out by *you,* with the assigned gun number of your Gun Log Book (BK, PG and NO). That way, if the Feds ever check your 4473 forms and they arbitrarily pull one out of the pile and hand it to you, asking when, where, and who the gun came from, you won't go into shock with the idea of finding information on a gun that came and went ten years ago.

In that event, all you will need to do is make a notation of the number and go right to your Gun Log Books where you will pull the correct book and turn immediately to the firearm they are questioning. You will be able to give them all of the information that they need and you will be marked on their records as being accurate and cooperative.

Finally, fill our Sections 11 through 15. Sections 16 and 17 should be pre-stamped with the store name, address, and gun license number. In Sections 18 through 20 are the name and title of the transferor and the date the firearm was released ... *out the door.*

I repeat the information about the 4473 form here as I said I would earlier and perhaps you can see that with a certain established routine, one is far less vulnerable to making serious errors.

The only routine I know of that has worked for us is the one I just outlined here in this chapter. It would be a shame to lose your license to deal in firearms because of negligence or the lack of establishing a method whereby the fewest errors are made.

The firearms trade can be financially rewarding. Don't blow it because you haven't taken the time and effort to find a way to keep from being continuously negligent. One or two errors is acceptable. Develop a pattern of errors (both in firearms and in collateral lending) and you will be looking for another business venture.

I would bet my hat that you won't find any other that is nearly as rewarding in income, in interesting people, in unusual stories, and in a whole lot of fun. The aggravation is there, as it is with anything that is worth doing. The down times are so-so. The up times are the best!

YOUR STATE LAWS

Please remember that the Federal laws are *only part* of the picture. Your State laws must be adhered to as well. Some of the states like California, who has had to deal with arsenals of illegal firearms, are very strict on their gun legislation. This creates a myriad of paperwork for both the gun dealer and for the bureaucracy. These laws are in place to make purchasing firearms much more difficult. Whether or not these laws are significant in curtailing the possession of illegal firearms and/or keeping the firearms out of the wrong hands, is a constant subject for debate.

If you live in California or in a state that is as strictly enforced as California, your legislation is probably very detailed and complicated to understand. It is my suggestion that you contact your State Collateral Loan Association and they will be happy to help you understand the step-by-step procedures that you will need to follow in order to be in compliance with your laws.

Perhaps your state isn't so strict on their requirements for gun ownership. In that case, you are very fortunate. But you still must know and understand the laws that you *are* governed by. Don't make the mistake of assuming that you already know the law. Check with your state and with your association to be sure.

* * *

More men than women have at least a smattering of education in the handling and workings of various firearms. When our Victorville store had an all-girl crew, it didn't take them long to get the hang of handling firearms.

Needless to say, there were a lot of hard lessons to be learned along the way. Even with the expert coaching that was available consistently via telephone, they still encountered problems and made their share of errors.

They never got hurt too badly on a deal and some would attribute this to the possibility that they had no gun experts available to them in their midst.

Painfully aware of their limitations, they lent conservatively. Consequently, the worst that ever happened was that they broke even on the worst of their transactions. Even then, those times were few and far between. As the store progressed, so the girls progressed.

Opening a pawn shop and dealing in merchandise that one knows little about is a very brave endeavor. Doing it successfully is a super achievement.

By playing a conservative role, it is not an a typical finding that ignorance can be profitable. It can be a pleasant surprise to find that the firearm so conservatively lent upon turns out to be a rare collectible. Every once in awhile, there is that twenty-five dollar investment that brings hundreds of dollars in return.

This is not the norm, but it happens. It's bound to if the pawnbroker keeps up a good pace of lending and doesn't get the 'over loan jitters'.

One of the most important things to know is that it is imperative to make sure that all of the pieces of the firearm are in place and there is nothing broken or missing (like the clips). If you don't know what you are looking at, it is difficult to tell if it has something missing or broken on it!

Antique value on guns have a lot to do with parts that have different serial numbers, indicating that a defective or missing part was replaced. If serial numbers don't match on a collector's piece, the value plummets in a downward spiral!

A good rule of thumb is to take no 'wall hangars'. If you do, lend no more than $15 on them. Then they are pretty easy to sell if the prices are kept around the $50 to $75 range.

When you do know what you are looking at, either from experience or from your gun catalogues, a loan of up to half the actual trade value can be made. The usual ten cents on the new dollar doesn't apply to firearms. Usually, we lend around one-third of the trade value in the Gun Trader's Guide.

At first, try making low offers in order to see what your business will generate. This will give you an indication of what your competition is doing. If the customer walks at your offer, let him go. If he returns to take what you offered, you know that the competition is bidding even less than you are.

Remember, if a pawner objects to the small amount of the loan you are offering him, remind him that it's only a loan and you don't want to be stuck selling the item.

On the front of our gun catalogue, there is a reminder noted: ***...IF YOU CAN'T FIND IT IN THE BOOKS AND YOU ARE NOT SURE, THE ANSWER IS NO!*** Far better to allow the good deal to walk than to stick yourself with an unsalable item.

We have a sign posted at the door: ***PLEASE CLEAR ALL WEAPONS BEFORE ENTERING STORE.*** This sign works well with men who have a full understanding of their weapons. It does not work well with most women who bring in their husband's firearms for pawning. I am a full equal rights advocate, but it is apparent where women are lacking. They seem to feel that if it isn't in their area of interest, then they don't want to obtain the information for themselves.

Guns are just not an area of interest for most women. Their ignorance isn't out of the inability to grasp the information, they simply are not (as a whole) motivated to learn about destructive weapons. I think women are more 'life givers' and instinctual, they are not inclined in any direction that would be destructive to life in general.

Enough philosophy ... men usually don't know much about jewelry, either. That's not to say the world isn't full of male diamond experts ... it's simply to say, in the ordinary general scheme of things, we don't usually find an overabundance of female gun experts nor do we find an abnormally large ratio of men who have much knowledge of gemstones. This is an observation and not a 'chiseled in granite' statement. Some pawnbrokers might find the exact opposite to be true in their stores.

For the above reasons (I believe), women are more inclined to bring in a loaded weapon ... and this information is not included in any sense of bias. Rather, it is incorporated in this writing in order to keep the recipient of the weapon alive and healthy as possible!

In other words, check the weapon in ALL cases for ammunition in the chambers. I've found that in some bolt action rifles, I actually had to stick my little finger down into the barrel because sometimes I couldn't see the shell that was, indeed, lodged in the chamber!

In our first store, we have a few tell-tale signs of improperly checked weapons ... like a couple of dents in our safes and a few bullet holes in the ceiling! Because of the fear factor that seems to be present in many women, they are leery of guns. You might be surprised to know that virtually all of our accidental discharges were set off by men! In two and a half years with an all-girl store, there was never even one incident of an accidental discharge.

Revolvers should be opened upon handing them to customers for inspection.

Semi-automatic handguns must be handled just as carefully. Remove the clip and lock the weapon open.

Hand all weapons to customers butt first, barrel pointed toward the ceiling. Some gun stores have gone the extra distance by placing a lock on the trigger mechanism before showing the weapon. In this day and age, this is not a bad idea.

We do not carry any ammunition in our stores ... just a slight extra precaution. I might get shot with one of my own guns, but I won't give them the ammunition to do it. It is strictly b.y.o.a. (bring your own ammo) to the holdup!

In all the years we've been in business, we have never been held up at knife or gun point. I believe the way we handle our own weapons has something to do with this. Nothing will get our clerks in trouble faster than careless treatment of weapons.

There is a lot of money to be made in the dealing of firearms. Many pawnbrokers refuse to handle them. That is understandable.

It is my recommendation that if a pawnbroker is unfamiliar with firearms, go get an education. Get familiar with handling firearms.

You can read all day long,but just like you can't learn to drive a car until you get behind the wheel, so it goes for firearms. Once one gets the feel of what a firearm is like in their hands, the initial fear is overcome and replaced by knowledge. We fear only the unknown. A pawnbroker can virtually cut his business in half by not dealing in firearms.

If you just want to 'make a living,' then handling guns is not crucial. If you want to be 'successful,' handle firearms as well. If you want to be 'super successful,' handle every conceivable item with which you can familiarize yourself.

USE SIGNS AND PROTECT YOURSELF. Signs posted in a store can save a lot of grief for the proprietor in the long run. Some states require signs like these to be posted:

HANDGUNS WILL NOT BE SHOWN TO ANYONE UNDER 21 YEARS OF AGE.

WE ARE NOT OBLIGATED OR QUALIFIED TO TRAIN ANYONE IN THE HANDLING OF FIREARMS. IT IS, THEREFORE, ASSUMED BY THE MANAGEMENT THAT PERSONS WHO ARE PURCHASING FIREARMS HAVE HAD, OR INTEND TO SEEK OUT, PROPER TRAINING.

IF YOU LEAVE A LOADED FIREARM WITHIN THE REACH OR EASY ACCESS OF A CHILD, YOU MAY BE FINED OR IMPRISONED, OR BOTH, IF THE CHILD GAINS ACCESS TO, AND IMPROPERLY USES, THE FIREARM.

The last sign is not only mandatory in the state of California, it must also meet the strict California requirements. The letters must be in the form of a minimum of three-inch blocks and the sign must be posted in a conspicuous place. Three-inch block lettering makes up for a pretty big sign to place inside of a retail establishment. And, unless it is posted in the back room, the size of it alone creates conspicuousness. This sign takes up a very large area in some of the smallest pawn shops where every square inch of display area is critical for their survival.

The ability to survive when being named in a lawsuit of such magnitude could depend solely on the above posted signs. The inconvenient and unsightly signs could turn out to be the one and only thing that has insured the survival of one's livelihood. In that light, they aren't quite so inconvenient and unsightly.

We are living in a country that has become sue happy. We see it all the time. I cannot believe the number of people who are running around with pending lawsuits. It seems like every third customer lets us know that they are expecting a settlement any day now.

This kind of talk makes me leery. I don't care for signs cluttering up my store either. Perhaps out in Podunk people are much friendlier. A man's word is his bond and his handshake is still an honored contract. Unfortunately, this is no longer so in the metropolitan areas.

Things used to be that way right here in Southern California. I am old enough to remember when right was right and wrong was something you didn't do ... and if you did, you were shamed. Either I was very naive, or people took pride in playing by the rules.

Everyone knew the rules. Tell the truth. Keep your word. Play fair. Be polite. Never take what isn't rightfully yours. Keep your hands to yourself and treat others as you would like to be treated.

If I could assign every single person in the United States one piece of homework, I would make it mandatory to read one chapter out of one book, one time each day for one year. The chapter would be the first chapter out of a book entitled, *"All I Really Need To Know, I Learned In Kindergarten,"* by Robert Fulghum.

Over the past several years, I have discovered that no matter how well one plays by the rules, those rules can be distorted and used as ammunition. The perpetrator becomes the victim.

It used to be that one could always tell the difference between the good guys and the bad. The good guys wore white hats! I feel like a dinosaur strolling through Times Square!

Well, times have changed and it looks like the

rules have, too. I would never have believed that *I* could do anything that would give a person cause to file a lawsuit against me. New rule. *I* don't have to!

Suddenly, I'm in the middle of one lawsuit and another is pending. They have nothing to do with firearms or even with anything I did that was wrong. Nevertheless, there it is. I've been told there is an *up* side. They say one isn't truly successful until they can tell these litigious parasites to go to the back of the line and wait their turn like everybody else!

So there is a choice. Don't post signs and stand the chance of being sued and a 99% chance of losing in a court of law. Post signs and lower your odds to 75%! I choose the signs.

An even stronger tool that can be used is on the next page. But it isn't any good unless you put it to use. No one purchases a firearm in my stores without signing the following form.

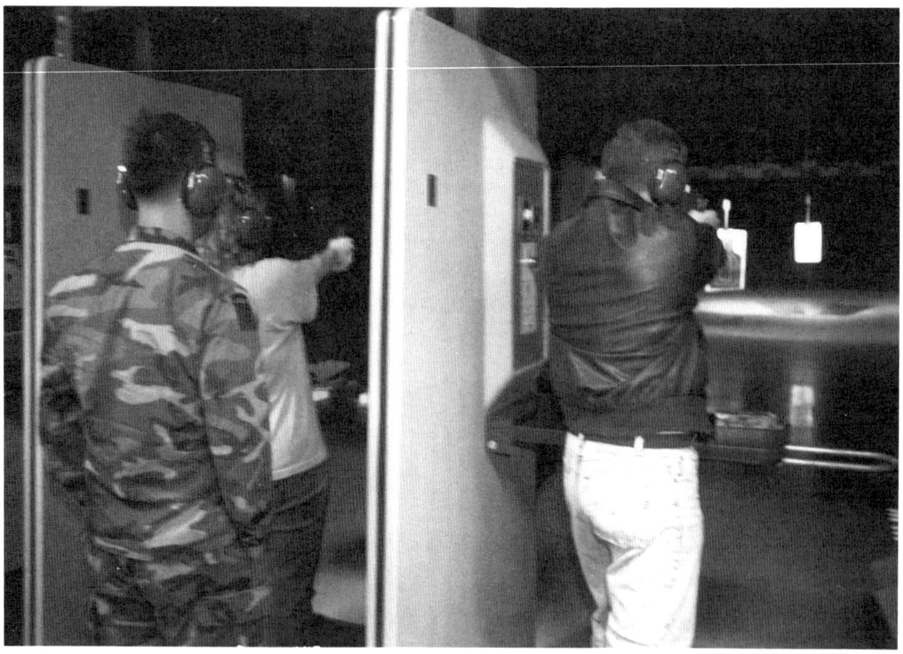

YOU HAVE PURCHASED A DANGEROUS WEAPON

1. The person who sold you the gun you have just purchased is *not* a gun expert and is *not* qualified to advise you on loading, firing or transporting the gun.

2. Do *not* load or use the gun without special training from a gun expert.

3. All guns sold in this store are "used" and sold "as is" condition. This gun should *not* be loaded or fired until it is examined by, and approved by, a gun expert.

4. Each gun is designed to fire ammunition that meets certain specifications. Do *not* load or fire any ammunition in the gun unless assured by a gun expert that the ammunition meets its requirements.

5. The gun should *always* be stored unloaded in a location inaccessible to children and unauthorized persons.

6. Upon purchasing the gun, you are required to complete the Federal Gun Registration Form #4473. This is NOT a permit for you to use, carry or transport this gun. You must ask the local police or sheriff in the jurisdiction where the gun is located about when and how you may transport and use the gun.

--o0o--

I have read all of the above and acknowledge that the person who sold the gun to me, is ***not*** an expert. **I agree to,** and assume full responsibility for, obtaining expert advice and instruction elsewhere before loading or firing the gun.

Dated:_______________ Signature_________________________________

Form Approved: OMB No. 1512-0006 (8-31-92)

DEPARTMENT OF THE TREASURY
BUREAU OF ALCOHOL, TOBACCO AND FIREARMS

REPORT OF MULTIPLE SALE OR OTHER DISPOSITION OF PISTOLS AND REVOLVERS

INSTRUCTIONS

1. This form is to be used by licensees to report all transactions in which an unlicensed person has acquired two or more pistols and/or revolvers at one time or during five consecutive business days.
2. A separate form is to be submitted for each such person.
3. The report is to be submitted to the ATF Law Enforcement Office for your area not later than the close of business on the day that the multiple sale or other disposition occurs. See **State Laws and Published Ordinances-Firearms,** for the office nearest your business premises.
4. Complete Items 1 through 7, fold, seal with tape, affix postage and mail.

PAPERWORK REDUCTION ACT NOTICE

The estimated average burden associated with this collection is .20 hours per respondent or recordkeeper, depending on individual circumstances. Comments concerning the accuracy of this burden estimate and suggestions for reducing this burden should be directed to Reports Management Officer, Information Programs Branch, Room 7011, Bureau of Alcohol, Tobacco and Firearms, 1200 Pennsylvania Avenue, NW, Washington D. C., 20226, or the Office of Management and Budget, Paperwork Reduction Project (1512-0006), Washington, D.C., 20503.

(Fold on this line)

1. TRANSFEREE'S NAME *(Buyer) (Last, first, middle)*	
2. RESIDENCE ADDRESS *(Number, street, city, State, ZIP code)*	3. DATE OF BIRTH
4. TOTAL SOLD IN FIVE DAYS	
REVOLVER	
PISTOL	
5. NAME & ADDRESS OF LICENSEE MAKING REPORT *(Hand stamp may be used)*	6. DATE
7. FEDERAL FIREARMS LICENSE NUMBER	

ATF F 3310.4 (11-89)

FEDERAL

REPORT OF MULTIPLE SALE OR OTHER DISPOSITION OF PISTOLS AND REVOLVERS

Form Approved: OMB No. 1512-0129

DEPARTMENT OF THE TREASURY — BUREAU OF ALCOHOL, TOBACCO, AND FIREARMS **FIREARMS TRANSACTION RECORD** **PART I — OVER-THE-COUNTER**	TRANSFEROR'S TRANSACTION SERIAL NUMBER

NOTE: Prepare in original only. All entries on this form must be in ink. See Notices and Instructions on back.

SECTION A — MUST BE COMPLETED PERSONALLY BY TRANSFEREE *(BUYER) (See Notices and Instructions on reverse)*

1. TRANSFEREE'S *(Buyer's)* NAME *(Last, First, Middle)*	☐ MALE ☐ FEMALE	2. HEIGHT	3. WEIGHT	4. RACE

5. RESIDENCE ADDRESS *(No., Street, City, County, State, ZIP Code)*	6. DATE OF BIRTH			7. PLACE OF BIRTH *(City and State or City and Foreign Country)*
	MONTH	DAY	YEAR	

8. CERTIFICATION OF TRANSFEREE *(Buyer)*—An untruthful answer may subject you to criminal prosecution. Each question must be answered with a "yes" or a "no" inserted in the box at the right of the question:

a. Are you under indictment or information* in any court for a crime punishable by imprisonment for a term exceeding one year? **A formal accusation of a crime made by a prosecuting attorney, as distinguished from an indictment presented by a grand jury.*		c. Are you a **fugitive** from justice?	
		d. Are you an unlawful user of, or addicted to, marijuana, or any depressant, stimulant, or narcotic drug, or any other controlled substance?	
b. Have you been convicted in any court of a crime punishable by imprisonment for a term exceeding one year? (NOTE: A "yes" answer is necessary if the judge could have given a sentence of more than one year. A "yes" answer is *not* required if you have been pardoned for the crime or the conviction has been expunged or set aside, or you have had your civil rights restored and, under the law where the conviction occurred, you are not prohibited from receiving or possessing any firearm).		e. Have you ever been adjudicated mentally defective or have you ever been committed to a mental institution?	
		f. Have you been discharged from the Armed Forces under **dishonorable** conditions?	
		g. Are you an alien **illegally** in the United States?	
		h. Are you a person who, having been a citizen of the United States, has renounced his/her citizenship.	

I hereby certify that the answers to the above are true and correct. I understand that a person who answers "Yes" to any of the above questions is prohibited from purchasing and/or possessing a firearm, except as otherwise provided by Federal law. I also understand that the making of any false oral or written statement or the exhibiting of any false or misrepresented identification with respect to this transaction is a crime punishable as a felony.

TRANSFEREE'S *(Buyer's)* SIGNATURE – EXECUTE AT TIME OF ACTUAL TRANSFER OF FIREARM(S)	DATE

SECTION B — TO BE COMPLETED BY TRANSFEROR (SELLER) *(See Notices and Instructions on reverse)*

THIS PERSON DESCRIBED IN SECTION A: ☐ IS KNOWN TO ME
☐ HAS IDENTIFIED HIMSELF/HERSELF TO ME IN THE FOLLOWING MANNER

9. TYPE OF IDENTIFICATION *(Driver's license or identification which shows name, date of birth, place of residence, and signature.)*	10. NUMBER ON IDENTIFICATION

On the basis of (1) the statements in Section A; (2) the verification of identity noted in Section B; and (3) the information in the current list of Published Ordinances, it is my belief that it is not unlawful for me to sell, deliver, transport, or otherwise dispose of the firearm(s) described below and on the back to the person identified in Section A.

11. TYPE *(Pistol, Revolver, Rifle, Shotgun, etc.)*	12. MODEL	13. CALIBER OR GAUGE	14. SERIAL NO.	15 MANUFACTURER *(and importer, if any)*
1.				
2.				

16. TRADE/CORPORATE NAME AND ADDRESS OF TRANSFEROR *(Seller)* *(Hand stamp may be used)*	17. FEDERAL FIREARMS LICENSE NO. *(Hand stamp may be used)*

THE PERSON MAKING THE ACTUAL FIREARMS SALE MUST COMPLETE ITEMS 18 THROUGH 20

18. TRANSFEROR'S *(Seller's)* SIGNATURE – EXECUTE AT TIME OF ACTUAL TRANSFER OF FIREARM(S)	19. TRANSFEROR'S TITLE	20. TRANSACTION DATE

ATF F 4473 (5300.9) PART I (4-91)

ILFORD

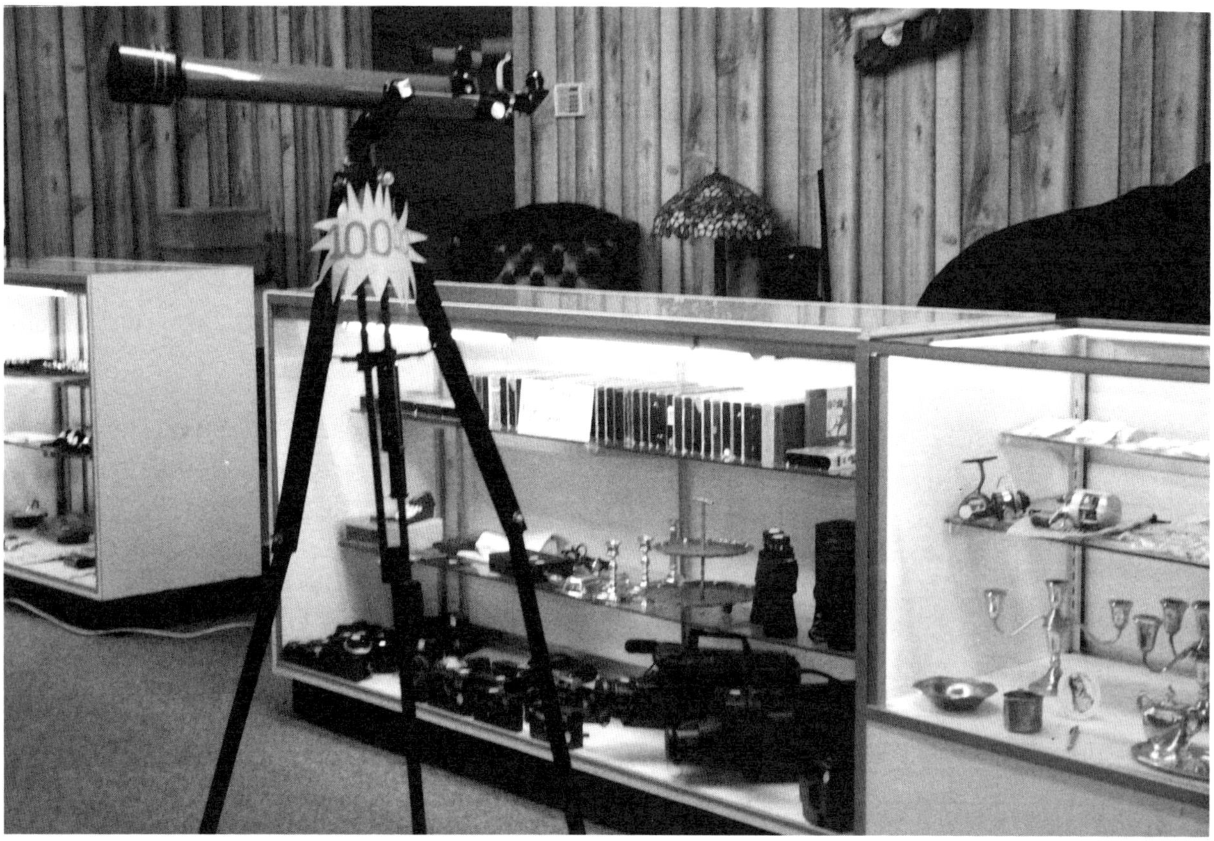

CHAPTER 14

CAMERAS AND OPTICS

SINGLE LENS REFLEX CAMERAS

Cameras can account for increasingly good profits as the pawnbroker makes himself aware of some general principals and guidelines regarding such merchandise and secondly, as the pawnbroker broadens his knowledge by keeping aware of the ever-changing technology in the photography equipment industry.

There are three kinds of cameras that interest the pawnbroker who is NOT a camera buff.

These are the ***Single Lens Reflex*** (SLR) cameras which operate with mirrors, allowing the photographer to peer directly through the lens to view the subject matter.

These cameras are easily identified by the pyramid shaped top over the lens on top of the camera. The mirrors are built within the pyramid structure. These cameras are generally used by the camera buffs and professional photographers.

Two decades ago, *SLR* cameras required a certain amount of knowledge in order to operate the equipment successfully. Today's SLRs can be operated by just about anyone.

They are equipped with two kinds of functions ... the function that a knowledgeable photographer wants to have accessible to him in the ability to manually control all of the elements that are required for creative and artistic results.

The same camera can be operated with excellent results by a novice. Many photo buffs like these features so that their spouses and children are able to use the camera almost as effectively as the pro.

How can we tell if the camera is in good working order? The element of risk is high in this area of pawnbroking. A camera can pass all scrutiny of testing and visual inspection and still not be functionable where the actual results count ... i.e., the picture.

A pawnbroker once took in a beautiful Minolta 35mm SLR. It was the top of the line at the time. The camera originally cost nearly $500 new. It looked immaculate. The pawnbroker almost turned it away because he couldn't test the shutter. There were no batteries in the camera. He took a chance and bought it for twenty-five dollars. The pawnbroker later found that the camera was a total loss because it had apparently been submerged in water at one time. It must have been dropped in a pool and then recovered immediately and aired to dry. Of course, no rust or corrosion was visible and the broker chose to take a chance. Had the camera proved to be functionable, the broker would have paid up to $50 for it.

After twelve years of experience in the pawn business, I can safely say that the probability factor was in the favor of the pawnbroker on a scale of 90 to 1 odds!

In this particular case, the pawnbroker made a good decision. It didn't work out and he suffered a twenty-five dollar loss, but the chances of the camera turning out to be good weighed heavily in the broker's favor and had that been the case, the pawnbroker could have easily gained a return of a thousand percent ... probably more.

In checking out an SLR camera, the first rule of order is to be sure the camera has the above described alternate functions. These functions can be determined by a switch on top of the camera that says 'program' or 'auto' on the older cameras. The letters AE often identify the camera as an automatic focus piece.

The newer computerized models have the function displayed in LED crystal. These multiple program AE cameras with dual metering systems are the most costly and, consequently, the most desirable.

New models are coming out all the time, making the camera business one of the most competitive markets in the world. New innovations that make use of computer modules allow these cameras the greatest versatility ever.

Keep up on the latest innovative cameras as they come out because sooner or later, you will see one come across your counter and you won't want to miss out on a good buy because you lacked awareness.

Make sure the camera is in good condition. A thorough visual inspection will give tell-tale signs of mishandling.

Mars, scratches and dust or grime tell the story of what general maintenance and care (or lack of) the unit has received.

Indications of critical blows are easily spotted by the lens rings. Many times a dropped or mishandled camera will have a dent or ding on the outside perimeter of the lens.

Many cameras will come in with several lenses. It is wise to scrutinize each lens rim for signs of dropping. Dropped cameras usually land lens down because the lens (in many cases) is heavier than the camera body. If a camera is dropped with the standard 50mm lens, then the signals can be found on the sides of the camera's body as well.

The camera looks clean and unmarred by dings and scratches. Now the inspection will turn to focusing.

Make sure the camera will focus on subjects near (three to five feet distant), mid-range (ten to twenty feet), and infinity (subjects in the distance).

What is seen through the SLR "eye" is what will appear as the end result. In other words, if what is seen through the viewfinder is blurred or out of focus, then the photograph will appear the same way. This is the reason most photographers won't use anything other than an SLR (single lens reflex) camera.

The bulk of SLR cameras that the pawnbroker deals in are the thirty-five millimeter film cameras.

There is another kind of SLR that will be a rarity, but one the pawnbroker should be aware of because of their tremendous value. These are the 'roll film' cameras. They have a boxey look and they are focused by looking 'down into' the camera from above rather than through the back of the camera.

These, along with the same kind of *roll film* cameras that are professional *twin lens* cameras (more exceptions to prove the rule) carry the same boxey look. Do not confuse these professional models with the old 1950's box-like cameras. This is where a camera guide from a good, reputable dealer comes in very handy. Information on how to obtain complete camera guides will be found at the end of this chapter.

Until you get the feel of your store and you are familiar with a good cross section of merchandise, there will be doubt. The doubt lessens with time and experience. So while learning the ropes, keep the first rule of pawnbroking. ***When in doubt, pass!***

Later on, you will find you are a bit more encouraged to make a few gambles on certain items as you familiarize yourself with those items. We all make mistakes. They just get fewer and further between.

After visual inspection and focusing, shake the camera to see if there are any loose pieces floating around inside the mechanism. Pass if you hear any rattles or loose parts.

The next step is to open the camera. Look for any signs of breakage. Every camera should look clean inside. If there are any signs of dirt, dust or scratches, turn it away. It has not been cared for properly.

The camera is a delicate piece of equipment and the slightest sign of abuse is a good indicator that it will not function properly. No amateur photographer with the slightest knowledge of cameras will purchase any camera in such condition.

The next test is to smell the insides of the camera. Turn it away if it smells moldy. It has been exposed to dampness.

Check the lenses for mars, marks and scratches on the glass. Something as simple as an innocent fingerprint can etch its way permanently into the lens if not cleaned within a certain period of time.

Keep lens cleaner solution and paper wipes made especially for camera lenses on hand. These items are readily available at any retail camera store. Any local pharmacy that deals in photo equipment will have cleaning kits for sale in their camera department.

Clean the lenses thoroughly with the cleaner and wipes to see if the lenses come clean. If any marks remain on the lenses, give a low ball price on them ... or better, make your offer based solely on the value of the camera body, taking no account of the lenses whatsoever. This way you get the camera and the lenses are 'freebies.'

Close the back cover of the camera body and focus on an object that is shadowed in a darkened corner. Snap the shutter button.

The shutter should click and stall then click

again, suggesting a longer exposure because of the lack of light that was reflected into the lens.

Cock the camera again (if there is no automatic film advance built in or added onto the camera) and direct the lens this time toward the brightest lit area (close up or distance) and click the shutter once again.

The shutter should click twice in a row with no pauses. This indicates that the shutter is now correctly reacting to the overabundance of light by making the film exposure much shorter in time span. This action is what separates the older, manually controlled cameras from the modern, computerized version.

A manually controlled camera requires the photographer to take a light reading on a special meter and to adjust the camera lens (f stops) according to the amount of light that is indicated on the meter. Some older models have a light meter built into the viewfinder. As far as a pawnbroker is concerned, the older manual cameras are obsolete and nearly impossible to sell ... even if they are considered collectable.

COMPACT CAMERAS

The new compact cameras are the most popular by far among rank amateur photo enthusiasts. The compact camera is an international boon to the tourist population, as well as to the ordinary folks who just want a nice photo for a momento of the occasion.

There are literally hundreds of designs that are available on the market today. These cameras offer the pawnbroker a good profit because of the markup that is possible, coupled with the fact that almost everyone who doesn't own one wants one and they are the most affordable of good cameras available.

Compared to the SLRs, they are inexpensive, they are far easier to handle and store and they are absolutely foolproof ... all this while offering incredibly good results as well.

This camera can be checked in much the same manner as the SLRs. The most common error pawnbrokers make when it comes to this kind of camera is that they don't check the brand to make sure that it is a good name brand.

Outfits like the television shopping clubs sell copies of these cameras at greatly reduced prices.

Most mail-order outfits that offer compact cameras for free or for sale at low prices, deal in large shipments of look-alikes. These look-alikes are most distinguishable by their heft.

When picked up, they seem very light ... almost hollow. The more expensive of the compacts feel solid and well built. Refer to the end of this chapter for the most desirable camera brands and models.

Compact cameras are often quite unique. Some of them come with all of the bells and whistles to allow the same versatility of photographers who are experienced and own the most sought after equipment on the market.

They are automatically focused and they have automatic zooms. Some will allow multiple exposures for artistic license. There are even automatic loading, automatic advance and rewinding cameras. Many utilize an alternate flash as the camera decides for the photographer whether or not the flash is needed.

There are compacts that come equipped with five year lithium batteries so that the owner doesn't have to concern himself with battery replacements. They can shoot photos from as close up as 1.8 feet and range to perfect focus on infinity shots.

Some are equipped with quartz dates and they record the date or time directly onto the film.

There are telephoto and extra long telephoto automatic lenses.

Then there are the aqua compacts that allow underwater photography and will shoot close-ups out of the water as well.

There are even several cameras out that talk to the photographer!

The possibilities on the automatic cameras are almost limitless.

Almost all of these cameras begin their retail prices at around one hundred dollars (sometimes they are on sale for as little as seventy-nine dollars) and can range as high as three hundred dollars.

The desirability of these compact, thirty-five millimeter cameras is apparent. Obviously, every precaution against a failed photograph has been eradicated by the manufacturers. If an individual has a 'brown thumb' when it comes to taking photographs, the days of overexposed prints are a thing of the past.

The pawnbroker can do quite a brisk business when it comes to these compacts. The trick is in buying them right.

They will sell with no problems. Many people cannot afford or they just don't want to put out over one hundred dollars in cash for a small camera.

If the rule of thumb for pawning (or buying) a compact is ten cents on the dollar, fifteen dollars is offered for a one hundred and fifty dollar camera. The same camera is set out retail at around seventy-nine dollars. They don't stay on the shelf very long when they are just like new and cost half as much as new!

Who would pawn or sell their one hundred and fifty dollar camera for fifteen dollars? You would be surprised! At either end of the retail spectrum, there is always room for bartering. This bartering capacity is what keeps the successful pawnbroker sailing in smooth waters.

VCR CAMERAS

Learn how to run a VCR camera. They are usually very simple and can be figured out in a matter of a few minutes. An hour spent with a VCR camera teaches the student just about everything he needs to know in order to operate it effectively.

Basically, the VCR camera has the same setup as a VCR player and both are similar to an audio cassette player. They offer the same setup in common.

There are the *forward, rewind, play, pause, record* and *eject* buttons. Record a minute or two, then pop it out and play it on one of your VCRs that you have hooked up to display. If it is a mini-cam, it can usually be hooked into any VCR and re-recorded on a regular VHS tape that can be played back right away.

Asking the customers to demonstrate any kind

of equipment or musical instruments for you is a good way to judge whether it really belongs to them. If they can't figure it out, it's a pretty good indication it might not belong to them and it isn't theirs to pawn anyway. This doesn't always hold true. Spouses often don't operate certain household equipment. Use your own good judgement. Sometimes you get a *feeling*. After they check it, go over it yourself to be sure.

Video cameras are not as critical in design as still cameras. Video cams can look banged up and still work very efficiently. Also, the privilege of viewing immediate results takes some of the guesswork out of the pawning. Of course, if they look rough, you won't be able to get much for them. So if you are thinking of making an offer on such a camera, take this into consideration.

Familiarize yourself with the latest video equipment regularly. The Sunday papers often offer the weekly sales on such items. Ten cents on the dollar is always safe and it is the second rule of thumb when pawning.

Turn it around for half or less than the original value, depending on the age and desirability of the camera. Mini-cams are the 'in' cameras today and it is difficult to turn the large bulky video cams unless the price is right.

POLAROID INSTAMATICS

These are good sellers. They retail for around $150. Be sure it is the Polaroid and not a Kodak. Kodaks were recalled in 1987 because they were infringing on the patent rights of Polaroid. They are worthless because there is no film available for sale anymore.

BINOCULARS AND SCOPES

Binoculars are a sure-fire seller in a pawn shop. You can get them in for very little money and if you keep your prices right, you can turn them right around.

When testing binoculars, peer through them and focus them in on an object at the farthest distance. Then bring the focus in to the nearest object to see how they perform.

If they feel like they are pulling your eyes in uncomfortable directions, there is something wrong with the lenses. Usually, the binoculars have been dropped when double vision is experienced while peering through them. Binoculars are supposed to magnify distant objects comfortably for the human eye.

Do not take binoculars that create any kind of eye strain. It is tempting to take some very expensive binoculars at a cheap price if the sighting is off just a little bit. The pull might seem slight, even barely perceptible. Don't be tempted. You'll have them forever!

Telescopes are good sellers in areas where there isn't a whole lot of smog and haze. They are a little slower moving in areas like Los Angeles, but they will eventually sell if the price is right. Like the binoculars, if the telescope doesn't focus properly, pass.

Rifle scopes are best left alone. It has been my experience that not many people are interested in rifle scopes unless they are already mounted on the weapon.

I learned the hard way when a fellow came in to my store with a box full of brand new .22 rifle scopes. He wanted $3 each. I counted the scopes. There were 30 of them.

I told the guy I'd give him $1 each. He left, returning in about an hour.

"I'll go ahead and take the $1 each for them," he said as he set the box down on my counter. I bought them.

I just knew I could get $12 each for the things. When the 30-day waiting period was up, I priced them out and distributed some of them in my gun showcases and the rest with the binoculars.

I didn't sell one!

I dropped the price to $9.95 and I *still* didn't sell one.

I dropped the price again, to his original price of $3 and I will be darned if I could sell just *one* of those worthless things!

I came to realize that what I thought was a great deal didn't even spark the interest of one of my customers in two years.

The Salvation Army wound up with them and I got a write-off.

It is strange, but of all the very good deals I've made, by wit and by pure luck, the deals that stand out most to me are the deals where I turned out so absolutely wrong when I just knew I was absolutely right!

BRAND NAMES

It is crucial that the pawnbroker knows the brand names of all these above items. So many times counterfeits are accepted across the pawn counter by accident. The counterfeits bear names that are similar to the name brand items. If a pawnbroker is not on his toes, he could find he paid good money for a Time-Life camera!

Bear in mind, as well, that there are many price ranges within the name brands. To say "A Nikon camera is a Nikon camera," is to say "A Chevrolet is a Chevrolet." There are many models that range the field of pricing. For instance, a Nikon FE-2 (body only) retails new for $269, as opposed to the Nikon F3AF (body only) retailing new for $1,169.

*　　*　　*

MOST SOUGHT AFTER NAME BRANDS

Hasselblad .... (500 Series, rare and desirable)
Nikon .... (N Series and F Series)
Leica .... (R4, M Series)
Canon .... (AE-1 Program)
Minolta .... (Maxxum)
Olympus .... (OM Series)
Pentax .... (Superprogram)
Yashica .... (Program Models)
Vivatar .... (Lenses and compacts only)

* Note: Models listed are just the models we've found to be best sellers in our stores. These cameras offer many models that are equally desirable. The same cameras also offer models that are not so desirable on the market today. For instance, the Nikon Company – a model called the EM. The Nikon EM was a very cheap version of Nikon and remains virtually untouched by camera buffs on the whole.

OTHER BRANDS ARE:

*Bronica .... *Usually not in demand
*Konica
*Tamron
*Tokina
*Contax
Omega
Mamiya
*Nikonos .... Made by Nikon
*Kiron .... Lenses only
*Sigma .... Lenses only
*Soligor .... Lenses only

DO NOT TAKE IN:

*The old 8, super 8 and 16 millimeter movie cameras.
*Old flat top compact cameras.
*Antique cameras of ANY kind.
*Lenses without cameras.
*Slide projectors.

(Unless you are a camera buff and know what you are doing, it is wise to follow the DON'T list.)

TELESCOPES, BINOCULARS AND RIFLE SCOPES

Brand names include:

Nikon ... Minolta ... Soligor ... Bushnell ... Celestro ... Baush 6 Lomb ... Tasco ... Pentax ... Trijicon ... Steiner ... Simmons ... Weaver

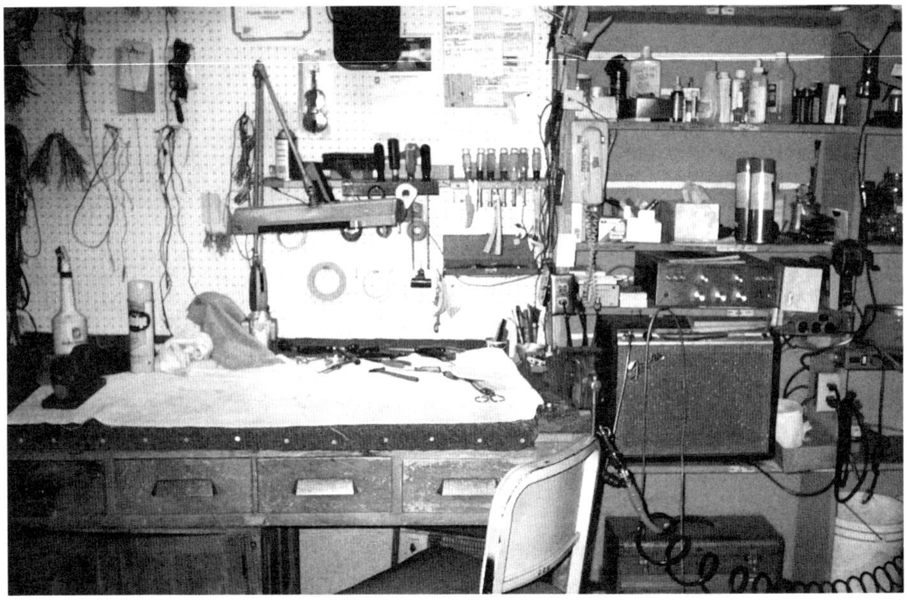

Don't forget a nice work area with all of the necessary tools at hand. There is always something to tighten, to mend, or just give a good polishing. It's much easier to sell a shiny guitar than one that looks like someone ate over it.

(Speaking of keeping merchandise clean, here's a neat little sales tool to use when selling diamonds and gold. Keep a nice clean polishing cloth under your display counter. When a customer asks to see a piece, take it out and gently wipe it off before handing it to them. When they give it back, do the same thing before you return it to the showcase. This keeps your jewelry looking clean all the time and it shows the customer that you value your own fine selection. Very psychological!)

CHAPTER 15

ELECTRONICS (SIGHTS AND SOUNDS)

The basic rule for pawning anything that runs on electricity is that everything must be tested. If, for some reason, the item was taken in without being tested, the pawnbroker or the clerk must write 'untested' on the pawn ticket. This saves any problems when the pawners redeem their merchandise and it doesn't work properly.

It behooves the pawnbroker to test every item because he might just be setting it out for sale before very long.

Whenever an item comes in, the pawnbroker looks at it as a buy ... because if the pawner doesn't return, that is just exactly what the pawnbroker has done. Is the item clean or can it be cleaned up? Is the item outdated or obsolete? Is it an item that is in demand all the time? Or is the demand based on the season of the year? Are all the pieces, parts, doors, hinges and knobs in tact? What is the age of the item? Does the item work well?

All these are questions that should be answered to the pawnbroker's satisfaction before making an offer or a loan.

It is easy to get lazy and allow an item to come into the store untested, especially when the same pawner has had the same item back into the store with great regularity.

TELEVISIONS

The greatest television demand in a pawn shop is the thirteen-inch color television. Many people purchase these televisions for a second set, more likely for a child's room.

The nineteen-inch color televisions with remote controls are the alternate favorites. People like to place those in their own bedrooms and they want remote controls so they don't have to get up to change channels.

The huge consoles sell relatively well, but they take up so much space that unless the pawn shop is of relative size, it is a difficult item to display and sell.

AC/DC color TVs are great little sellers. Make sure the cord that plugs into the car lighter is with the television.

The poorest sellers are the small one to six-inch screens.

Pocket televisions are almost *no sells* unless the pawnbroker is willing to take fifteen dollars or less for them. They really aren't worth the effort.

Another poor seller is the little black and white sets. If someone brings a twelve to nineteen-inch black and white portable TV into the store and the TV works very well, it is our policy to offer to purchase the set (not a loan) for five dollars. Those small black and whites sell okay if the prices can be kept down around nineteen ninety-five. If you try to get any more, it just won't happen.

Make sure the date on the back of the television is within four years or newer on those sets that warrant a twenty dollar loan or more.

The more you lend on a TV set, the more picky you should be. It is pretty hard to get much money for a nine-year-old TV set. If an old TV comes in and it seems to work well, an offer of five or ten dollars is good.

If the price is right, anything will move. Imagine the find a forty-nine dollar, twenty-one inch color TV is, especially if it works very well.

Many times people don't want to spend much money and they are willing to risk the higher probability that the TV might quit on them. Many times, they just need it temporarily and plan to make a larger purchase later on.

Keep a close eye on the local discount store in your area. You want to maintain abreast of the most recent sales prices on televisions. You don't want to be offering a used television for the same price or more than the customers can purchase brand new.

Again, ten cents on the dollar is the rule. If a television sells new for two hundred and sixty-nine dollars, then the offer to pawn or buy should be around twenty-five dollars. That same television will go out for sale for around one hundred and forty-five dollars ($145), depending on the desirability of the unit. The price could go up to one hundred and ninety-five dollars ($195) and if it is a very nice set, it should turn over in a relatively short amount of time.

Once a deal has been negotiated, the pawn ticket or the buy ticket will be filled out by the pawnbroker or the clerk.

A trick of the trade is to leave the television running while the ticket is being written. Sometimes a television will not tell the true tale right away. If you see that the picture is beginning to not reach across the screen on any of the four sides, that means it has a weak picture tube. In order for this to happen, sometimes the set needs to be warmed up well.

A deal is not a deal until the cash is in the customer's hand. More than a few times, we have had to back out on an offer after it was written and even signed and thumbprinted by the customer.

Just apologize politely and tell them that you will have to renege on the deal because of a faulty picture. Many times, they will argue but it is better to be the bad guy with your cash intact than good guy who's the proud owner of a broken television that can't be sold.

The most desirable sets come cable ready and equipped with remote control. Digital display is far more desirable than the twist-type knobs. If the sound system is in stereo, the set should not stay on the shelves very long at all. Newer model sets such as the one just described can stand loans of up to fifty dollars.

VCRs

THE AVERAGE LIFESPAN OF A VCR IS FIVE (5) YEARS.

VCRs have gained such popularity in such a short period of time that it is rare to find a person who doesn't own at least one. Many people own and use two or more. VCRs are frequently used as loan collateral. But, as on televisions, there are conditions to be met. *The most important thing to know is that the old Beta VCRs and the top loaders are obsolete.*

Sometimes we will buy a Beta from a customer if it is in *immaculate condition.* But that's it! **Buy JUST ONE!** Pay ten dollars for it and set it out for sale at fifty to seventy dollars. Eventually, someone will come in who is looking for a Beta because they still have all their old Beta tapes. When you sell the Beta, wait for another one to come in that looks like new.

Neither lend on nor purchase any VHS top loaders. They are old dinosaurs looking for a place to rest their weary bones. They're too new to be called antiques and they are too old to sell! Some of them are only a few years old. You might want one for yourself, but selling it is another story. Steer clear for now.

Because the VCRs are so plentiful, a pawnbroker can afford to pick and choose the ones he wants to deal in. But remember ... VCRs are the first to be pawned and they are the first to be redeemed! Rejoice when one comes out for sale!

Every VCR must test out well. Keep a television at your testing station for this purpose. Sometimes there is a run on televisions and it is tempting to sell the last one on the shelf. But then VCRs cannot be tested. So don't give in to greed here. VCRs should be three years or newer.

Slightly beat up VCRs (nothing broken or missing) that work well with no remote and no instructions can bear a ten to fifteen dollar loan. Add a remote, add another five dollars. Add the original box and instructions, add another five dollars.

A lesser brand name VCR (nothing broken or missing) that works well and is in good condition, with no remote and no instructions can stand a twenty dollar loan. Add five dollars for a remote. Add another five dollars for instructions and original box.

A name brand VCR (nothing broken or missing) that is in fair condition and works well will stand a thirty dollar loan. Add five dollars for remote and add another five dollars for the instructions and box.

A name brand VCR (nothing broken, nothing missing) that is in good condition will stand a loan up to fifty dollars. Add a remote, add five. Add the instructions and the original box, add another five.

A name brand VCR (nothing broken, nothing missing) that is in brand new condition will stand a sixty dollar loan. Add a remote, add another five. Add instructions, add another five. Add the original box, add another five.

You can see how you can enable yourself to create a system of guidelines to follow. It isn't long before you begin to utilize your own formulas for just about everything that you pawn or buy. Simply revise your formula as you need to. Formulas should change as the years progress. This is especially true for equipment such as TVs and VCRs.

New innovations continue to outdate the older models and the public demand is for the most updated item available on today's market. By using this philosophy, you will overcome the worst pawn shop nightmare of a dank old shop filled with grimy and obsolete merchandise. It's time we separated the junk shop from the updated, and yes ... even trendy, pawn shop.

Today, VCRs are updated to the point where stereo VCRs have been around for a few years. A stereo VCR is ALWAYS worth more than a regular VCR.

Somewhat new on the market are the VCRs that can be paused and then a large knob located on the front of the VCR can be rotated so that the exact frame or pose can be selected. These sell for top dollar on the retail market. They are very desirable to pawnbrokers and the buying public.

Keep a television at your testing station at all times. Today's VCRs have no clock or digits to show what channel is set or which way the tape is winding. Instead, this information is projected on the screen of the television. There is no way to test these without hooking them up to a television.

Take a few trips to a Circuit City near you. Keep your eye on what's going on in the electronics market. New things are coming on the scene all the time, and if you don't know what you are looking at, you might be passing up a great opportunity to buy or loan on a very desirable item.

Many pawnbrokers make the mistake of turning away all VCRs that don't have a remote with them. This is silly. People come in all the time with a VCR that is a few years old and not the top of the line brand. Often, they forgot the remote or the kids broke it.

As long as they function from the front of the unit, offer $10 to $20 on it. I can't think of a reason in the world why a pawnbroker couldn't sell a VCR like that quite easily for $59.95 to $79.95. Where are you going to pick up a VCR anywhere for that kind of money?

People love them for their kids. Mom and Dad have the good one in the living room and the kids have one of their own in their room. The parents don't care if the kids don't have the convenience of a remote box ... and neither do the kids. Half the time the kids lose them or break them anyway.

STEREOS

In order to effectively pawn stereo components, a complete system must be available in order to test individual components and speakers. Again, I must caution you to make sure you do not sell your testing system.

There are several obsolete components. The first is the record player. No record players at all!

The second obsolete item is the single cassette component. All of the new cassette components are dual.

The third item is an eight track. If a system comes in that has an eight track incorporated into it, the answer is absolutely not.

After you have your feet wet and you get a feel for your market, you will know which taboos you can break and which you must maintain.

There are literally hundreds of makes and models. Stereo components are some of the most difficult to pawn. It's important to understand the difference between a Kenwood from a Sony and a Pioneer from a Yorx in order to make the very most money on each invested dollar. Because it is assumed that the reader has little experience in this field, another grid type scale is presented until time builds experience.

Divide stereo components into three categories according to what you feel are the most desirable makes and models. For instance, I might group Kenwood with Pioneer and Sony with Sansui and I would definitely place Sound Design and Yorx in the lowest price ranges. If a customer comes in with one or two Kenwood components, I might lend twenty dollars apiece.

In California, each unit must be placed on a separate pawn ticket so that the serial number and model can be individually investigated.

If the Kenwood was comprised of an entire system, i.e., amplifier, tuner, cassette deck, CD player and two high-quality speakers, it would be no problem for me to lend twenty-five dollars on every single unit. They would have to be picked up together and the total loan amount would be one hundred and fifty dollars.

If the units were of lesser quality but in new condition, the loan would drop to twenty dollars per component or one hundred and twenty ... personally, I would round it out to one hundred dollars.

On the Soundesign and Yorx, the loan should not be more than five dollars per unit. Thirty dollars would be a very good loan for the six pieces. If one were to go back to the original formula of ten cents on the dollar, it would be right in the ballpark of the original retail prices.

The condition of the components would weigh heavily on the loan amount. For instance, let's say the Kenwood was a couple of years old and it showed some minor wear and tear. The loan amount would drop to one hundred. If the Sansui was in similar condition, fifty to seventy-five might be good enough for a loan. If the Yorx were to show the same wear and tear, fifteen dollars would be the ceiling on that loan.

It takes some time but pretty soon you begin to develop a feel for what you want to loan on any given item. The day will never come that the pawnbroker isn't thrown for a loop on the amount of the loan or whether to even loan anything or not. That is what keeps the business so interesting.

Take that nice Kenwood that warranted a one hundred and fifty dollar loan and set it out for sale at a nice fat sales price of maybe six hundred and fifty to seven hundred dollars and watch a clever shopper steal it from you for only six hundred dollars and they even got you to pay the tax on it for them! I love a clever shopper.

A four hundred and fifty dollar price tag on the Sansui components will make those units disappear. Seventy-five to ninety-nine dollars takes the Soundesign out the door.

Keep catalogs of everything on hand. If you are an orderly person, the catalogs could be indexed and filed away.

Sears, Best, Montgomery Ward and JC Penny's offer complete catalogs of everything.

Radio Shack has weekly specials that can be collected and put back for references. Glean out the old information as it is replaced by the new.

Keep your store neat and tidy as possible. Nothing looks worse than a backlog of old catalogs and sales fliers. It is also very inconvenient to have useless references to dig through in order to find what you need.

BOOM BOXES

Yesterday's 'ghetto blasters' are now obsolete. Long gone are the big JVCs that look like complicated suitcases! Today's boom boxes are low, black and sleek. They offer many features such as dual cassettes with speed dubbing and detachable speakers. Many have a single cassette and a CD player incorporated into the system.

Again, depending upon the make and model ... so go the prices. The top dollar to loan on a boom box that offers many features and is in excellent condition is around thirty dollars. Remember, ten cents on the dollar. You won't see many boom boxes retail for over two hundred and ninety-nine dollars.

Stay at or below the thirty dollar ceiling and you shouldn't make any mistakes. Set the nicest boom box out for sale priced around one hundred dollars and watch it sell!

Good merchandising dictates the one hundred dollar figure be translated to ninety-nine dollars or one hundred and seven-fifty.

The one hundred and seven-fifty is easily bartered into one hundred dollars and you pay the tax or one hundred and seven-fifty and I'll pay the tax. Most people don't necessarily want a good bargain. They just want to say they got the item at a better price than originally quoted.

THE WALKMAN

Five dollars. Sell for twenty to twenty-five. Remember that there are similar units available that sell for as little as twelve to fifteen dollars new. This item is generally not a good investment. Take one or two if they are the original Walkman and then wait and see how they turn over.

COMPACT DISKS

In order to be truly successful in turning the compact disks, a lot depends on the artists and what kind of music is preferable within the area the disks are being sold. Country is always big on the west coast, as is rock and roll. Of course, in the Hollywood area, the heavy metal groups are always good sellers. Any of the old standards that are in the area of soft rock seem to sell well. Avoid Christmas and children's CDs. Reggae and soul are also steady sellers.

Check the CD against a bright light. If you see light coming through tiny holes, the CD is defective. CDs are a good item to take in. Pay anywhere up to three dollars each for CDs and sell them for around seven-fifty each.

RECORD ALBUMS

Records don't move very well because the few people who have record players hesitate to buy used albums because they are so easily damaged. There are still many people who refuse to give up their record collections in favor of tapes or CDs. If some nice albums happen to come in that have been popular in the past, they will sell pretty well, especially if they are collectibles such as Elvis Presley Albums.

Give a quarter a record and sell the less popular recordings for a dollar each. The more collectibles can go for up to ten dollars apiece, depending on the album.

The old seventy-eights rate the same as an LP album.

CASSETTE TAPES

Pay twenty-five cents to fifty-cents each and sell for three dollars each. The same criteria applies for the artists and the type of music they play. Check each cassette recording for use and/or damage. Do not take in home recordings. Take only the original tapes that were sold out of the music stores.

The old standbys that everybody knows are steady sellers while the newer artists like Taylor Dane, Mariah Carey and K.D. Lang go over very big in a wide variety of age groups. New Kids On The Block, U2 and the Police are biggies with many age groups. Just tune in to your local soft rock stations, the country stations and you will hear the updated artists as well as the best of the oldies.

Cater to the youth by taking in the heavy metal and hard rock. They will spend their money if they see what they like. The heavy metalers like Def Leperd, Pink Floyd and ZZ Top.

The most difficult kind of music to sell is the New Age. I would suppose it is because most people who frequent pawn shops are not into meditation and enlightenment. It is popular in a culture within a culture (the Yuppie group), but it is not generally desirable in a large cross section. Kitaro is one of the most renowned artists of the New Age Movement.

Rap music is still another style of desirable music that is being sold on the popular market today.

If you don't mind messing with CDs, tapes and records, there is money to be made in that area of the business. It might not pay the rent, but it will definitely cover the lunches and maybe even the electricity bill once in awhile.

If you enjoy it, do it. If you don't, it's not worth the hassle.

NINTENDOS

I would be remiss in neglecting to cover these great little sellers. Many pawnbrokers don't deal in them because they don't want to mess with them.

Here's the deal. Every Nintendo that comes in usually has a few games with it. If there are only one or two games, I offer between $15 and $20 for the whole thing. (This means that all of the equipment must be with it, like the control sticks, the gun and the control boxes.)

We can sell the Nintendo for $49 which isn't so wonderful. Leave 1 Nintendo tape with the set for the sale. The other Nintendos sell for $9 if they don't have the covers and the instructions. If they do have the covers and instructions, you can get up to $15 for some of them.

Sometimes customers come in and sell all of their Nintendo games because they bought a new Super Nintendo and none of the older games will work in the new Nintendo. You can buy the games for $2 to $3 apiece. Check your local competitors to see what they are giving for them and you can match them or do a little better.

Some pawnbrokers don't want to take the older games because of the new Super Nintendos. The new Nintendos are selling for $200 and not many parents are interested in buying another Nintendo plus pay for all of those games they bought before. A Nintendo game sells for around $25 to $35 depending on what it is and where you buy it.

The original Nintendo games are going to be around for a long time. I believe pawnbrokers will get at least another five years out of them before they phase out. During that time, the Super Nintendos will be coming in and the good business will continue.

VIDEO TAPES

$3 to $5 only if still sealed in original wrap. Some pawnbrokers will pay $ .50 to $1 for a tape that has been opened. It's worth that if it is blank.

A BIG DON'T ON STORING VIDEO TAPES. **DO NOT store them anywhere near car speakers. You will magnatize your tapes and they will be ruined.**

DON'T LIST

1. VCRs or televisions that have a rental company written on the back of the units. These are rentals and they belong to a rental company. Some are purchased by the customer as used units. Take them ONLY if the presents the receipt with the unit.
2. Electrical units that have missing parts such as knobs, levers, covers, etc.
3. Electrical items over 3 years old.
4. VCRs that are top loaders.
5. Beta VCRs.
6. Video tapes that have a broken seal.
7. Speakers that hiss.
8. Tuners that won't tune all the way to either end of the dial.
9. Stereos that won't balance when manually operated.
10. Units with missing serial numbers.
11. Units with altered serial numbers.
12. Items that are inscribed with names and personal ID numbers.
13. A pawner's 'personal guarantee' that the item works.
14. Untested merchandise.
15. Merchandise that displays signs of poor treatment.
16. Damaged merchandise.
17. Obscure brands over one year old.
18. Electrical units with broken or crudely repaired wiring.
19. Any piece of merchandise that you honestly don't want to have to sell.

This pawnbroker lined his jewelry showcases along the aisle that leads to the loan counter so that his view of the most expensive merchandise is unhindered. The track lighting for the displays is mounted on a frame of 2'' X 2''. Even with its lack of refinement, this large, open and well lit store lends an air of ease to the customers.

14 PC COMBINATION WRENCH SET
75-Watt Soldering Gun
ANY CRAFTSMAN TOOL - YOUR CHOICE $1.00 - $5.00
AEG

CHAPTER 16

TOOLS (HAND AND POWER)

Tools, like all other merchandise, are taken in at ten cents on the dollar. Make sure they are not broken or abused. Take only the clean tools and let the grimy tools walk back out the door.

Pawnbrokers have no extra time to be cleaning tools. Make sure all the parts are in good condition and nothing is chipped or broken. Look for signs of heavy wear and pass on those that look like they have been used heavily and often.

HAND TOOLS

Avoid any tools made anywhere other than the United States. Top of the line hand tools are Snap On, Mac, Proto and Craftsman. If the tool says Taiwan or Japan, they won't sell nearly as well as the American names.

Sets of tools are far more reasonable than individual items. This runs true in Sears, Builder's Discount and Home Depot among others.

If a person has an entire set of sockets and is missing one or two, it will cost five times as much to buy the individual socket than it runs per item by purchasing an entire set. But who wants another entire set when they need only one or two items?

That's why the discount stores can make so much more by selling these items in individual packages for many times more than they can get for them in sets. This is what the pawn shop is very good for.

When a good set of sockets come in, the pawnbroker will go through them and price them to buy at about twenty-five cents apiece (this is considering that they are in good condition and clean). The larger ones he prices three for a dollar and so on up the scale.

If they are lost to pawn, the sockets can be placed in bins and priced from fifty cents apiece to several dollars each, depending on size.

Some pawnbrokers capitalize on tools and earn handsome profits. Other pawnbrokers just don't want to mess with them and they offer the entire tool box for sale at a price that is around half of what the replacement value would be. (Again, this is if they are in good, clean condition.)

A copy of the Sears Tool Catalog should give the pawnbroker all the information he needs in order to deal in hand tools. A quick trip to a local discount store tells it all in the individual pricing that this kind of item commands.

Tool bins are very effective in order to generate a good steady stream of customers. Not many days go by that the same buyers double back from time to time, looking for good buys for their workshops.

It's especially nice when the wives tag along and spot a piece of jewelry that they'd like to have. Many a sale was made to those Saturday afternoon browsers who came in for a pipe wrench and left with a diamond ring!

POWER TOOLS

Power tools are good sellers provided the prices are right and they are of good quality. Brand names play a large role in this arena of tools as well.

American made are not the only desirable brands. In fact, Makita is far more desirable than Black and Decker. Craftsman and Skil are good sellers as well. Circular saws that are wurm driven are far more in demand than the smaller version.

Take in the most basic of tools and stay away from the tools that are more specialized. For instance, it would be preferable to take in a wurm drive circular saw over a refrigeration amp meter.

Carpet laying tools seem to be a good seller. A lot of people are turning to this kind of business because of the popularity of wall-to-wall carpeting in American homes today.

Be sure to plug in all power tools that come in and make sure that the workings run smoothly. Make sure the cords are together and intact. Look for signs of wear and abuse. Listen for bearings that can go bad. If the sound isn't smooth, no one else will want to buy it either. Pawn and buy each item as if you were going to take it home and use it yourself.

DO *NOT* TAKE IN CAR PARTS!

What are your chances of selling specialty rims? Stop and consider an auto parts store. A huge inventory is needed in order to satisfy each individual customer. The chance of selling a 1987 Chevrolet carburetor is pretty slim.

Walking into a pawn shop that has a set of chrome wheels sitting out for sale is always good for a chuckle.

I feel for the unwitting pawnbroker who made a loan on custom chrome wheels only to find out that anything custom must go to an equally rare, *custom customer*. My only advice to such an unfortunate pawnbroker is to try and fall in love with those chrome customs because chances are they are going to be in his possession for a very long time to come!

It's quite tempting to make a low ball offer on such an item because they are originally priced at ten and twenty times more.

Remember that a good buy is only a good buy when one of two things can happen.

Either the item can be turned over fast for a reasonable profit or it is something that the pawnbroker wants personally for himself. Other than those two reasons, nothing is a good buy.

The most successful pawnbrokers have an almost immediate market for everything they buy. Merchandise that sits on shelf space and collects dust is worth nothing. In fact, the space it takes costs the pawnbroker every day. Space is money as time is money.

That's why items like bulky air compressors and generators are not good unless they can be turned over quickly.

PNEUMATIC TOOLS

In order to test pneumatic tools, an air compressor is needed. If there is plenty of room for the pawnbroker to keep such an item for testing purposes, then air tools are good to take in. (See local tool catalogs for prices.)

DON'T FORGET TO PICK UP A SEARS TOOL CATALOG.

You will find that a good old Sears Tool Catalog will help you in pawning and buying. When time comes to sell, they are invaluable as a pricing guide.

Craftsman are always good sellers because some of the Sears stores are still making good on them. Check your local Sears Center.

We didn't know what we were going to do with an entire record store full of LP bins, but they were cheap so ... we bought them. Now, I don't know what we would have done without them!

CHAPTER 17

MUSICAL INSTRUMENTS

Musical instruments vary in popularity as much as they vary in size, shape, method of play and tone emitted. Listed here in this chapter are the most common and sought after instruments. Any instruments other than the ones listed are considered to be exotic in terms of pawnable items.

Pawn shops sell instruments to basically two categories of people. These are *country/rock groups* and *standard band students*. Other groups that are involved in music are usually of the orchestral variety and the quality instruments they seek are purchased either new or are bid for in a specialized market.

The reasons for remaining out of the exotic instrument area are many fold.

First, the pawnbroker usually doesn't know what he's looking at.

Second, chances are excellent that the instrument is stolen.

Third, it would be an uncommon buyer who would happen into the store by chance and spot such a rare item.

Fourth, the value of such an item is left to pure speculation.

Fifth, unless the customer is able to demonstrate the instrument, its state of repair might remain a mystery. Unless you are interested in a unique wall decoration, you would probably be wise to pass.

One last, but most important piece of information regarding musical instruments is this:

MAKE SURE THAT EVERY INSTRUMENT YOU TAKE IN HAS THE CASE WITH IT.

With the exception of guitars (guitars are normally sold with cases if they came in that way) and other instruments that are usually NOT sold with cases such as keyboards, your chances for turning over the most stunning of musical instruments dwindle down to just above zero without the cases. Even if the case is run down and worn, it is by far and away in your favor to have it with the instrument. Tag each case with the brand and/or some code that will help you to locate it easily.

STRING INSTRUMENTS

ACOUSTIC GUITARS

Acoustic guitars are also called *flat tops.* All acoustic guitars are hollow so that the sound of the instrument can be enhanced. The vibrating strings are magnified by the hollowness creating full resonant tones which are emitted from the instrument.

There are several kinds of acoustic guitars. The ***standard six string guitar*** is usually strung with metal strings.

The ***classical*** guitar tends to be a bit smaller and is strung with plastic strings to prevent unwanted noises as the player runs his fingers up and down the frets. A classical guitarist must make many more keying motions, consequently it is impossible to keep the fingers from lagging on the strings. Many classical guitarists still opt for the finer sounds of metal strings and the price they pay for the higher tone quality is the distracting keying rasps.

The ***twelve string*** guitar isn't quite so common. These are the large acoustics that are strung with metal strings that run down the neck in two pairs of six. Each string has its own tuning knob and can be adjusted individually as necessary.

The brands most commonly prized in acoustic guitars are the Martin, Fender, Ovation, and Gibson. Applause, Yamaha, Hondo, Guild, and BC Rich are also some good contenders among many others.

Like cars and cameras, many top brand names offer lesser, low priced models in an effort to attract the consumers who are working with a much lower budget. This is the reason for obtaining the best pricing catalogs possible. Orion's Blue Books are, by far, the most desirable in listing the finest cross sections of musical instruments.

There are as many brand names and model numbers, not counting limited editions and collectible colors, as there are makes and models of automobiles!

Even if I were an expert in the music industry, it would be virtually impossible to list every single category of price indexing here in this piece. That's where building your price listing library comes into play.

No attorney is able to know every law written and every precedent set by judicial process. That's why their offices are decorated with handsomely bound editions of reference guides. Those *decorations* are the tools of their trade and the attorneys value their law library as the surgeon values his precision tools.

In the same manner, pawnbrokers maintain up-to-the-minute references for every imaginable item that could possibly come across the loan counter. *It is one of the costs of doing business.*

WHAT TO LOOK FOR IN A GUITAR

1. *Neck of guitar out of line or warped.* Peer down the line of the guitar neck to be sure it is straight and true. Check the base of the neck to be sure it is not lifting from the body. Make sure it is securely fastened.

2. *Check to see if the frets are worn down.* Flattened frets indicate much use and they become very difficult to key. The frets that show most wear are usually the top five or ten.

3. *Look for hairline cracks and fractures* on the front and back of the body.

4. *Check for broken or missing pieces.*

5. *Make note of the general care* and maintenance that has been given to the instrument over time.

6. *Make sure all the pieces are together and intact.* The last thing you have time to worry about is finding missing parts for a guitar.

ELECTRIC GUITARS

As with acoustic guitars, there are several basic kinds of electric guitars. There is the **standard six string electric** guitar. The bass guitar and the fancy double neck with sets of six string on each neck.

Here again, we open the door to a maze of confusion. The price settled on to pawn must be one that meets with catalog buying prices or lower, or in the event you can find no reference, a price that you are willing to gamble. Remember, **'when in doubt, send it out,'** or **'don't pay more than you are willing to lose.'**

Generally, a better electric guitar is one that offers three or four adjustment knobs and that has three or four pickups. A pickup is a bar that runs under the strings on the base of the guitar body. Most pickups have a nail-head size piece of metal under each string.

Accept no electric guitar that has missing pieces and this includes strings. How can you know if the guitar works if there are no strings?

Many times a plate is missing off the back of electric guitars. Do NOT take them in.

An expert in the field might disagree. Of course, rules do have their exceptions. In this case, if you have access to a person who is handy at guitar repair, you would base your decisions on which guitars to take in a little differently. Unless you are in such a position to make that exception, the answer has to be NO.

If you can spot the flaws, so will the customer that is considering it for purchase. Think about it. If you were a buying customer in search of a good guitar, would you consider *this* guitar?

Have an amplifier ready at your testing station for the customer to demonstrate his electric guitar. Most customers don't think to bring in the cord, so be sure to have a spare handy. If they don't know how to demonstrate it, it might not be theirs to pawn.

Be sure to have a bass amplifier for the bass guitars AND a guitar amplifier. If you allow a customer to plug his big bass guitar into a small guitar amplifier and he turns up the volume, your guitar amplifier won't be fit for anything but the trash!

If you must be limited to one amplifier, use a bass amp because a regular guitar can't hurt it. If you only have access to a guitar amp when testing a bass, turn the volume down as far as possible and then plug the bass in. As the pawner plucks the strings, slowly turn the volume up until you can test the bass satisfactorily.

BASIC GUITAR PRICES

Paying out cash for musical instruments can be very tricky ... so it is best to cover yourself in this area. A general rule is that 'no name' 'cheapie' import acoustic guitars can be purchased through the wholesalers for around $45 to $50.

By knowing this, when a pawner brings in a guitar that has a name brand on it, you can feel reasonably sure that your investment can be around $20 to $30 if the condition of the guitar warrants an offer to pawn or buy. A name guitar will easily sell for $75 to $150 with not much problem.

The 'cheapie' electric guitars wholesale for around $130 to $140. It doesn't take a genius to figure out the fact that money is there to be made if a name brand electric guitar is pawned or purchased for from $30 to $50 and sells for $90 to $190. If you don't know what you are looking at and you can't find it in the book ... and the instrument is in good condition (no major gouges, cracks, warps, dirt and all pieces intact), it is safe to offer up to half the wholesale prices of the most inexpensive guitar on the market.

Figure the electric bass guitars around the same area as the standard electric guitars. The bass guitars are probably a bit more expensive but the difference is not a vast one.

ACOUSTIC BASS GUITARS

These rare guitars take up buckets of space but it is always fun to own one and keep it on display. Smaller stores sometimes display a cello because of the size factor in the huge stand-up bass. They are great attention grabbers.

Acoustic bass guitars are worth a lot of money. If I were making the purchase for my store, I would go around $100, especially if a case is included. Chances are, it won't sell or you won't *want* to sell it. So keep your investment within reason of your budget. This is the kind of item where one is fine. More than one is far too many.

VIOLINS

Forget everything you ever heard about Stradivarius. *A fiddle is a fiddle where the pawn shop is concerned.*

Few concert violinists look for their instrument in a pawn shop. Violins are solely for the student, no matter what it says on the inside. Therefore, pay out your cash for a fiddle ... and unless you have the kind of luck that it takes to hit the big one on the state lottery,you will probably have purchased just that ... a student model.

Check for condition and then offer $10 to $30 for the violin. You will be able to sell it for $49 to $99 and probably not a penny more. There are two basic sizes — full and three-quarters. An oversize violin is probably a viola and not standard collateral in pawn shops. The cases to violins are mandatory to sales.

CELLOS

An unusual pawn shop item. The cello is an orchestral instrument. Normally, a pawn shop does not deal in them. They are not rare and not in great demand. Here, I make the exception because I do buy them. They might linger around my store for a year or so. Eventually, they sell.

Students looking to buy cellos are forced to pay extremely high prices for new student models. One must own a cello to play a cello. This is the proverbial exception that proves the rule.

If the instrument were in reasonably decent condition and it was complete with strings, bow and case, I (personally) would invest up to $100. If I wanted to sell it as soon as I could, I would contact the local schools and see if the music department or one of the students might be interested in a good buy. Nothing ventured, nothing gained!

A case with the cello is much more desirable but I would take one without the case, if necessary. Just cut the price by half.

MANDOLINS

Like bass guitars, keep one on hand. It's not that they are so big, they just aren't in very much demand these days. Pawn or buy for $15 to $30. Sell for $75 to $95. Cases not mandatory.

BANJOS

Two banjos at any given time are plenty, according to our experience in both locations. Pawn shops rarely get more than $150 for the nicest of them.

Keep your bidding around $15 to $25 for loan or buy. Your area may dictate that you may deal in banjos more effectively than has been our experience. Don't overlook this possibility. Banjos are such difficult sellers that we prefer to take them with the cases.

AUTOHARPS

Autoharps are commonly seen in pawn shops. They can be taken in 'new' condition (in the original box with instructions and tuning key) for around $10 to $20. They can be sold for around $75. Do not accept autoharps with rusty or broken strings.

PIANOS

For obvious reasons, pianos are a difficult item in a pawn shop. We've taken in one piano on a trade simply because we wanted it for our home. Otherwise, there was no room for it to be displayed or stored in the pawn shop. For around $500, we were able to obtain a baby grand (not to be confused with the concert grand which is enormous). The brand was an obscure one, but for $500 we weren't going to quibble.

Uprights and spinets can be taken in, but remember that if the instrument is in poor repair or impossible to tune, chances are (unless you are a pianist), you won't know the difference and you will be stuck with a piano that is unsalable.

The four top names in pianos are *Baldwin, Steinway, Rowland* and *Yamaha*. If one of these names were to be presented to me in the pawn shop, I believe I would risk $100 and if I were sure about the instrument being in a good state of repair, $300 would not be unreasonable. A good piano of these quality names could resell easily for around $800 to $1200 and possibly more, depending on the condition.

ELECTRIC PIANOS

No longer very popular due to the updated keyboards that can mimic the piano plus a myriad of other instruments. Only the newest of electric pianos are in stereo. Clearly, no one wants a mono electric piano. The newer ones are marked with *stereo*. As far as you are concerned, if it doesn't say stereo, it isn't.

Electric pianos have no speakers and they must be hooked into a stereo system or into amplifiers in order to play. Be sure you test them thoroughly. Pay up to $50 but remember, they are very slow to sell.

KEYBOARDS

Although these instruments are electric, I include them in the stringed category. *Rowland, Casio* and *Yamaha* are the standard brands that are big on the market today.

Several years ago, the small keyboards were quite the rage and they became a good pawn item. The market is now flooded with them and the demand has dwindled.

It would be best to take only the more sophisticated keyboards that are equipped with a MIDI.

The MIDI is a feature that allows the keyboardist to channel the music out to other sound systems. Bear in mind that the nicest keyboards can sell for quite a bit of money, new. Getting a buyer to shell out a small percentage of that figure in a pawn shop is difficult at best. Offer $30 to $50 on a pawn or loan for the nicest ones and let the rest of them go. If they don't take it, consider it your gain!

Do not take any keyboard that is not equipped with a MIDI. You can tell this by simply looking at the instrument. It will indicate that it does include a MIDI, usually right on the front near the brand name. Keep sale prices down in the low one hundreds unless you happen to know that the keyboard in question is a real specialty item that would be instantly recognized by a knowledgeable keyboardist.

Test every single key to make sure there are no dead keys. Test volume and the various sound effects.

Every keyboard that doesn't feature a MIDI can be considered to be a toy! If you feel like you could turn a profit on those models that don't feature a MIDI, give between $5 and $20 for the best of them. This is the only way a profit can be turned on these items.

WIND INSTRUMENTS

The most common brands are listed below. Almost every horn that comes into the pawn shop is a *student model.*

Parents purchase these instruments in hopes that their child will take an interest in the instrument. Nine times out of ten, the instrument winds up back in the pawn shop.

Many times pawnbrokers feel obligated to repurchase these instruments for nearly what they sold them for. This is not how it works! Offer only one-third of the price they paid to buy it from you and offer that ONLY if the instrument is in the same (or better) condition than when the customer first bought it.

By offering a third, you will probably be giving the customer more than most other pawn shops would.

Don't be afraid to take the more common wind instruments. They will clog your shelves from the day after Christmas until the Fall of the year when school begins and the music classes meet. Look for musical band instruments to move quickly in September, October and sometimes into late November. You won't have enough of them.

There are two categories of horns: Woodwinds and Brass.

WOODWINDS

Woodwinds are broken down into two main categories. The first category includes the **reed instrument family.**

Clarinets, saxophones, bassoons and oboes along with other more exotic variations fall into this category.

A small wooden reed is fitted to the backside of the mouthpiece. The sound of the instrument originates with the player creating vibrations by passing air between the reed and the mouthpiece. The player controls the amount of air while manipulating various valves and valve covers in order to produce desired tones and pitch.

The alternate category of woodwinds consists of the **non reed** instruments. These consist of flutes, piccolos and recorders.

Basically, all woodwinds were made of wood at one time and what made them similar are the fingering positions. Today, most of the woodwinds are made of metal (except clarinets, some piccolos and recorders). Most of these exceptions are considered *exotic* in nature.

INSPECTING THE WOODWIND

When considering a loan or purchase of a woodwind, make sure that all the springs on the instrument are in working condition.

Some valves remain open, others have covers that are opened and closed when certain keys are pressed. Other covered valves are meant to remain closed and open when other keys are pressed. If the cover is open, there should be a key that will close it when pressed and open the valve again when released.

The alternate is true with covered valves that remain closed. Find the key that lifts the cover and then release the key to make sure the cover drops back down covering the valve securely.

Every key that is pressed should have an action and an alternate reaction when released. No key should cause an action without an alternated reaction upon its release.

Another important area to check are for dried up and/or crumbling pads. Under each valve cover lid is a white pad. These pads should look puffy and clean. There is a natural ring on the pad that is ridged by the valve.

When the pads are browning and crumbled, this is a sign that the instrument is in need of repair.

A woodwind instrument relies on proper closure of the valves in order to create the proper sounds. This means the pads should be resilient and pliable. Age darkens and dries them. Poor care of the instrument such as neglecting to dry it properly after each use shortens the lifespan of the valve lid pads.

When inspecting clarinets, look closely at the cork that surrounds the male ends on each piece of the instrument. The cork should look healthy and unscarred.

Blackish cork that is crumbling is a sign of deterioration from age and/or poor care and maintenance.

Usually, a small container of cork wax comes

with the clarinet. Cork wax is a covering that keeps the cork moist. Most well cared for clarinets include a container of cork wax in the case. No cork wax included alerts me to be suspicious of cork damage.

Saxophones don't have the significant cork problems but inspection of the valve springs and pads is as vital as for the clarinet.

Check for dings and dents in the saxophones. The metal on saxophones erodes when improperly cared for. The metal on all instruments should look bright and shiny.

The clarinet's exterior ebony should have a lustrous sheen to it. Plastic pieces on a clarinet reduce the value immensely.

Check to make sure all the pieces of the instrument are together. Clarinets have five pieces – the mouthpiece, a small connection between the mouthpiece and the first half of the valve section, the second half of the valve section, and the bell of the horn to finish the five piece set. Flutes, piccolos and saxophones are in two pieces.

The easiest way to check for all pieces is to have the pawner assemble all the pieces in front of you. If the customer is not knowledgeable about how the instrument is pieced together, put it together yourself.

If you can't figure it out, don't deal on the instrument. It won't be long before you understand how the instruments are supposed to look. They are normally not very complicated in this manner. Take some time and browse through a music store and don't be afraid to ask questions.

ALWAYS make sure each instrument has its own case. Horns of all kinds need their cases in order to turn them over for any profit at all. Without a case, a horn is virtually unsalable.

THE WOODWIND FAMILY

CLARINETS

There are two kinds of clarinets – the common 'licorice stick' of Benny Goodman fame and the bass clarinet that is very hard to get rid of. Bass clarinets look like black ebony saxophones. Obviously, pass on bass clarinets. Pay from $15 to $30 for clarinets and sell them for $99 to $199. Common brands ... Selmer-Bundy, Pierre, and Elkhart. Must include case.

SAXOPHONES

Soprano, Alto, C-Melody, Bass (the alto sax is by far and away the most popular. Avoid taking C-Melody saxes. C-Melodies are recognized by the unusually long piece that extends from the mouthpiece.) Saxophones in good condition can stand a loan of $30 up to $100, sometimes more ... and they sell from $125 to $550, depending on the brand and the style. Common brands are Selmer-Bundy, Conn, Elkhart, Yamaha, and Armstrong. Must include case.

FLUTES

Flutes are another good seller in September. Pay $15 to $30 for average to good flutes. You can go up to $50 for a pretty silverplated flute. Sell them for $79 to $145. Common brands ... Selmer-Bundy, Armstrong, Elkhart. Must include case.

PICCOLOS

Piccolos are always good sellers. Offer $20 to $40 on nice instruments. They can be sold for $95 to $225. Piccolos can demand a little higher price than flutes because of their rarity in pawn shops. Inspect piccolos much the same as flutes, clarinets and saxophones. Must include case.

BRASS

Brass instruments include the trumpet, coronet, bugle, slide trombone, french horn, tuba, and sousaphones.

These instruments are much easier to check out than the woodwinds. All of the brass horns (with the exception of the trombone, bugle and sousaphone) have three valves. The trombone is 'noted' with a long slide while the bugle and sousaphone require different mouth pressures and combinations of air pressure entering the mouthpiece in order to fluctuate the tones.

Brass instruments are the most simplified of horns. They are played by the musician placing both lips on a circular funnel-like mouthpiece.

The mouthpiece is designed in such a fashion that the vibrations of the musician's lips are funneled into a condensed space that allows the sound ot the vibrations to be translated into smooth even tones.

Although brass instruments are varying in extreme size, the basic principals remain the same. Brass instruments have either three valves or they have no valves. Most of the tones are created by the pressure and intensity of the musician's lips and the wind velocity he chooses to create.

The structure of brass instruments consist of variations of single tubes. Different sizes create different tone ranges. The small instruments emit the higher tones while the larger, more cumbersome of the class, emit low frequency vibrations.

The instruments with no valves are regulated by the player's lips and wind pressure. The instruments with three valves require the same amount of effort to play but offer the musician more octave options.

INSPECTING BRASS INSTRUMENTS

The simplified design of the brass instrument offers the potential lender/buyer easy access to inspection.

The most commonly overlooked faults lie with the valves. The valve buttons should feel silky smooth as they are pressed down and released.

The release action should be quick and the button should return to the original position without any hesitation. If the valve hesitates, it is 'sticky' and will require repair before it can be resold. It is much easier to turn away an instrument with such a problem than it is to worry about who can fix it and for how much.

Make sure all the pieces are there. French horns are more complicated and there is a piece of the piping structure that can be removed for saliva draining. The best way to make sure everything is included is to have the customer assemble the pieces or assemble them yourself. The missing pieces are obviously glaring.

The condition of these horns depend on the manner in which they have been maintained. Look for scratches, dents and signs of wear and tear in order to establish the horn's value. Cases are mandatory except for the bugle and the souzaphone.

THE BRASS FAMILY

TRUMPETS

These are the most popular of brass band instruments and they are always a good seller. Most common brands are Conn, King, Yamaha, Yvette, Blessing and Bundy. Buy for $30 to $50 and sell for $140 to as much as $350 in rare cases. Trumpets must be accompanied with mouthpieces and cases. Sometimes a cleaning shammy, mutes and an occasional trumpet stand are included and usually those items make for an easier sale.

CORONETS

Coronets are simply a down-scaled trumpet. They are nearly obsolete and it is a rare coronet that is still in mint condition. If a *mint* coronet happens to come across your path, invest no more than $20. It might sit on your shelf for a long time, but it will sell eventually. Price it around $100. Do NOT take in another until the one you have is sold. Mouthpiece and case are essential.

TROMBONES

The trombone is one of the variations of brass that doesn't have the three valves. Instead, it features a slide that can be adjusted according to the desire of the musician and the different notes and octaves are emitted with a combination of mouth and wind pressures and the slide.

Do not take many trombones in. One or two is sufficient. They are not fast sellers, but they will sell. Pay $30 to $50 for them and sell for $150 to $200. Must include mouthpiece and case.

FRENCH HORNS

Used french horns are hard to come by and sell easily when the price is right. New, the lower priced student models run around $1100. Some stores feature sales prices as low as $950.

A beautiful french horn complete with mouthpiece and case can be pawned or purchased for $100 to $150.

A sales price of $450 to $750 will turn the horn over quickly. The larger baritone french horn sells *new* for around $1300 and up. $100 to $200 should show a good return when the horn is priced from $600. Common name brands are *Yamaha, King, Bundy* and *Blessing.*

BUGLES

Own one for fun. More is a bore. A bugle is a great conversation piece. Buy it for $5. Price it at $30. Enjoy its aesthetic value. Mouthpiece is a must. With or without the case, it sells or it doesn't.

TUBAS

The tuba is a three valve instrument. Although the tuba is an orchestral instrument (its weight could not allow the tuba to be carried very far in a marching band), it is not unwise to take one if opportunity arises.

While the tuba is certainly not an exotic instrument, there still aren't many tuba players. As in the case of the french horn, the demand is not great, but when someone wants a used tuba, they are ready to pay good cash for a slick one. Any brand is acceptable. With case and mouthpiece only. Pay from $50 to $200. A tuba in mint condition can sell in a pawn shop for $500 to $800.

SOUZAPHONES

There is an interesting history attached to the invention of the souzaphone. The souzaphone was invented by none other than John Phillip Souza. Souza was (as most of us know) the composer of many of the moving pieces that are commonly played today by all marching bands.

Souza loved the deep oom pahs of the tuba and he wanted to find a way to recreate those powerful low tones for his marching band.

At first, he tried carrying the tuba and its player on a horse and cart and although the effect was the effect he was looking for, it still was not a complete marching band. Souza tried several metals until he came up with the first crudely made giant tin horn bell with three valves taken from another instrument (probably the tuba).

He wound up with an instrument that equaled the tonal qualities of the tuba while, at the same time, being light enough to carry.

The new oom pah horn was so cumbersome that it had to be designed in such a manner that the player virtually had to climb into the instrument and carry it in a 'wrap around' fashion.

Today, these instruments are made of a lighter and more cost effective fiberglass. A marching band just wouldn't be the same without the subtle oom pahs of the familiar souzaphone.

If you can find a place to put it, this rare musical instrument is a real find. There are very few souzaphone players, but the souzaphone can command a healthy price. Any brand in reasonable condition can sell for as much as $1500 in a pawn shop.

Pawn or buy for $100 to $200. If you price the souzaphone under $1000, it would be an excellent buy for an aspiring player. Many marching bands provide the player with the instrument.

PERCUSSION INSTRUMENTS

Obviously, drums are the first percussion instruments that come to mind. There are many variations of drums. Many are exotic or strictly orchestral, such as congas and kettle drums. Other percussion instruments that come to mind are cymbals, zylophones, marimbas, tambourines and bongo drums.

INSPECTION OF PERCUSSION INSTRUMENTS

If you decide to take them, make sure all the skins are intact and in good condition.

Many drums are equipped with springs and knobs that hold the skins in place. Make sure that all of these items are together and in place.

Keep the loans and buys low. The more exotic the instrument, the more caution should be taken when lending. In many cases, the competition has turned them away because of their uncertainty. Sometimes you can use this to your advantage by making a low ball offer. If they accept it, you might have an opportunity to make a lot of money, but if you don't, you won't have lost much.

DRUM SETS

Good to take in if space permits. Pawn for no more than $100 for a complete set. Complete sets include one or two bass drums, a floor tom, one or two upper toms and a snare drum. Drum sets are difficult to sell if the set is not complete.

There is only one drum that can be bought and sold out of the set and that is the snare drum. *Do not loan on or purchase any part of a drum set individually EXCEPT for the snare.* One bass or one tom is no good unless the rest of the set is included.

A complete set of drum hardware includes 2 cymbal stands, one hi-hat stand (if drum set consists of 2 bass drums, then the stand for the hi-hat consists of an extension bar and 2 clamps to attach the stand to the bass drums). If there is only one bass drum, the hi-hat stand must have legs. The snare stand opens up and has 3 prongs that hold the snare drum.

The upper tom (sometimes 2) doesn't have a stand, therefore there should be a mount coming off the bass drum that will allow the upper tom to sit at the proper angle. The floor tom has its own legs attached at the bottom. Then there is the drum stool or the drum throne. There should be one foot pedal for each bass drum.

You can tell the top of the line drums by looking inside the drum. If the drum is made of wood or clear plastic, they are usually the best on the market. The cheaper lines are made of pasteboard or cardboard.

Top of the line brands are: *Sonar, Slingerland, Gretch, Yamaha, Ludwig, Pearl* and *Tama.* A less expensive well known brand is a CB.

Cymbals sometimes don't come in with the drums, but if they do, the standard cymbals required to fill out a complete set are the ride cymbal which is 18″ to 20″, the heavier crash cymbal 15″ to 20″, and the hi-hats (an upper and a lower) that measure 14″ to 15″. The Zildgen is more desirable with the Pastie as a close second.

CYMBALS

Don't take in cymbals over 16 inches in diameter. Any cymbal 16 inches and under may be purchased for $10 to $20 and sold for $60 to $75. Take in only the Zildgens and Pasties. Hi-hats can be purchased for $15 and sold for $60 to $75. Make sure they are not bent and full of dings. A distorted instrument creates distorted sound.

TIMBALES

The timbales look like two flattened snares attached together with a cowbell in the middle. They are usually shiny chrome color and are gaining enormous popularity with latin bands. I haven't had any experience with them as of yet, but I believe I would go around $20 to $30 on a buy or pawn and then check them out in a music store. They should sell easily in a pawn shop for $75.

CONGA DRUMS

The congas sell new for around $200 for the smaller size and the price ranges upward by the size. The larger ones can sell new for as much as $500 or more. Buy or pawn for $20 to $75, depending on the size and condition. Sell for $100 to $300.

KETTLE DRUMS

No. Very expensive and almost impossible to sell. Kettle drums are strictly an orchestral instrument.

XYLOPHONES

Made of metal. Bordering on the exotic. The

band type xylophones that can be carried could be purchased for around $25 and resold for about $75.

MARIMBAS

Made of wood. Too exotic and takes up too much space for the desirability factor.

BONGO DRUMS

Common item in music stores. Buy for $5. Sell for $15 to $20.

MISCELLANEOUS

ACCORDIONS

Interestingly enough, accordions are becoming popular once again. This time the large, custom models aren't in so much demand as the smaller, cheaper versions that are colored in hues of reds, golds and whites. The Mexican Mariachi bands buy them regularly.

These accordions sell for around $100 to $190 in a pawn shop. This gives plenty of leeway to buy them for usually around $25 to $50.

The accordion must always come in its own case and it is best to keep clear of the large models. Although the larger models can be very expensive in a music store, they are difficult to sell in the pawn shop.

ACCORDION INSPECTION

In order to be sure that the accordion is in playing condition, it must be demonstrated. One of the tests to insure that the bellows are functioning correctly is to slowly pull the accordion apart. This should be difficult to do without a depressed chord. If there is no difficulty in opening the bellows without depressing a note or chord, there is an obvious leak in the bellows. No whistles or sounds of escaping air should be evident.

In order to check the keys, depress a chord button and allow the accordion to open from the top. Play each key until you are sure that every key works correctly.

CONCERTINAS

These are the little hand-squeeze boxes that were so popular among folk groups of many ethnic cultures. The Spaniards, Mexicans, Germans, and Swiss use them frequently in their music. They are becoming increasingly rare.

There are some new concertinas being manufactured in Taiwan but they are not quality like the older models made in Italy, Germany and Austria.

A concertina from Taiwan or Korea can be purchased for $10 to $15 and sold for $35 to $50.

If you are fortunate enough to have one of the older European models that is in decent shape come in, it is safe to offer $50. $150 or more could be realized from a sale. Chances are slim that one will cross your path but in the event it does, I would advise taking it. I wouldn't be too quick to sell it either.

HARMONICAS

May not be sold used. If you wish to stock harmonicas, stock them new. The cheaper harmonicas sell at a very good pace. Do not allow the customers to 'try them out.' This is a violation of health and safety laws.

Your MM Merchandising catalog sometimes lists harmonicas wholesale. If you decide to carry them, invest in a bellows that will demonstrate the harmonica sanitarily. The bellows are usually offered in the same catalog. Bellows are an investment in your store. They seldom need replacing so it is pretty much a one-time expense.

* * *

The above listed instruments are not, by a long shot, all of the instruments there are that exist. They are, however, the instruments which we have found to be some of the best money makers in the business.

It is not our suggestion that anyone ignore the more exotic like the steel guitar and even the ukulele. Every instrument of every kind should be taken into consideration.

For instance, pawn shops normally carry ukuleles. But they sell used for around $10 to $15. They are $39 new. Clearly, they are an instrument that could be deleted from the list for the new pawnbroker until he can get his bearings on the market and not spend money unwisely.

The same goes for such instruments as the steel guitar. Except for the Pacific Islands, I would say that this instrument is not the central core of any top ten tunes of the day. They are very expensive and they are very hard to sell. You really have to find the right buyer.

In order to develop your clientele, order a few imports from some wholesale company and display them at cost plus 10%. Everyone loves a good buy and the word gets around.

When people see you are willing to deal in musical instruments, you will begin to do business with sellers and pawners, as well as buyers.

At first, it seems as if you'll never have enough merchandise and then one day you will look up and every shelf will be full and every nail will have something hung on it.

Assure yourself plenty of space
for bulky musical instrument storage.

CHAPTER 18

COMPUTERS, TYPEWRITERS, AND FAX MACHINES

Should I Pawn Them?

There are many things involved when taking in computers. Keep in mind that computers can become obsolete within only a year or two. I purchased my 286 for my own personal computer which has 4 megs of hard memory in 1990. I felt that a 286 would be enough for me because our computer at the pawn shop was a 386 and there was no way I would need anything like that.

Well, my 286 is not only obsolete, but I have outgrown it as well. I have a flatbed scanner that only allows for scanning documents and is not capable of performing well with photographs as you can clearly tell in this book.

I am ready for a scanner with more capabilities than mine has, but my 286, with all of its memory, is not capable of storing more than two or three pieces of art at a time.

The more one works on a computer, the more capable they become and the more they want to expand their abilities to do more and to do better.

Personally, I know little to nothing about computers as far as computers go. I just know my job would be very difficult without one ... both at the pawn shop and in my home.

Pawning computers is another story. This is an area that many pawnbrokers shy away from ... and for good reason. If you know nothing about computers, you might be wise to get your feet wet with items that you can readily familiarize yourself. As you become more comfortable with your business, I would encourage you to expand your knowledge into every conceivable area.

Computers ARE the future. They are integrated into our lives, whether you know about it or not. Even if you never did much more than glance at one, you depend on them. Your car probably wouldn't operate without a computer. Everything is becoming computerized, from home thermostats to industrial giants.

Almost everyone has used a hand calculator (I don't mean your fingers), a microwave oven and a versateller.

If you think you are ready to begin dealing in computers, unless you are a real whiz at them, I would advise purchasing Orion's Blue Book of Computers. I wouldn't consider taking in a computer without my blue book!

I'm not sure if FAX machines belongs in this chapter or not. Since there is no chapter dedicated to office machines, I will incorporate them here.

I only have a few pointers on these items outside of recommending Orion's Blue Books for Computers and Office Equipment.

1. FAX MACHINES: Test FAX machines by telling the customer they must bring some FAX paper with their machine so you can test it. Sometimes a roll out of my FAX will work in other machines long enough for a test to be run.

After you plug the machine in, turn it on and feed a sheet of paper with something written or pictured on it into the feed rollers. The rollers should accept the document just enough to hold it in place ... about ¼th of an inch. Next, push the start button and the document should feed in and as it goes through, the FAX paper should roll out with a copy of your document.

If this fails to happen the first time you send the document through, try it one more time on the other side. Some FAX machines feed document side up and some feed document side down. If you get nothing either way, refuse the machine.

If you get a clean copy from the FAX, unplug your telephone and connect the FAX machine to your telephone line. Listen for a dial tone. Then place a local call. You can call anywhere ... or just call for the time. If the voice transmission is good, then the FAX machine works.

It will send and receive because it made the copy and the way it sends is through the phone system.

Some FAX machines sell for as little as $299 new and others sell for as much as $3,000 new. That is why it is important to have your blue books handy.

2. TYPEWRITERS: The small portable electrics don't sell much at all. If I take in one of the small portables, it is only when it offers a correction tape feature. Anything older than that, I turn away. On those that I do take in, I give $10 to $15 on them. Most of them are new at $100 to $150.

The more goodies the typewriter has on it, the better. When it offers a spell check, I will go up to $40 if it is practically brand new and works well.

If the typewriter has a word processor in it, that's good for about $40 to $75.

The Brother Word Processor runs around $350 new. Anything in that category I pay no more than $125, depending if it is new and complete with instructions and with the demo floppy disk that comes with the package new.

A lot of customers complain that they didn't bring the instructions and the demonstration floppy because they just want a loan and they are not going to leave it.

They might be telling God's truth. Don't believe it. No one can predict the future. The one time you break down and let something like that come in to your store, that is the very time someone gets run over by a beer truck and (for reasons beyond all their control) you become the owner.

If you know nothing about a Brother Word Processor, how do you plan on demonstrating it without any means to do it? If you go out and buy a blank disk, how will you understand what to do next?

If you know nothing about word processors and your customer knows nothing about word processors, you are going to be left with a word processor while your customer gives up looking for a deal and winds up in Sears with a salesman (who may or may not know anything about word processors) but who doesn't care because he has a demo floppy that tells the customer exactly what to do!

All word processors come with demonstration floppy disks. They can walk anyone through the system. There are little test programs that are built in to the word processors. NO! All the test program does is show the capabilities. The demo disk teaches the user HOW to use those capabilities.

3. PHOTOCOPY MACHINES: Do NOT take any photocopy machine that requires toner or special paper for copying. Those have been antiques for twenty years!

Do NOT take any old *granddaddy* hulks unless you are certain that you are looking at a new and updated version. Few photocopy machines are the hulks they once were. The old bulky machines are machines that print on both sides of the paper, that print in living color (not ONE color ... that's just a colored ink cartridge which is available for almost any photocopy machine) and which collates as it prints.

TEST EVERYTHING! As soon as you don't, that will be the one thing that doesn't work and you will become the proud owner.

Any item that you cannot understand is sure to become a permanent fixture on your display shelving! If you cannot demonstrate the merchandise, how can you possibly sell it? Waiting for the right person to come along isn't good business.

CCH
weekly alert
federal tax coordinator
INCOME
U.S. TAX CASES

CHAPTER 19

KEEPING THE BOOKS

Bookkeeping for a pawnbroker is sometimes the worst of his nightmares ... but it doesn't have to be.

Maintaining a simple and easy to understand system is the key to keeping your records straight and in good order. At the end of this chapter, I have included three worksheets that are utilized during the course of each day.

You might have some better ideas. Maybe you could improvise my system into one that would be more tailor-fitted to suit your needs.

The best recordkeeping system is the **KISS** system. I know that it is my favorite because it certainly suits me and my brain capacity for numbers.

Keep It Simple, Stupid

The more complicated the system, the more lost I become in it. It's kind of like a Twilight Zone of calculators for me.

I devised this method because I am acutely aware of my limitations. It's bad enough getting nailed by an audit from the IRS without having to realize that my own miscalculations were the sole reason for my dilemma. If I can keep my categories straight and maintain a continuous carrying forward of simple addition and subtraction, I am peaking out at my level of competency. I have no interest in breaking through the ceiling!

At the end of this chapter, you will see two sample worksheets and one sample Daily Report. After the samples I have included some blanks in case you would like to use them. You can photocopy them easily.

The first two worksheets will be kept by your register. The Daily Report will be filled out by you as you copy from your completed worksheets at the close of each working day.

Beginning with the *Loans and Buys* worksheet, look it over from left to right. The worksheet pretty much explains itself.

Everytime you make a loan, write the item (such as jewelry, TV, guitar, etc.) in the far left column. Move over one column to the right and write in the amount of the loan. That's all you need to do when you make a loan.

Whenever you take a loan redemption, you will utilize the third *item* column. Again, moving to the right, enter the amount of the loan that was repaid. *Do not* add in the amount of the loan charges (which are any charges incurred over the original loan amount). The next column over is reserved for those charges. The next column over is another *item* section. This is where you will enter what you bought *outright* from your customers and last, of course, the amount you paid for the item.

At the end of the day, total up each column and enter the figures in the designated boxes below.

The next worksheet is for *Sales.* The left column is again reserved for the item. The next column is where you will enter the price you had marked on the tag. To the right of the *tag price* column is where you will enter the actual price you settled on with the customer. To the right of the sale net column is the *tax* column. Always enter the tax, even if you told the customer the tax was included in the price. If your state has a sales tax, you will find this column very handy at the end of each quarter.

The last column is for *code.* The code is any series of letters you choose which will indicate what you originally paid for the item you sold. There are two codes that are popular with most vendors.

You can use either one of these or find a word or a series of words which are made up of ten letters with no two letters alike.

B L A C K H O R S E
1 2 3 4 5 6 7 8 9 0
P R O F I T A B L E

When you place your merchandise out for sale, make a *code tag.* Each code should consist of the first letter of the person who sold or pawned the merchandises' last name. The next thing is a series of numbers that are the numbers which were assigned to the pawn or to the outright buy. Following those numbers write a symbol you make up to distinguish a pawn from a buy. For instance, a star can be a pawn and an outright buy can be a plus or a dash. Some people just use P for pawn and B for buy.

So your code tag might read S01237*BK. If you need to look up any information on that particular piece of merchandise, you will look in your Pawn Sold To Stock File under the letter S. Next, you will have to sort through the tickets one by one until you come across the number. Usually, you will have a pretty good idea about when it came out. It doesn't take long to get familiar with your inventory.

Or if you are trying to just figure out if you want to take an interested customer's offer on the item, you can see by the BK that you have $15 invested in it. If your sales price is $60 and a customer offers you $50, it is a big help to be able to glance at the tag and know what you paid for the piece.

So when you make your sale, be sure and enter your code letters (or translate them into numbers if you choose).

At the end of the day, after you close your store, you will take out the last worksheet called the *Daily Report.* Some pawnbrokers prefer to begin this sheet an hour before closing the store if they have clerks to wait on the customers. If this is how you wish to do it, it can be done only if you pick up the two daily worksheets with the loans and sales and replace them with two fresh worksheets. Begin your new day one hour before you close.

In our case, we've closed our day and collected the day's numbers. We've added them up and now we will take out a blank *Daily Report.*

See the three samples with the figures incorporated.

The first thing we will do is date our *Daily Report* so the dates match with the two worksheets.

Now, the first row, reading from right to left, we see LOANS. Write in the number of your tallied loans for the day in that box. Our loans tally to $435.00. Next, fill in the tallied REDEMPTIONS (or loans picked up). Today we had $420 redeemed.

Moving to the left to FORFEITS, we see that we had $200 that was lost to pawn. This number is not incorporated on the worksheets. You will have come by this number because each day some of the loans are going to be forfeited.

You will know which loans these are because every day you will be looking in your current pawn file. If you are filing your tickets in the order of the first letter of the last name and then each ticket filed one behind the other in order of coming in ... then the oldest ticket will always be in front of your file under the name of the pawner. The newest ticket will be placed in the rear of that file under the pawner's first letter of his last name.

The A file will be oldest first and newest last. The B file will continue and so each letter will carry pawn tickets, oldest first, newest last.

Every morning, you will be going through your file and pulling the forfeits. In some states (California), the pawner must receive a 10 day notice. Each day, we go through our files and pull the ones in front that have matured beyond the redemption date and are now in the (30 day window) time frame when they must be notified. As the letters are mailed, those names go in a recipe card file and as they expire, are pulled and the forfeit figure is listed in the forfeits box in the upper right hand of the *Daily Report.*

Next row down is the *Stock Status.* This row is to let us know about how much money we have invested in inventory.

The first box is for BUYS. Obviously, everything we *buy* is going to become our inventory. Inventory is always listed for what we pay for an item and not what we want to sell it for. You will understand this at tax time when you realize that it is far to your advantage to have your inventory listed on the low side.

Today we bought $70 worth of new inventory.

Now we come upon FORFEITS one more time. We will enter the same $200 from the upper right box. Remember, we are *forfeiting* the merchandise from our loans, but we are *adding* it in to our stock.

Another thing we want to do is to *deduct* from our inventory that which we have sold. We can't deduct the price we sold it for, so we must deduct what we paid for the stock. By incorporating our codes into our *Daily Reports,* we automatically know what number to deduct. Simply translate your profitable or your blackhorse (or whatever you choose for your coding) into numbers, add them up and enter that number into the code box on the *Daily Report.* In our case, we had $96 invested in the stock we sold today.

The third row is easy. This is the INCOMING CASH. Of course, our sales are incoming cash. DO NOT INCLUDE TAX ON THESE FIGURES. IF YOU DO, YOU WILL FIND YOURSELF PAYING TAX ON YOUR TAX.

We sold $401.95 today. Next, we took in our LOAN CHARGES. This is all of the money we took in (over and above the loan amount) when a pawner picked up his loan. Today we earned $89.50 on our loans. The last box in the third row is for extension fees.

If you allow for your pawners to extend their loans when they can't redeem them, this is where you enter that fee. Today there were no extensions.

Glancing downward, there are five categories: YEAR TO DATE LOAN STATUS – CURRENT CASH ON HAND STATUS – YEAR TO DATE SALES STATUS – STOCK INVENTORY – YEAR TO DATE LOAN CHARGES.

If there are any other records you wish to keep, incorporate them in the additional areas. You might want to include your taxes on the *Daily Report.* Since we pay them quarterly and the sales are all totaled at the end of the month, we didn't see a need for it. But the form could include a QUARTERLY TO DATE TAXES category.

It's always good to sock away your taxes in a separate account so they don't hit so hard when they come due.

On the YEAR TO DATE LOAN STATUS, we see that we had $1,000 out on loan.

Today we had $420 in redemptions. This means that our total loans are down to $580, and we loaned our $435. Now our loans are at $1,015. The $1,015 is the number that we are going to carry over to tomorrow's *Daily Report* and enter in the LOANS FORWARD box.

Moving down to CURRENT CASH ON HAND STATUS, we see that we started with $1,000 cash in our store this morning.

We sold $401.95. Our subtotal is $1,401.95. Then we paid out $70 in outright buys. Now our cash is at $1,331.95. We collected loan charges of $89.50. Add that to the cash for a subtotal of $1,841.85.

We had no extensions today but we had $435 in new loans. That takes our cash on hand back down to $1,406.45.

Some Girl Scouts came in selling cookies and we bought $6 worth. This is a deduction for income tax purposes as well. If you have many expenses like that in one day, you will keep a separate list aside for your bookkeeper to itemize and tally the total for this area.

Bills paid out of your checking account do not have a place here. Regular monthly expenses are in your check register, which you will hand over to your bookkeeper with your *Daily Reports* for the month.

We drew no money out of the bank for our store and we had no deposits. Our total CASH ON HAND is $1,400.45. Remember, cash on hand *includes* the checks you took and the credit card receipts you have. Once they are deposited, they become CASH OUT.

Carry the $1,400.45 over to tomorrow's *Daily Report* and enter in BEGINNING CASH.

Now we travel up and to the right to the YEAR TO DATE SALES STATUS. So far, this year we sold $500.

Our sales today were $401.95 (this does NOT include tax). We had no cash refunds so our total sales this year were $901.95.

Carry figure ($901.95) forward to tomorrow's *Daily Report* in the NET SALES YEAR TO DATE box.

Down one more is STOCK INVENTORY. We started out with a GROSS STOCK FORWARD of $10,000 and we added $70 to our inventory with the outright merchandise we purchased today.

Next, we added once again to our stock by pulling the FORFEITED LOANS of $200. This brings our stock up to $10,270.

But we sold some stock, too. Translating our PROFITABLE or our BLACKHORSE codes, we know that we sold $96 worth of merchandise. We deduct this from our STOCK INVENTORY. This leaves us with a total inventory of $10,174.00.

Last on our list of categories is the YEAR TO DATE LOAN CHARGES. This is how you are going to tell what kind of a return you are getting for your loan investment. Your year to date loan charges were $500 and you collected $89.50 today. If you had any EXTENSION FEES, you would add them in to the $89.50 loan charges.

Today, there were no extension fees so your charges of $89.50 are added to the $500, making a total of $589.50.

Carry this figure over to your new *Daily Report* that you are beginning for tomorrow and enter it in the GROSS LOAN CHARGES FORWARD.

Now, you are finished with your daily books and ready to go home. At the end of the month, submit every *Daily Report* to your bookkeeper. You don't need to give him the worksheets. They are only for your use.

Along with the *Daily Reports,* you will submit your check stubs or photocopies of your month's check stubs. It's a little more work, but I prefer to photocopy them. It's not so bad when you reduce them 75%.

A FAX machine works wonders as well.

A bookkeeper is well worth the little it costs. Be sure to go over everything carefully with him before you submit your quarterlies and your tax returns. Bookkeepers are the least expensive, but they can't appear for you if you are audited by the IRS.

I prefer to pay a little more for a good CPA. It might seem like too much now, but it is little enough if you wind up owing back taxes to the Federal and State governments.

Fair warning: We were spoiled and we kept our bookkeeper long after we were doing well enough to make a change to a CPA. He got us into some hot water (actually, it was in our favor), but try and tell the IRS that they owe you more money and see how fast an audit comes down on your head!

Now, rather than a CPA, we have moved up to a $100 per hour MBA and we are glad to pay it!

As your business grows, resist that new car or that remodeled kitchen for just one more year and put your money into a good CPA or even an MBA who knows the pawn business. Your State Association should be able to steer you in the right direction.

Even if the CPA is a distance away, invest in a FAX machine and make your annual trip out there to do your taxes. It costs money now, but it can save you an untold amount of money and a whole lot of heartache down the road. Take it from someone who's actually been there.

These pull-out drawers made wonderful jewelry displays. This pawnbroker locks his displays with padlocks to insure their safety. Note: A wonderful hint I picked up from another pawnbroker concerns round inset locks. Often, one can't tell if a showcase is locked or unlocked. Painting the top half of the lock with red nail polish when it is in the locked position will insure that one glance will tell you if your showcase is locked or unlocked. If the red polish is facing down, someone forgot to relock the showcase.

DAILY WORK SHEET: LOANS AND BUYS

DATE: *April 1, 1990*

ITEM	LOAN	ITEM	PICK UP	CHRG	ITEM	BUY
Television	*50.00*	*Jewelry*	*20.00*	*6.00*	*Jewelry*	*50.00*
Jewelry	*5.00*	*Stereo*	*50.00*	*18.50*	*Camera*	*10.00*
Jewelry	*15.00*	*Jewelry*	*50.00*	*9.50*	*Radio*	*10.00*
VCR	*50.00*	*Guitar*	*100.00*	*17.50*		
Drums	*75.00*	*Jewelry*	*100.00*	*14.50*		
Tools	*100.00*	*TV Console*	*100.00*	*23.50*		
Jewelry	*50.00*					
Jewelry	*15.00*					
Basbl Cds	*30.00*					
CD	*20.00*					
Jewelry	*25.00*					

TODAY'S TOTALS

LOANS *435.00*	PICK UPS *420.00*	CHARGES *89.50*	BUYS *70.00*

DAILY WORK SHEET: SALES

DATE: *April 1, 1990*

ITEM	TAG PRICE	SALE NET	TAX	CODE
Jewelry	*59.95*	*50.00*	*4.13*	*BE*
Radio	*29.95*	*29.95*	*2.47*	*K*
Golf Club	*10.00*	*10.00*	*.83*	*A*
Jewelry	*379.00*	*300.00*	*24.75*	*RK*
Tool Box	*15.00*	*12.00*	*.99*	*A*

TODAY'S TOTALS

TAG PRICES *493.90*	*SALES NET* *401.95*	*TAXES* *33.17*	*CODE* *96.00*

DAILY REPORT

DATE: *April 1, 1990*

LOAN STATUS	LOANS *435.00*	REDEMPTIONS *420.00*	FORFEITS *200.00*
STOCK STATUS	BUYS *70.00*	FORFEITS *200.00*	CODE *96.00*
INCOMING CASH	NET SALES *401.95*	LOAN CHGS *89.50*	EXT FEES *None Today*

YEAR TO DATE LOAN STATUS	
LOANS FORWARD	*1,000.00*
LOAN P/U TODAY -	*420.00*
SUB TOTAL	*580.00*
NEW LOANS TODAY +	*435.00*
	1,015.00

YTD SALES STATUS	
NET SALES YTD	*500.00*
NET SALES TODAY +	*401.95*
SUB TOTAL	*901.95*
REFUNDS -	*None*
	901.95

CURRENT CASH ON HAND STATUS	
BEGINNING CASH	*1,000.00*
SALES +	*401.95*
SUB TOTAL	*1,401.95*
OUTRIGHT BUYS -	*70.00*
SUB TOTAL	*1,331.95*
LOAN PICK UPS +	*420.00*
SUB TOTAL	*1,751.95*
LOAN CHARGES +	*89.50*
SUB TOTAL	*1,841.45*
EXTENSIONS +	*None Today*
SUB TOTAL	*1,841.45*
NEW LOANS -	*435.00*
SUB TOTAL	*1,406.45*
MISC. CASH PAID OUT -	*Donation 6.00*
SUB TOTAL	*1,400.45*
CASH IN/OUT +/-	*No Deposits No Withdrawals*
TOTAL CASH ON HAND =	*1,400.45*

STOCK INVENTORY	
GROSS STOCK FORWARD	*10,000.00*
OUTRIGHT BUYS TODAY +	*70.00*
SUB TOTAL	*10,070.00*
FORFEITS SOLD TO STOCK +	*200.00*
SUB TOTAL	*10,270.00*
CODE FROM TODAY'S SALES	*96.00*
	10,174.00

YTD LOAN CHARGES	
GROSS LN CHGS FWD	*500.00*
TODAY'S LN CHGS +	*89.50*
	589.50

ALL GUNS
10%
OFF

CHAPTER 20

COMPUTERIZED PAWN SHOP

A word about computers is in order being as most pawn shops are now running their business on them.

If the budget is very tight, a computer is an expense that the new pawnbroker can prolong ... usually not for very long. Actually, as your new business progresses, the opposite becomes true. For a busy pawnbroker, a computerized system is the most financially and organizationally expedient move he can make.

A good time to think of investing in a computer is when the pawnbroker and one clerk are kept pretty busy most of each day. Often, that happens within the first few months, depending on your location and the demand. With this recession, the demand looks to be rising rapidly and with no end in sight.

You will want to get with a good system when you are ready and you will want to know what that system is and where to find it.

Because each state carries its own individual laws, specially designed computer software must be used. It is important to find a company that deals specifically with your state.

Don't try to do it yourself. Unless you are a whiz at computer programming, *and* you have a thorough understanding of your state laws, this is a job for the experts. You are an experienced pawnbroker.

Programs are available for the mega-pawnshop whose needs extend to multiple chain stores as well as programs that cater to the intimate *mom and pop* operation. The prices range accordingly.

If you are just starting out, keep your system basic and forgo all the bells and whistles. For instance, there is no reason to incorporate a bar coding system into a pawn shop that can be run by one pawnbroker and a couple of clerks. On the other hand, if your business expands to five or six clerks, and/or more than one store, the bar coding feature could become a feature that would be hard to live without.

As you expand your business, you can upgrade your system. If you start out with a good computer firm that specializes in pawn shops for your state, they will be able to continue working with you in an ongoing capacity. They understand your special needs because they know when you started and how far you've come. It won't be necessary to educate them to your way of conducting your business.

As a new computer user three years ago, I found the computer to be an exasperating piece of equipment. Every time I couldn't get the program to do what I wanted, I called my computer man. Each time I called, he walked me through another phase of the program and soon I began to catch on.

I admit, somewhat abashedly now, that (not unlike the automobile) the problem was caused more often by the nut behind the wheel – the *steering* wheel, that is.

Today, I can't imagine my world without a computer! By learning to work my pawn shop system, I felt secure enough to inquire about other programs that could prove helpful in other areas of my life. Now I have expanded my computer to do many of my time-consuming tasks. I pay all my bills on my checkwriting program, I conduct much of my correspondence by computer modem, and I even wrote this book on my word processing program.

You will be able to identify qualified computer firms by attending a National Pawnbroker's convention. It is at those conventions that you are able to meet with all of the vendors who deal with pawn shops. They are there to explain and demonstrate their products. The computer firms bring in their hardware with the various programs for you to try out.

Your state collateral loan president is also a good source of information. He/she will be happy to assist you by giving you the name of those computer companies that specialize in pawn shops.

Call each of the companies and ask for references. Be sure to let them know the size of your pawn shop and how long you have been in business. They will try to direct you to their customers who are on a system similar to the one you will probably be needing.

Then call those pawnbrokers and ask them their opinion. Do they like the program? Is it easy to run? Did the clerks find the program difficult to learn? What kind of service does the company offer? Does the company offer computer support and if they do, is it readily available at all times? If the computer goes down, can the pawnbroker pick up where it left off, manually? How long does it generally take for the company to respond on a service call for repairs?

Anyone who calls his state association will be able to acquire the names of several companies that have created software for pawn shops. Call each of them and ask them for references.

Don't call anyone newly on their system. Chances are, you'll get a frustrated new user like I was and they will scare you off.

Rather, call a few people who have been using their systems for two or three years. Ask them how they like it. Ask if they have many problems. Most of all, ask if telephone support is available to them. Unless you are computer wise, you will need a whole lot of support in those first weeks.

Ask me about my system. I can tell anyone in all honesty, working with a computer and without one is two different worlds.

A computer is like driving a fine, new Farrari ... in the sunshine ... down the autobahn ... after a repaving ... with silk.

Compare that with driving behind a mule ... which is old ... and sick ... in a cart ... a wooden cart ... an old, wooden cart ... with square wheels ... on a muddy road ... in the rain ... on a bad day.

You WILL computerize.

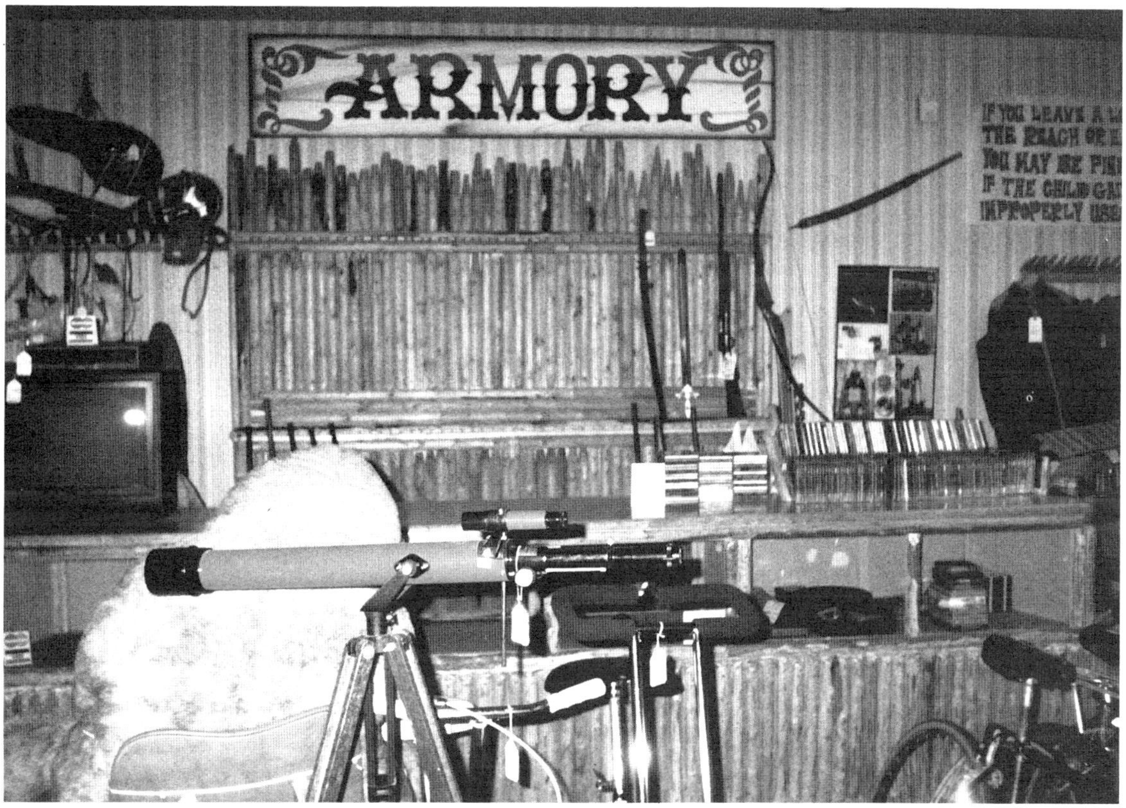

The creative energy that went into this store carried over to the gun displays as well. The showcases in front house all of the handguns while the back wall is used to display the rifles and shotguns. The long guns were removed for a better view of the background.

The two most important things to you are your family and customers. Treat them both well and you'll be successful.

CHAPTER 21

CUSTOMER RELATIONS

I decided to add this chapter because of the importance of the perception of pawn shops by the general public.

During these times of recession, we are seeing new people come into the store who have never had the experience of pawning. They are feeling a bit frightened because of the false images of pawnbrokers that have been presented to them over the years.

They need to borrow some cash and they are wary of a con artist pawnbroker who might want to steal their merchandise.

I don't like to do business with anyone without developing some kind of understanding as to what I am about as a person.

It is important to let them know, first off, that I am a human being who understands their plight. Once they feel I am not out to hurt them, they relax and gain confidence in me, as the pawnbroker.

I begin by explaining what pawn shops are about. I let them know that we are here to make small loans that are intended to help them over a few rough spots. I make them understand that pawn shops never give the full value of any item because it is the pawnbroker's intent that the merchandise will be redeemed. When too much money is lent on any item, the item stands a good chance of being lost to pawn.

This is a good time to point out all of the merchandise that is for sale in the store and let the customer know that it is preferable for the pawnbroker if the items are redeemed rather than risk becoming overstocked with unsalable merchandise.

It is important that the customer completely understand the contract so they can be at ease about their items. They must know that their items will be cared for to the best of our ability.

Once the new pawner understands that I bear him no ill will and that I am genuinely concerned for his plight and I am interested in helping him out of it, he begins to develop a trust toward me and his fears subside.

These are the customers who are the best advertisement for the pawn shop!

Sometimes gold prices drop and it is not feasible to lend the same amount of dollars on the same item that has been coming into the store over and over again. Many times, the customer gets his/her feelings hurt. They kind of feel like you are insulting them.

Assure them that it has nothing to do with the quality of their merchandise. Tell them that the gold market is dropping and you must lend accordingly, even though you know that they have been good customers and that they do pick up their items all the time. Let them know that you truly appreciate their business and that you will be happy to lend them more when the market turns back around.

There are other people who don't come in to pawn or to buy. After awhile, it becomes easy to spot the person who was a victim of a theft.

Their poor image of pawn shops leads them to believe that pawnbrokers purchase hot items and put them right out in the showcases for sale. They are afraid that if they tell the pawnbroker they are looking for stolen items, the pawnbroker will run to the showcases and pull out the stolen items before the victims can spot them!

When the pawnbroker's initial approach to help them is rejected, it is wise not to pursue it any further. I simply let them look as long as they like. When they don't see what it is they are looking for, they timidly approach the counter and ask if a certain ring or item was taken in lately.

There's no point in trying to explain that there are so many customers and items that any pawnbroker would be hard pressed to recall any particular incident. Instead, I ask them if they experienced a theft. They are usually surprised that I suspected they were victims of such a crime.

Then, ask them if they reported their loss to the police department. If they did, I explain that all of our merchandise descriptions are sent into the police department every day, along with the identification of the person who borrowed on it or sold it to us. I go on to tell them that they will probably be wasting their time looking in all of the showcases in all the pawn shops.

Pawnbrokers are required to hold items for a given amount of time so that the police can investigate any suspicious people or merchandise. In the state of California, we are required to hold all items for a minimum of thirty days before we can sell them.

They are usually quite surprised to learn how closely we work with the police department.

Do not reveal any information about pawned or sold merchandise as this is a violation of confidentiality to the customer.

I explain that it is as important for me to keep all transactions confident as it is for the local bank to not share depositor's information. After all, that's what we are. A bank. Just like the Savings and Loans, except we don't service savings and checking accounts. We do make small loans.

If they have any reason to suspect that their items have been pawned to our store, I ask them to go to the police department and I will fully cooperate with any police officer or deputy. I will give any information that the officer tells me to give. This way, the officer is responsible for the breaking of confidence and not ourselves. Many officers shy away from taking on such responsibilities unless there is good cause to suspect there is some foul play going on with a pawner.

I try to explain just exactly what it is pawn shops do and when these people begin to understand that we are a perfectly legitimate operation, they even start looking around the store to do some shopping of their own. This is a good opportunity to point out the fine deals that can be had in pawn shops.

Another good way to develop customer relations is to join the local Chamber of Commerce and become active within the Chamber. The Chamber is always looking for volunteers to participate on committees. If you don't have the time to spend, then offer to donate a small piece of jewelry for a raffle or a door prize.

Attend the functions so that when your donation is auctioned off or raffled, your name will be announced as the donor and people will be interested in asking you more about the pawn business.

Invite other members of the Chamber to come in and visit you in your store. Offer to hold a Chamber mixer in your store after hours. This creates a wonderful opportunity for the other local merchants to see what wonderful bargains you have to offer. Mixers are always a lot of fun. Make a large pot of coffee and mix some wine coolers and serve these with some chips and dip and maybe some homemade cookies.

Always *take the time to explain* your business to anyone who is interested enough to ask about it.

Be a part of the solution by helping all pawnbrokers to change their negative images. If you are not a part of the solution, then you are a part of the problem!

DON'T KNOCK THE COMPETITION.

Instead, tell the customers that most all pawnbrokers work the same way you do. Explain that some people work better with certain people and some people do experience personality conflicts.

NEVER accuse another pawnbroker of shady dealings.

Those accusations have a way of bouncing back and reflecting on you. Speak for yourself and let the other guy answer for his mistakes.

Join such organizations as the Kiwanis, the Rotary Club, the Optimists, Elks, Lions, etc. These clubs are an excellent means of promoting your business. If you are not a natural joiner, join anyway!

Developing a good public image will pave the way for your business to become a successful, integral part of your community. Don't be ashamed of what you do. Instead, take pride in the fact that you are in a business that is designed to be a credit to your community and to the public in general.

ALL YOUR COMMUNITY NEEDS IS A LITTLE EDUCATION.

If you remain remote and aloof from the business community, then the common misconceptions will propagate and you are the one who suffers in the long run.

Get excited! Your vocation is more than honorable. Remember, there once was a time when excommunication was the punishment for those who dared to defame the honorable profession of pawnbrokers!

There's no end to the creative ideas for displaying merchandise. This pentagon showcase circle was assembled and then lined with cheap wooden tree stakes which were split in two and nailed to the sides. The edges were smoothed down and burned with an old circular sander wheel. (If you are handy and opt for doing something like this, be sure to protect your lungs from the fine particles that are created while sawing. This wood is treated with powerful chemicals to prevent it from rotting easily in the ground.)

Here is another angle of the same showcase. It is centered directly beneath a skylight in the middle of this store. Note the same theme carried through with the rustic/safari look ... even to the wooden barrel filled with golf clubs.

CHAPTER 22

STOCKING YOUR STORE

Word-of-mouth (WOM) is the best advertising and the *only* advertising that no amount of money can buy. It travels with lightening speed, it is the most effective, and (best of all) it's free!

Large corporations allocate millions of dollars for the sole purpose of seeking ideas that would motivate consumers to recommend their products.

Ironically, this form of advertising (while out of reach for most mammoth conglomerates) is available, with little effort, right at the pawnbroker's fingertips and best of all, it's free! It is a smart pawnbroker who understands the value and availability of this advertising gold mine.

The initial outlay for good inventory should be viewed as *advertising*. Advertising is just exactly what it is!

A good inventory is the best advertising for a pawn shop. Advertising is a necessary expenditure for every business. Few businesses have the capacity for generating WOM advertising. A pawn shop is one of them.

Most pawnbrokers use several avenues of advertising, and wisely so. The most common are the Yellow Pages. Some run display advertising in the local newspapers. Others buy billboard and bus bench space. Many pawnbrokers use radio and television to carry their message.

Alternately, I know many pawnbrokers who have never spent a nickel on advertising. Their lucrative stores run solely on WOM advertising!

Traditionally, pawn shops develop most of their best clientele through the borrowing customers and lookey-loos.

Quantity, quality, condition, and fair pricing; this combination tells prospective consumers all they need to know. Before long, word gets out.

What the word turns out to be depends solely on the proprietor. Is there plenty to choose from? Is the merchandise of good quality? Is it clean, well displayed and in good repair? Is the store well lit and clean? Are the prices fair? Is the proprietor clean, neat, and friendly?

Every business must maintain an advertising budget but precious few are able to generate WOM as well as a neighborhood pawn shop. The beauty of this kind of advertising is that money spent is money retained in inventory equity.

Due to limited budgets, many small pawn shops have been initiated with very little to no retail inventory at all.

The probability of ultimate success *seldom* depends on the quantity of the initial stock. The amount of time it takes to launch the pawn shop into a thriving business has, however, a lot to do with first time inventory.

When the shelves are empty, the lookey-loos drop out. The only customer base that builds are the borrowers. Eventually, as the shelves begin to fill with forfeited loan collateral, word spreads. As this happens, the buying customer base begins to form.

Some pawnbrokers start out by stocking their shelves with items that are only a step or two above junk. Something to sell is certainly better than nothing to sell.

Older items have a more positive effect than broken and/or dirty items. Even junk can look pretty good if no parts are missing, it's clean, and nicely displayed.

Retail sales move at a snail's pace for the first year or so, picking up as the forfeited loan collateral (which should be of better quality if the pawnbroker is doing it right) replaces the initial inventory.

Ideally, a new pawn shop offering a well-rounded inventory that is good quality, clean, in decent condition, and reasonably priced, will create the strongest customer base in the shortest period of time.

Stocking the shelves with a nice inventory may not be as expensive as one might believe, at least not if one knows where to shop for good deals!

The most important thing to know is that one cannot expect to make much profit on the initial stock. That's okay. Breaking even puts the first-time pawnbroker ahead of the game!

The goal here is to create a store that is well stocked with the nicest looking and lowest priced merchandise possible.

The first-time inventory is not going to be the inventory that will fill the shelves this time next year. There is bound to be some small loss on some of the initial inventory but there will be profits as well.

Once the entire inventory consists of forfeited loan collateral and outright buys, a tidy profit will be realized on nearly every item.

One must keep the big picture in mind. Overall, there will be a substantial profit. The worst thing one can do is lock into the idea that a profit must be made on each individual item. That is losing sight of the forest by focusing on one tree!

A loss of $50 on a new television purchased at a wholesale house is offset by the $100 profit gained on a diamond ring that was purchased in another pawn shop.

The initial stock depends on your budget and how much time stands between today and the new pawn shop. If the grand opening is projected six months to a year into the future, there is plenty of time to accumulate a nice inventory.

If the projected opening is only a few weeks from today, the selection of inventory and the amount one can afford will be, most probably, limited.

Before you go out on your treasure hunt, be sure to re-read any of the chapters in Part Three that pertain to items with which you are not familiar. Keep this book with you as a reference tool when you embark upon your travels.

BEGIN YOUR SHOPPING.

Of course, the more time one has to shop, the better chance he has of finding excellent buys.

The first inventory to begin accumulating is the *timeless* inventory. The last thing on the shopping list will be dated items.

I have a philosophy about selling.

If I give you a perfect orange and I challenge you to sell it for a quarter in Grand Central Station, could you?

You certainly have enough foot traffic for many potential customers. Your product is top quality. The orange is beautiful, large and succulent and it exudes a fragrance of sweet orange blossoms and honey. In fact, this orange is the most perfect speciman ever grown. On top of that, it's priced right. It's a good deal!

You are honest, clean, impeccably dressed, well groomed and manicured. Your manners are polished, you hold degrees in nuclear fission and law, you are a charter member of Toastmasters, and of course, you are very good looking!

Let's build one of those cutesy stores for you and your orange right in the busiest part of Grand Central.

Your store is filled with old world charm right down to brass fixtures and a candy cane fringed awning.

Above the awning is an elaborate neon sign forming your own handwritten signature embossed over a neon orange.

Your store is as charming and attractive inside as it is out. It is well lit and well equipped, right down to a brand new computerized cash register.

In the very center of your little store stands a beautiful antique mahogany showcase. The glass is beveled with delicate etchings of scrolled designs. The showcase is a masterpiece, crafted by the loving hands of a great artist.

Right in the center of this magnificent showcase rests a royal blue velvet pillow trimmed with four golden tassels.

Spotlights and special effect lighting are trained on the showcase.

Inside the showcase, in the very center, is a plush velvet pillow. The pillow is royal blue and it is decorated with four golden tassels. In the center of the pillow rests the perfect orange.

Do you think you could sell the orange now? Well ... maybe.

Naaah! I don't think so.

Now let's create another scenario. This time, instead of one orange, you have twenty truckloads of oranges to sell. They are the same quality and just as appealing as the first and priced exactly the same, 25 cents apiece. You are the same well versed, impeccable, good looking person as before.

You can have all the same advantages as before. You have the foot traffic of Grand Central and your store is just as elaborate. In fact, we will increase the size of your store, making it a giant supermarket.

Oranges fill every showcase, every shelf, every bin, and every tray. Oranges are stacked to the ceiling and oranges spill out into the aisles.

Will customers be milling around, selecting the best oranges? Will they be lined up at the cash register waiting to pay for their oranges? Will you be able to sell all those oranges? How about half of them? One truckload? A crate?

It's possible.

Probable?

Not really.

How about a dozen?

Could happen.

In truth, you probably won't sell even one!

Why not?

In the first scenario, there is nothing to choose from. It is human nature to be selective. When there is no selection, there is no interest.

How is the second scenario different from the first?

It isn't. You still had nothing to choose from! Too much of the same thing is as bad as only one thing!

Unless a person is in the market for bushels or truckloads of oranges, such a quantity is overwhelming.

Grand Central Station is where one would find the average consumer and the average consumer would have no interest in the purchase of one item where there is no selection. Certainly, the average consumer has no need for twenty truckloads of oranges.

Those who deal in oranges by the truckload don't care about attractive displays, about picking and choosing; how well the salesman presents himself is not an issue. The only concern would be quality and price.

WHERE TO LOOK FOR INVENTORY

Where else? Pawn shops!

Of course, you won't deal locally. Why would your future competitor give deals on his inventory that is earmarked as stock for his competition down the street?

Shopping for inventory is a business venture, but it can also be a whole lot of fun!

Why not make this business venture a vacation as well? This way you can see some nice countryside and take care of business at the same time. It's fair and it's deductible!

Travel as far and as wide as time allows, checking out the pawn shops, thrift stores, any secondhand dealer or thrift store you see along the way.

MAKING ACCEPTABLE OFFERS

When you first walk into a pawn shop, make a mental note of which items might be considered as overstocked for the store.

For instance, a pawnbroker whose store is stocked with twelve flutes but only three guitars is probably going to be open to negotiation on his flutes.

Perhaps the showcases display many trays of ladies' rings and only a few of the larger men's rings. You can assume that you might do well by making an offer on several rows, or even trays, of the ladies' jewelry.

Normally, a pawnbroker will be open to offers 10% to 20% under his marked prices. If he has an opportunity to get rid of some of his inventory glut, he will entertain even lower offers, probably even half of the marked prices according to how much he can sell.

I usually browse around the pawn shop for awhile before I try to meet the pawnbroker. Sometimes there is no need to bother introducing oneself if the store has nothing to offer.

The first determination is to ascertain if the general pricing of the merchandise is in the ballpark. Some pawnbrokers overprice every item in the store in hopes of selling at those inflated prices but willing to negotiate them down. This is a waste of time for him and for his customers. Certainly it is a waste of time for you.

Try to get him to make the first commitment by asking him if he would be willing to deal with you if you were to buy two flutes instead of one. Point out two of the lower end flutes that are in average to poor condition.

One of the secrets is not to be greedy. In the pawnbroker's eyes, you are asking him for a favor, you are not doing him one. Be humble.

One way to put off a pawnbroker is to select his best merchandise then make him a low ball offer! Learn to take the good with the bad. If he has a flute that is in poor condition, include it in your selection.

The pawnbroker is delighted to get rid of his culls and is willing to give a generous discount on them. If he does, then ask if he would be willing to do any better if you were to buy three flutes. Then ask if he would give an even better price on half his flutes.

When you point out which flutes, choose the half on the left or the half on the right, taking care not to pick and choose. Leave the best flute for the pawnbroker to sell at top dollar.

Try to negotiate for half price. If he won't budge from your last offer, walk over to the jewelry display and point to those trays of ladies' rings.

Ask, "Could you do any better on your prices if I were to buy some of this jewelry from you as well?"

You want to get the pawnbroker as close to half price as possible.

Once you have arrived at a suitable figure, like 40 to 50% off, then you can start widening the selection by asking if this camera or that television could be included in the deal.

Don't change your mind on what or how much you've already selected. If you take him up on his discount, you are committed to the flutes and that tray of rings you pointed out earlier.

If you think you won't be able to do anything with two of the six flutes, then look around the store and select some nicer items.

You couldn't have expected a 50% discount on a top-of-the-line video cam or a color television before, but now it might be possible.

Ask if he will do the same on each item you select, always adding to the pile. If you wind up spending $5,000, you will have made his day and your retail inventory base will be off to a good start and already marked at his original prices, around $10,000 total.

Chances are, you won't be discounting any of your purchases over 20%. The worst case scenario: you will realize a 30% markup on your initial inventory.

TIMELESS INVENTORY

Timeless inventory consists of items that don't age. Most things lose value over time. But there are many things that don't.

For instance, a socket wrench is a socket wrench and the only purchasing considerations that apply are brand, size, condition, and price. The age of a socket wrench is not a factor.

Jewelry is another timeless item. The only factor that must be considered in selecting your new stock is style. All fine metals and precious stones are valuable.

Consumer consideration for investing in fine jewelry are style, condition, size of the diamond or other precious stone (not ring size), and price.

DATED INVENTORY

Dated inventory consists of items which depreciate in value over time – televisions, stereos, cameras, VCRs, office equipment, and/or anything computerized, such as word processors, games, and computer hardware.

The age of the equipment is the prime consideration for consumers, but age is certainly not the only consideration. Brand, features, performance, condition, and price are all factors that weigh significantly into the equation of determining dollar investment.

Consumers often opt for older models that feature all the bells and whistles as opposed to new basic models devoid of all but the bare essentials.

SPECIALTY ITEMS

Unless you are into a hobby (such as coins, stamps, baseball cards, comic books, etc.), it is best to stay away from specialty items when creating your initial inventory. Stick to the basics.

While that beautiful Franklin Mint monopoly set trimmed in hand-rubbed woods and gold plate is collecting dust, socket wrenches, color televisions, and diamonds rings will be selling. Antiques are slow sellers as well.

SELECTING YOUR INITIAL INVENTORY

JEWELRY:

I list jewelry as the first category because jewelry is the mainstay of any successful pawn shop. Fully 80% to 90% of a pawn shop's cash investment, in purchasing and in loan collateral, is secured in diamonds and gold.

In an emergency, jewelry is the most accessible and readily available collateral. Nearly everyone owns a piece or two. Jewelry isn't cumbersome and difficult to carry. People can justify spending money on jewelry by calling their purchase an investment.

Most customers who frequent pawn shops do so for the purpose of finding good buys on jewelry.

Remember the oranges! Glutting your showcases with an excess of inexpensive pieces is just as unrewarding as investing everything you have in one magnificent bauble.

Keep your jewelry inventory well rounded and basic. Stay away from pieces that are very unique, no matter how attractive you might think they are. These pieces will come into your store as outright buys and as loan collateral.

It's perfectly alright to have them as part of your retail inventory, but (because of their uniqueness) they are very slow sellers.

In the beginning, select inventory that is up to date and commonly sought after. Don't buy too much of any one thing. Fifty wedding bands and no gold chains doesn't make for a well rounded inventory.

It is better to invest in more moderate to low priced pieces and be able to display a wider selection, rather than only a few expensive pieces that are outside your usual customers' price range.

The best sellers are the small ladies' rings that are priced under $100.

Incorporating antique jewelry or jewelry that is crafted from platinum and/or white gold is probably not good for your initial inventory if that inventory is going to be very limited.

While these items are lovely to look at, in today's market they are not as popular as yellow gold. They will eventually sell as there are always those who are particularly interested in antique and white gold jewelry. The market, however, is much more limited.

A smart pawnbroker keeps himself current on jewelry prices and the most current trends. An occasional perusal of a few updated jewelry catalogues put out by local stores (like Best, Sears, or Montgomery Ward) will help the pawnbroker keep his prices regulated well under new retail.

Catalogs also help determine whether a particular piece brought in by a customer is worth a few extra dollars because it's in Vogue.

Any yellow gold ladies' rings that are set with baguettes, pave settings, and channel settings are very popular now.

DIAMOND POPULARITY

1. ***Round Cut:*** The Round cut diamonds are the most common and sell the best. They are more durable and they have more fire than other cuts. Ladies often think they want a more unique cut, but when they see them placed next to an equally graded Round, they usually concede to the Round.
2. ***Marquis Cut:*** Marquis seem to be the next most sought after cut. When considering a Marquis for your stock, stay away from those that are chipped (the tips are vulnerable to breaking), contain obvious feathery inclusions, and a milky or shattered appearance.

3. ***Oval Cut:*** Ovals are cut very much like Rounds. When compared to an equally graded Round, they display the same brilliance and fire. The similarity is due to the similar faceting. Ovals are less common than Round and the Marquis cuts.

4. ***Emerald Cut:*** These diamonds tend to have the least fire and brilliance. They are difficult to sell unless the customer is definitely in the market for such a cut. I am more selective when purchasing an Emerald Cut. Color and clarity is much more critical due to the simplicity of the faceting.

5. ***Pear Cut:*** Or, Teardrop. This cut displays the traits of the Round and the Marquis because one end is Round and the other Marquis. On the Marquis end, be sure the tip is intact, with no shattering, milking, or heavy inclusions.

6. ***Heart Cut:*** These unusually cut diamonds are much more difficult to sell than one would imagine. The Heart often appears dead and is seldom cut well enough to display the fire and brilliance that naturally belongs to a diamond. Often, the table girdle is uneven.

7. ***Radiant Cut:*** This rare and beautiful cut is unique because it is a combination of two cuts. The table is Emerald Cut and the base is Round Brilliant. This allows for the maximum amount of fire to radiate upward through the larger table.

8. ***Trillion and Quadrillion Cut:*** These are the newest cuts. They are rare and very expensive.

9. ***Other Cuts:*** Diamonds have been cut into many unique shapes. The most unusual I have seen was a butterfly and a horse's head! These would be very expensive and the most difficult to move.

Chances are, you won't see the last three categories (7, 8, and 9) when you are shopping for your inventory. It is still good to be able to recognize other cuts in the event you are called upon to take them in as loan collateral.

BASIC JEWELRY STOCK:

1. 3 to 5 Rope chains over 20''.
2. 5 or 6 yellow gold wedding bands.
3. 3 or 4 diamond wedding sets, yellow gold w/small diamonds, $75 to $200 retail range.
4. 1 or 2 diamond wedding sets, $200 to $300 retail.
5. 5 or 6 ladies' diamond cocktail rings, $100 to $300 range. Free form and diamond cluster rings sell well.
6. 8 to 10 ladies' small rings with colored stones and diamonds, $75 to $125.
7. 3 or 4 pair gold hoop earrings, $30 to $75.
8. 1-2 pair .10pt. dia. stud earrings,$75 to $150.
9. 6 to 10 men's dia. rings, $100 to $300. Nugget style rings for men are still very good sellers.
10. 6 to 8 light weight gold serpentine chains, $25 to $50.
11. 3 or 4 ladies' gold link style neck chains, $75 to $150.
12. 8 to 10 ladies' gold bracelets, $25 to $150.
13. 3 to 4 men's lighter weight gold bracelets, $150 to $250.
14. 2 or 3 men's pocket watches.
15. 4 or 5 men's wrist watches (Seiko, Citizens, etc.), $50 to $75.
16. 4 or 5 ladies' newer design wrist watches, $20 to $50.

SILVER AND TURQUOISE

According to where you are located, New Mexico, Texas and Arizona are the naturally better markets. Unless you know for sure, invest in a very small inventory so that you can test your market.

Five or six ladies' and men's rings, a few bracelets and, if you can get a good deal on a nice squash blossom, add it to your inventory.

Sometimes in your travels, you will run across a squash blossom that won't sell because of the area. In this case, you might pick one up for $100 or less from a pawnbroker who is tired of looking at it! A decent squash blossom can fetch a remarkable price in Santa Fe or Taos. In Southern California, a pawnbroker can turn one over for $250 to $300.

Make sure the pieces are real silver. If you have a selection, choose signed pieces. Handcrafted pieces are usually signed by the artists who crafted them and are considered much more desirable than unsigned pieces.

Another type of silver jewelry that is currently popular is the heavy metal, punk rock style. This jewelry is noted for its macabre appearance.

Some pawnbrokers buy it over the counter for $1 per ring and $3 for the bracelets. It sells rather well at $8 to $12 for the rings and $12 to $20 for the larger, more intricate pieces.

NO PEARLS
NO WHITE GOLD
NO 50's or 60's STYLE WEDDING SETS
NO 40's, 50's, or 60's WRIST WATCHES
NO SMALL GOLD CHARMS
NO SHORT ROPE CHAINS
NO ANTIQUE JEWELRY

COSTUME JEWELRY

Pawnbrokers generally don't deal in costume jewelry for several reasons: 1) They don't want the customers to get the idea that any of their jewelry is not genuine, 2) They don't know anything about costume jewelry, therefore, don't understand that it can carry a certain value, and 3) They just don't want to be bothered.

All the above are valid reasons. We had been in the pawn business all of six months when I learned a valuable lesson.

One Sunday, I happened to notice a garage sale across the street from my brother-in-law's home where we happened to be spending the afternoon.

I walked over and saw a table full of costume jewelry, probably around fifty or sixty pieces.

I sorted through the pieces and made a mental note that although the jewelry was older and outdated (from the 60's and 70's), most was quality, in good condition, and still very pretty.

The majority was priced at twenty-five to fifty cents each. About ten pieces were marked at seventy-five cents and four or five pieces were marked at a dollar.

I mentally calculated roughly $32 to $35 for all of it. I asked the lady if she'd accept $20 for everything and she agreed.

Then I spotted a tall glass jug priced at $3 and added, "but you have to throw in that jug ... I need something to carry all this home in!"

I was actually kidding her, but she readily agreed and we filled the large jug with all of the costume jewelry.

On Monday, when we opened our doors, I emptied the glass jug out on my desk and began sorting and pricing the costume jewelry.

A very nice cameo copy broach looked like it might fetch the highest price. I attached the first tag bearing $19.95.

As I sorted and priced, a surprising number of pieces (eight in all) looked to be well worth a $12.95 price. Another six pieces I judged to be about a $9.95 value.

Ten pieces went for $4.95, ten pieces for $1.95, and twenty pieces for $ .95 cents.

All totaled, it came to a retail price of $286.20! Not a bad return for my $20 investment.

I cleared the plants and a few imported figurines out of an otherwise empty three-tier showcase, and filled it full with the costume jewelry. I made a nice sign which was placed in the middle of the top shelf that said: ALL JEWELRY IN THIS SHOWCASE IS COSTUME.

That afternoon, I ran an errand and when I returned, the cameo broach had sold for $19.95 plus the tax. I was already out of the woods!

Within just a few months, the costume jewelry display began to shrink until it had been completely replaced with forfeited loan collateral.

When only the smallest $ .95 and $1.95 pieces were picked over, I found a large crockpot and filled it with those pieces plus other small pieces I'd found over time and labeled the crockpot:

COOKIN' SALE
YOUR CHOICE
50 CENTS

Customers loved to dig through that crockpot and we were able to keep it full when word got out that for a few dollars, we would buy jewelry boxes if they were crammed with goodies.

Every shelf and showcase doesn't need to be crammed full. Beautiful displays can be made with just a few pieces of jewelry in a showcase.

Three to five ladies' rings, two or three men's rings, a pocket watch, two or three gold chains, and a wrist watch or two can make up a nice display.

FIREARMS

If you plan on carrying firearms, order a half dozen inexpensive .25 caliber semi-automatics to display in a showcase. These small handguns sell consistently well and you will find yourself ordering them by the dozens.

Twenty-two rifles are pretty common. The cheaper and most plentiful are the .22 Marlins. As a pawnbroker, you probably will wind up overstocked on them.

Pawnbrokers commonly give only $10 for a bolt action if it is in newer condition and maybe $15 to $20 on the semi-automatic Model 60 .22s. The bolt actions sell for about $25 and the Model 60s sell for around $59.95.

If you run into a pawnbroker who has racks full of these weapons, you can probably get the bolt actions for about $15 to $20 each and the Model 60s for somewhere between $30 to $40 each. This depends on if he is overstocked and on how many you are willing to take off his hands.

Pick up a few shotguns. You should be able to find some 12 and 20 gauges that are reasonable. Most pawnbrokers double (and sometimes triple) their money on firearms. Because guns are a very competitive commodity, the markup on them is not nearly so high as other items like jewelry or cameras.

Be sure you know what you are looking at when dealing in firearms. If you are not familiar with them, take a Gun Trader's guide along on your shopping tour. Refer to it every time you make any sizable purchases. Ask questions.

A pawnbroker who knows anything about firearms and who is interested in selling them will be happy to help you find the gun you are looking for in your guide. After all, chances are he has one of his own and uses it to refer to when pricing his guns.

Remember, the Gun Trader's Guide quotes top prices on guns that are in excellent condition. A gun that features a part from another weapon (such as a bolt with a serial number that is different from the number on the weapon itself) has dropped its value considerably.

Look for signs of wear and tear, rust spots, looseness in the stock, grips, or barrel ... missing parts, etc. Every little flaw drops the weapon lower in value.

The best deal a person can hope to get on a used firearm from an experienced gun dealer is probably about 20% below asking price.

Because the firearm business is a competitive one, the markup is usually a lot lower than what can be generated on other items such as jewelry or television sets.

CAMERAS AND OPTICS

There are about as many types, brands, and models of cameras as there are grains of sand on the beach. When selecting a few cameras to place into your inventory, be careful to choose only those that are good sellers.

Nothing is worse than the embarrassment of finding out that the nice camera you just priced out in your showcase at $99.95 has turned out to be one of those free gifts given out for subscribing to *Time-Life* magazine.

If you plan to start out with just a few cameras, try to keep your selection honed to the Canon T50, T70, and the Canon AE1 Program. These are all very good sellers. Stay away from the older Canon A1 and AE1. The Minolta 3000i, the Minolta 7000, and 9000 are also top sellers.

Don't buy lenses, flashes, or any camera equipment that must be sold separately. Unless cameras are your specialty, you will get very tired of looking at them collect dust in your showcases.

Binoculars are good sellers. Be sure and check them to make sure they focus properly. Tasco is a cheaper brand that sells reasonably well because they are very affordable.

TELEVISIONS, VCRs, STEREOS, BOOM BOXES

As in pawning televisions, so it goes in purchasing them for resale. Most televisions have the year they were manufactured on the back of the sets. Often, the dates are behind by one year.

Many brand new, off the showroom floor televisions will be marked a year old.

For instance, a set purchased in December of 1992 might have a 1991 sticker on it. Basically, a year can be knocked off the age, making a four-year-old set actually only three years old.

The manufacturing dates are very important because this is the only way one can know for sure the age of the set. No set should be purchased if it is over four years old. This means that in 1993, if a set is marked 1988, it was probably new in 1989 and it is now around four years old.

Four years is about as old as you want your resale color TVs, unless you are able to find an older one in pretty good condition and the price is where you can make a good profit. I won't turn down a six-year-old Sony Trinitron in excellent condition if I can get it for $20 or $30. I know (if the gods smile down on me and I can keep it running until it's sold), I can easily turn it for $79.95 without any problem.

Stereos are a good pawn shop item if you know just a little about what you are doing. But beware! They can be *foolers* to the uneducated eye. Stereos with all the bells, whistles, and dancing colored lights are pretty, but they are also cheap and tinny when compared to the heavy duty Sony and Kenwood components.

Stereos are for *listening,* not for viewing! That's how you will sell your sound systems, so it makes sense that this is how you must buy them.

Of course, they should look clean and decent, and the newer, the better. I don't know many pawnbrokers who will buy the older models, but I have done pretty well on some of them.

Every once in awhile, if a super sounding older model dial tuner comes in (the old non-digital silver models), I will make an offer of $10 on it.

Usually, I get it and when it comes out for sale, I hook it up to some good speakers and display it next to a newer model. People often think the music is coming from the new components and are amazed to find out it is emitting from the *grandpa* model. The price tag that adorns it is $39.95!

It will sell. If not, the store has some good music at the affordable price of $10.

Use the same formula for all sound equipment. Remember, look with your ears!

VCRs

VCRs are a tough commodity. Everybody wants them and no pawnbroker has nearly enough. If you can manage to throw one or two in on one of your *bulk* transactions, you will be very fortunate! Test them first. A broken VCR is no VCR!

TOOLS

Visit your local Sears center and browse around the tool section. Note the prices on individual socket and open end wrenches. Check the prices on the individual sockets, screwdrivers, pliers, etc. You will notice that they are all extremely high when purchased individually.

Next, look at the larger tool sets that are offered for sale. You will notice that there is a dramatic price difference when tools are purchased in full sets. The fuller the set, the more reasonable the prices. Hence, a set that runs (on sale) for $500 can be broken down and priced out at

$1,600 to $1,700!

The largest socket wrench in a Sears set runs around $27 individually sold. $12.95 is a good price for it and it will easily sell in a pawn shop.

Try to select the sets with the most open and box end wrenches. The smallest wrench sells individually at Sears for $1.95. Those can be priced for fifty cents. Sockets can be sold in a pawn shop from $ .50 to $10, depending on the sizes.

All good mechanics have full sets, but each piece is a different size and if a piece is lost, it must be replaced. Obviously, it would be ridiculous to buy another entire set for the want of a few pieces.

Where do you think these mechanics go for their replacements? Pawnbrokers who understand the value of good tools know that the best customers are the repeat customers.

It wouldn't hurt to let the local mechanics know that your pawn shop will be featuring good tools at very reasonable rates. Once word gets around to mechanics, expect them to be drifting in and out of the store every single day.

I found it surprising to learn that there are a whole lot of pawnbrokers out there who don't know this little secret ... or they think it isn't worth the trouble. You will recognize these pawnbrokers because they will have entire boxes full of tools for sale.

Sift through the tools and see which boxes offer the most name brands in the best condition. If it is a treasure chest of goodies, and the price is right, buy the whole box. Chances are, he'll save a $200 price on tools that can be broken down and sold for $1,000.

See the Chapter on *Tools (Hand and Power)* for further information on power and pneumatic tools.

MUSICAL INSTRUMENTS

Musical instruments, especially guitars, clarinets and flutes are a pawn shop commodity. Stock the walls and shelves with five or six acoustic and five or six electric guitars. Don't forget the electric guitar amps.

Two or three flutes, a couple of clarinets, one or two trumpets, one or two violins, and a small accordion are good starters.

Musical wholesalers are important to pawn shops. They offer the cheaper imports at reasonable prices.

Pawnbrokers often order their guitars and violins from them when their own stock is getting low. Remember, something to sell is better than nothing to sell! It is better to have those empty spots filled with cheaper imports than with nothing at all.

Wholesalers are also good for shelf fillers. Harmonicas always sell very well. Order several dozen and display them all together in a showcase. Don't forget to order the bellows. It's against the law to sell harmonicas used. This means the customers can't try them out, so a bellows is needed for demonstration.

Other good fillers are guitar strings. Order several dozen packs to display, along with several tambourines, and lots of guitar picks. The picks come in three weights: light, medium, and heavy.

Find three bowls and fill them full to put inside the showcase display.

OFFICE EQUIPMENT

Unless you happen to have them or you can find them for practically nothing, typewriters, adding machines and other office equipment are items that may nor may not be good sellers where you are located.

Some pawnbrokers do very well, but it would be wise to wait and see how the store goes. This department will fill itself soon enough. Electric typewriters are one of the most commonly pawned items.

REFER TO THE PREVIOUS CHAPTERS PERTAINING TO PAWNING INDIVIDUALLY LISTED ITEMS FOR MORE DETAILED INFORMATION.

DISPLAYING THE MERCHANDISE

It is difficult to know where to start in setting up a store, especially when the setup is going to be sparse, at best. Naturally, the fuller the store looks, the better. But not everyone is fortunate enough to do this at first. Making a little go a long way requires a little ingenuity.

Jewelry doesn't have to be profuse in order for it to look nice in a display case.

Once, while browsing around in an exclusive Beverly Hills jewelry store, I noticed that the showcases weren't full at all. In fact, some of the showcases displayed only five or six rings! Albeit, rings that were well out of my league and nearly everyone else's save for the occasional lottery winner, they were, nevertheless, sparse in number.

It would be worth a new pawnbroker's while to check out a few exclusive jewelers and implement some of their display ideas. Jewelry displays can be very expensive and one certainly doesn't get much for their money.

The last store I opened had a circle of five jewelry showcases. This meant a whole lot of money to buy displays or it meant that I had come up with some pretty clever ideas.

I took a trip to a fabric wholesale house and found a huge bolt of burlap. It looked a little ratty and, worse, it had printed letters running through it. I suddenly had a brainstorm and I bought 20 yards of it.

When I got back to the store, I rounded up a pair of scissors and a hot glue gun and set about my work. When the showcases were finished, they were lined with the burlap, complete with the printed letters in plain sight.

I ordered some inexpensive black felt ring boxes and set up the displays. The idea was right but it just didn't look complete. The jewelry inventory, while not to be sneezed at, looked sparse when spread around five showcases.

A few days later, I happened to be grocery shopping and I found some tiny potted cactus plants on sale for a dollar each.

I bought up a dozen or so and took them to the store to see how they'd look inside the showcases. They were perfect.

The combination of the burlap and cactus gave the showcase a southwest desert theme and the plush velvet ring boxes contrasted beautifully.

Later on, we added some clear non-blinking Christmas tree lights inside the showcases just around the bottom of the burlap covered liners.

Taking care to hide the wires by tucking them under the liners made the showcases look like the lights were built in. It was a very pretty display for the price of burlap, some dollar cactus plants, and a few strings of inexpensive Christmas lights.

Look around your pawn shop or even at home for ideas. Items don't need to be sold in order to be an effective enhancement to the merchandise.

How about a nice figurine to drape a strand of pearls over?

Nearly everyone that was married and had a wedding cake has that little caketop bride and groom tucked away at home in a drawer. Dig it out! It will make the wedding bands in your showcase look much more enticing.

Purchase some plastic dish pans and line some wall shelves with them. Label them with different prices and toss your tools into them according to kind and price. Sockets fifty cents, a dollar, two dollars, etc.

Fill a pan with individually priced screwdrivers, another with pliers, etc.

If you don't have enough tools to fill the pans individually, separate the tools by price only. Mix all of the tools that are the same price in one pan.

Hook up the televisions and keep them running. This attracts attention and you will find they sell much faster. A television that is kept running in a display window is a wonderful attention-getter at night when the store is closed.

Display the cameras, binoculars, perhaps a flute, a Walkman, and a Gameboy computer all in one showcase.

Don't try to reserve an entire showcase with one kind of item. If there are only two cameras to sell, they'd look pretty silly sitting all alone in a showcase.

Another one of my little tricks is to buy a few nice, bushy plants and place them in strategic areas that look rather empty and barren. Get them in all sizes and place them wherever they are needed.

Plants are relatively inexpensive if one knows where to shop. If a price tag is placed on them, they can even become part of the inventory.

Take up bare floor space with one or two nice used bicycles, a power lawnmower, an air compressor, a few guitar amplifiers, or an old barrel filled with golf clubs.

SUMMARY

Always keep your eyes open for good bargains and don't automatically discount an item just because you haven't carried it in the past. Have you run across a great deal on a mint condition boat? Do you have a place to display it for sale without hindering your other merchandise? Is it coming on to boating season? Can you make a reasonable profit on it? Then, why not go ahead and make the investment? It sounds like a good one to me!

Keep your brain always on that investing mode. A good pawnbroker eats, sleeps, and lives his pawn shop! He always chews on the possibilities before discarding the ideas.

Learn to ask yourself the right questions. The question is never, *''Will it sell?''* but rather, *''How long will it take to sell and will it make a decent profit?''*

Just remember, everything sold at least one time before! If someone bought it once, odds are someone will buy it again!

CHAPTER 23

VENDORS

Show me a man who knows it all and I will show you a world class fool! Who said that? I don't know. Perhaps I did. Nevertheless, who would argue? It is a fundamental and universal truth.

There is no matriculation, no sheepskin, nor is there graduation for the collateral lending entrepreneur. The only gauge a pawnbroker has to guide him is his bank account and his integrity.

The most valuable and desirable commodity in any industry is EDUCATION! In the collateral lending industry, education is valuable and desirable. It is also extraordinarily scarce. What precious little of it there is is cost prohibitive and time consuming. Who should know that better than you? You invested no small pittance in this publication.

Now you have set time aside for reading and digesting the material in order that you might educate yourself on the pawn business.

Accredited schooling is available in nearly every category of a pawnbroker's interest. Everything from gemology and gold casting to firearm and musical instrument repair is made available somewhere in the United States.

There are many more unaccredited schools as well. If the aspiring pawnbroker were to educate himself in this manner, he would need to plan his pawn shop somewhere in the distant future ... like a decade or two! This kind of education is also very cost prohibitive as well. I am not discounting trade school education. In fact, I encourage it. I am merely pointing out the fact that often it simply isn't doable.

Another wonderful source of education is the *Today's Pawnbroker* magazine. It is filled with interesting and educational articles that are directed solely to the pawnbroker.

It is a quarterly publication and, although the numerous articles are filled with educational meat and potatoes, one must always wait for the next issue to be printed.

There is, however, another source of education that many pawnbrokers never consider. It is immediate, concise, accurate, and as close as the nearest telephone. Best of all, the price cannot be beat. It is absolutely *free!* Most often, one needn't even pay the cost of a phone call.

That's right! I mean the vendors.

The end of this chapter includes listings of vendors who have been doing business with pawnbrokers for many years. Most items utilized in pawn shops are ordered by telephone, fax, or computer network. This opens several doors to your education on products, supplies, equipment, and services.

If you are unsure about grading diamonds, call one of the diamond dealers. If you have difficulty testing gold, a precious metals dealer will be happy to answer your questions.

Call a dealer in timepieces to find the value of an unusual watch. If you have questions on firearms, direct your call to one of the listed firearm dealers. If you are weak on cameras, coins, or musical instruments, there is a vendor just waiting for your call.

Brochures and catalogs are an excellent source of education for every pawnbroker. While you are on the telephone, be sure to make a special request for all such vendor information.

This is one time you will *want* your name added to mailing lists. New innovations and methods are constantly being discovered by the products manufacturers that are made available by the vendors.

If it weren't for mailing lists, many pawnbrokers would still be using horse and buggy techniques that have long been outdated.

Besides, it is shameful to pay top dollar only because you weren't supplied with timely information on a vendor's special sale.

You will find the vendors to be friendly, knowledgeable, and eager to help. They will answer any questions you might have. If they don't know the answer, they can probably steer you to the person who does.

Mention that you are new in the business and that you found their name listed in *Business Under The Balls.* And, tell them P. Taylor Fletcher says, "Hello!"

Vendors commonly offer assistance even if they don't make an immediate sale. Of course, the vendors are interested in selling their wares, but they want your business when you are ready for it. How can you become ready if you don't know what you are doing?

It makes sense for vendors to assist the new pawnbroker. An unsuccessful pawnbroker can't create much business for the vendor. Hopefully, when it comes time to place his orders, the pawnbroker will remember the vendors who were most helpful to him.

Next to your customers, vendors are the most important people that will contribute to your financial success. They are the providers of products, equipment, and services that help you to create and maintain your customer base.

Much of your borrowing clientele become good buying customers. Conversely, many of your retail consumers eventually need to procure a loan in your store.

WARNING! Word travels fast. Negative words travel faster. The one thing you will want to avoid is a credibility problem with the vendors. Pay your bills on time and always live up to your word on any commitment or agreement.

Once you have established yourself, you can

arrange for a consignment of merchandise with many companies. Pawnbrokers with standing reputations of honesty, dependability, and integrity can stock their stores clear to the rafters with consignment merchandise. This is an excellent way of freeing up dollars for collateral lending and, at the same time, offering top of the line new merchandise to their retail customers.

IN CONCLUSION

I always feel a bit envious of new pawnbrokers. They have so many wonderful discoveries still lying in store for them.

Every minute of my fourteen years in the industry has been filled with excitement, happiness, and joy. There is always something to look forward to in this business.

Whether it is expanding the store to include another building or only rearranging displays, there are always new ideas to implement and better ways of doing things. For every bad day I've experienced, there have been months of good ones!

I shudder to think I might have chosen to buy into a Burger King or a McDonald's franchise. For the life of me, I cannot find anything exciting or creative about computerized hamburgers. Franchise owners can't make a meaningful change without the blessings of corporate *Big Brother*. Adding an extra pickle or leaving out the secret sauce on a hamburger could result in losing the franchise.

Franchises may be lucrative, but I'd rather own a business where I called all the shots ... a business that feels like it belongs only to me.

My own life experiences have been varied enough for me to fairly compare. I've been a nurse, a telephone operator, and a secretary. I've worked as a waitress, department store clerk, sales training director, and mail carrier. I've sold advertising, insurance, real estate, and once I even sold bowling lessons to blind people! I am now a wife, a mother, a writer, and a pawnbroker.

Out of it all, my greatest joys have been four in number. You've got it! Wife, mother, writer, and pawnbroker, in that order.

Wife, because I am married to a dinosaur ... an officer and a gentleman with a great big heart ... the original Texan!

Mother, because I have borne and bred a truly rare bird ... a daughter who is magna cum laude, who sings like Patsy Cline and Reba McIntyre, who is a knockout beauty, and who is humble, loving, and kind.

Writer, because writing is the very sinew of my fabric. I can't *not* write.

Pawnbroker, because of the diversity and the freedom of doing things *my* way ... besides, *I* have first dibs on *all* the goodies!

Congratulations and the very best of luck to you on your new venture into the pawn business. It's a scary move, but if you love people, diversity, and creativity, you'll never be sorry.

Most important of all ... be thankful for all you have. We tend to become more involved in things we most appreciate.

The more involved you become in making the very most of your new pawn shop, the more fun you will find it to be.

Let the juices flow! You have chosen one of the most lucrative, creative, and exciting businesses in the world. The rest is easy!

TRADE SHOW EXHIBITORS

VENDOR'S INDEX

(MANY VENDORS BUY AND SELL)

Eastern Smelting & Refining Corp.

37-39 BUBIER STREET • LYNN, MA 01901
TELEPHONE: (617) 599-9000 • TOLL FREE: 1-800-343-0914 • TELEX: 940108 • FAX: (617) 598-4880

Recovering Precious Metals Since 1896

Established in 1896, nearly 100 years ago, Eastern Smelting & Refining Corp. specializes in the processing of scrap in order to recycle and reclaim Gold, Silver, Platinum, Palladium, Rhodium and Iridium. Each refining lot is processed individually in an efficient, economical and environmentally safe manner. Assays are performed in our in-house laboratory, which is considered to be one of the finest in the world. Our expanded facilities include a Representation Division where customers may witness the weighing and sampling operations.

Quick Turnaround Time/Financial Stability

On readily meltable high-grade Karat Gold scrap, payment can be made within five to seven working days. If requested, we also offer prompt money advance upon receipt and verification of the material. Eastern Smelting & Refining Corp. is one of the strongest capitalized firms of its type.

Settlement Options

We provide a variety of settlement options for the purchase of your precious metal scrap.

- **Check by mail**
- **Check by express mail**
- **Wire transfer to your bank**
- **Cash delivered by registered mail**
- **Transfer of precious metal to a pool account with a 3rd party**
- **Leaving metal in a METAL ACCOUNT with Eastern at no charge**
  We offer a Metal Account arrangement whereby the scrap material is refined now and the recovered precious metals are credited to your account. When the market reaches an attractive level and you wish to sell all or any part of the metals, you may telephone us to request our current quotation.
- **Return of precious metals—bars, coins, sheet, wire, grain or sponge**
- **Return of equivalent value in any semi-fabricated form**

Specialized containers can be provided free of charge for your convenience in accumulating and shipping material to us.

Our account executives are prepared to maintain contact on a continual basis in order to check on the status of precious metal-bearing accumulations and to assist you in any way possible.

We Operate Our Plant So As To Assure You Of Complete Privacy

all your diamond needs
in a nutshell
Call for FREE
Diamond Clarity Grading
Booklet while supplies
last.
BLUESTONE TRADING
Company Incorporated
BUY • SELL • MEMO
1-800-321-8508
(216) 442-7280
P.O. Box 24126 • Cleveland, Ohio 44124 • FAX (216) 442-0026

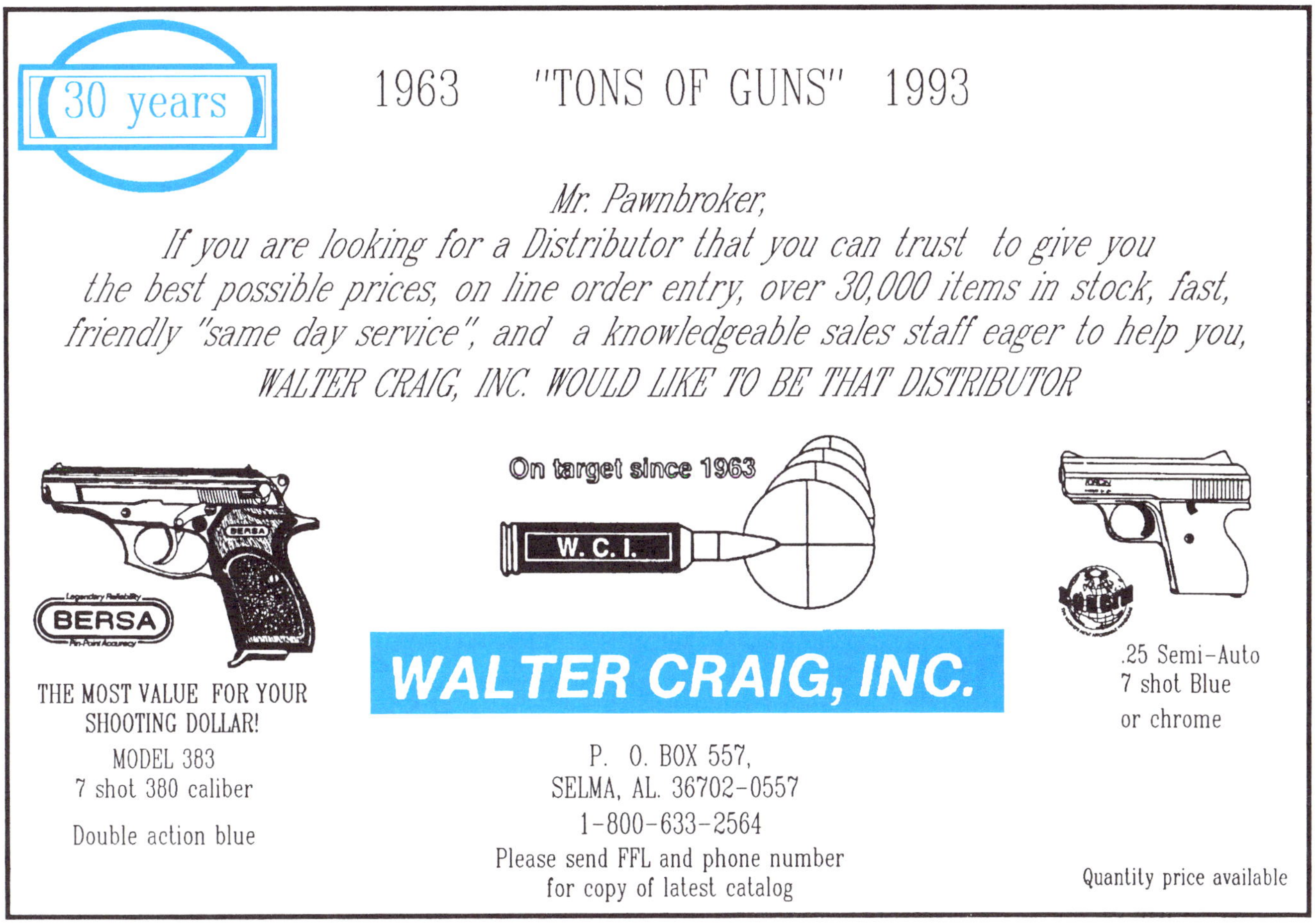
30 years
1963 "TONS OF GUNS" 1993
Mr. Pawnbroker,
If you are looking for a Distributor that you can trust to give you the best possible prices, on line order entry, over 30,000 items in stock, fast, friendly "same day service", and a knowledgeable sales staff eager to help you,
WALTER CRAIG, INC. WOULD LIKE TO BE THAT DISTRIBUTOR
On target since 1963
W. C. I.
BERSA
THE MOST VALUE FOR YOUR SHOOTING DOLLAR!
MODEL 383
7 shot 380 caliber
Double action blue
WALTER CRAIG, INC.
P. O. BOX 557,
SELMA, AL. 36702-0557
1-800-633-2564
Please send FFL and phone number for copy of latest catalog
.25 Semi-Auto
7 shot Blue
or chrome
Quantity price available

Let Us Be Your Warehouse
Your Full Service Pawnshop Supplier
Huge Selection, Great Prices, Fantastic Service
800-299-9035
M&M MERCHANDISERS
Serving Pawnbrokers Since 1976
Jewelry Displays, Tools & Supplies
Musical Instruments and Accessories
Closed Circuit TV Cameras & Systems
Telephones Audio/Video Accs.
Gold & Diamond Testers
Car Stereos
Orion Blue Books
Heres Just Some Of The Brands We Carry
Pyramid
Radion
Pioneer
CerwinVega
Power Acoustic
Legacy
Shure
Igniter
Thump
Precision Audio
Sabre
Guardian
Ohaus
Ceres
Gemini
Philips
Cougar
Hot Shots
Uniden
Huang
Audio Technica
TDK
Gibson
Black Diamond
Acculab
L&R
Telko
Panasonic CCTV
Renata
Bel Radar
M&M MERCHANDISERS 6611 ANGLIN DRIVE FORT WORTH, TEXAS 76119 800-299-9035 FAX 817-534-0153

IT'S NOT THE SIZE THAT COUNTS
IT'S HOW YOU
USE IT.
Use it to sell more diamonds ~ simpler, faster and with more confidence. With this preliminary consultation report, all we need is the stone number to generate a full certificate at any time ~ for you or your customer.
EUROPEAN GEMOLOGICAL LABORATORY E.G.L.
E.G.L.
SHAPE ROUND
STONE # LA16100572
WEIGHT 0.888 CTS.
CLARITY SI2
COLOR E
COMMENTS INCLUSION REFLECTS.
MEASUREMENTS 6.03 - 6.18 X 3.77 MM.
Actual Size
Member:
Diamond Club West Coast
Affiliate Member: AGTA
Associate Member: CJA
CHANGING THE WAY THE DIAMOND TRADE DOES BUSINESS.
550 SOUTH HILL ST. · SUITE 1310 · LOS ANGELES, CA 90013
(800) 235-3287 · (213) 622-2387 · FAX (213) 622-3138
EUROPEAN GEMOLOGICAL LABORATORY E.G.L.
E.G.L.

OVER A CENTURY OF SERVICE
GARFIELD REFINING COMPANY
PHILADELPHIA • PENNSYLVANIA
101st ANNIVERSARY CELEBRATION!
THE REFINER OF CHOICE SINCE 1892
NO LOT FEES
NO ASSAY FEES
NO HIDDEN CHARGES
Now!!
See for yourself how and why GARFIELD REFINING has remained the refiner of choice for 101 years! Just call for your FREE video tour, "INSIDE GARFIELD." It's fascinating to see how we process your scrap and pay you within 24 hours...
GARFIELD
VIDEO TOUR
■ CASH, BULLION, OR CASTING GRAIN PAYMENT.
■ THE GARFIELD GOLD WIRE IS FAST, FASTER, FASTEST!
■ ENVIRONMENTAL WARRANTY ASSURED.
■ STATE-OF-THE-ART PRECIOUS METAL REFINING.
■ PAYMENT IN 24 HOURS.
■ HIGHEST YIELDS.
CALL NOW...1-800-523-0968
DEPARTMENT "TP"
GARFIELD REFINING COMPANY • 810 EAST CAYUGA STREET • PHILADELPHIA • PENNSYLVANIA • 19124